Lousy Foreigner

Hushang M. Payan

Word Association Publishers

ISBN: 1-891231-10-3

Library of Congress Catalog Card Number: 98-75084

Word Association Publishers
205 Fifth Avenue
Tarentum, PA
www.wordassociation.com
724-226-4526

for
Irene

Table of Contents

Illustrations

Introduction

According to the Oxford Dictionary of Philosophy culture embodies attitudes, values, beliefs, arts, sciences, and habits of a given group of people. According to my experiences, however, it is a set of values that govern their behavior and develop the togetherness of any community.

Such pervasive rules cannot be taught. They must be experienced. The longer one lives with such customs, the better one understands them. The better one understands them, the more comfortable one feels practicing them. Necessity inspires adaptation, even complete change. It also contributes to the evolution of culture. The more familiar one is with the culture, the easier it is for that person to live in the community and become involved intuitively.

The younger a person is, the easier it is for him to accept the new culture. The best accultured immigrants are those who have been transferred to the new country before school age. What people experience in a new environment is as variable as their personalities. The difficulties that they encounter depend on their background and their preconceived notions of the new milieu. A willingness to accept the new mores makes acculturation less traumatic. Consequently, those who find the new ways intensely different suffer culture shock.

Since language skills are concrete and somewhat objective, one has a certain amount of control in understanding what is acceptable and what is not. Within the first two years of my stay in the United States, I became proficient enough in English to be able to assume the responsibilities of a young physician. Culture, on the other hand, is abstract. There are no written rules to dictate what is acceptable and what is not. There are no books that give lessons on tone of voice or body language in regard to greeting one's superiors, dressing for particular occasions, holding eating utensils, or moving in a crowd. Therefore only those who live within the culture are able to understand its innuendos and are able to assimilate more easily.

As a child in Iran, I grew up in a strongly paternalistic culture. From the moment I was born in Tehran, I was immersed in a hierarchy of values that stressed God, King, and country. In practice, one's life was devoted to fulfilling the expectations of ayatollahs, mullahs, dictators, police, one's father, and one's older relatives. In the United States, however, values focus on the individual, who in turn lives according to his rights and responsibilities. When I arrived in the United States in the early 1950's, a friend told me, "You are on your own. The harder you work, the better you live."

Later I learned that every citizen of the United States has the inalienable right to pursue life, liberty and happiness--as long as he lives within the framework of the law. The Constitution further affirms that "governments are instituted among men driving their just powers from the consent of the governed." As time went by, I noticed that in the United States, government belongs to people--in contrast with Iran, where people belong to the government.

Fifty years in the United States has changed me profoundly. I could no longer live without freedom, rule of law, and basic human rights. Arbitrary dictatorial powers of military kings or ayatollah clerics are archaic and unacceptable. Such strong convictions have prevented me from returning to Iran even for a visit. It has taken me many years-- a lifetime, in fact--to appreciate American values and ways of thinking. In this crossroads of the two cultures, I ran into many misunderstandings and difficulties. Because of such uncertainties, I have missed opportunities. On the other hand, I became involved with happy situations accidentally. The challenging experiences of this Americanization were many. Some are worth retelling.

Nevertheless, in spite of the fact that I have recognized and accepted the American way of life as best for me, I will always remember the associations of my early years in Iran.

As the expression goes, "You can take a boy out of the country, but you can't take the country out of the boy."

1
Birth

As the sky grew darker with shifting gray clouds, the cold wind reminded everyone that winter had definitely arrived. As the pains grew sharper with piercing contractions, the jolts reminded the mother that a baby was about to arrive.

When the snow started falling, Madar noticed that it was tea time and gathered her three children--two boys, ages 5 and 8 and one girl, age 11. As they hurried into the house, they first removed their shoes and then hung up their coats, hats, and mittens on hooks near the front door. The promise of cookies was incentive enough for them not to dawdle. Naneh, the servant so faithful she seemed like one of the family, had prepared a mixture of raisins, dates, berries, figs and nuts in a bowl large enough to hold a half dozen oranges. Along with these munchies each child enjoyed a small glass of hot, but diluted, Darjeeling tea and two small rectangular lumps of sugar. The children had to be careful not to touch the hot samovar.

Dusk soon turned to darkness which necessitated the kerosene lamp to be lighted. Madar sat down to join the family for tea, but had trouble finding a comfortable position.

"Oh, oh," she sighed deeply. "Naneh, will you please get my mother?"

Naneh gave her one knowing look, wrapped herself in her chador (the customary clothing for women which covered them from head to toe), took the lantern, and left.

Within minutes Grandma and her 15-year-old son Jamsheed joined everyone in the family room. As the mother of thirteen children she certainly had experience along these lines. Assessing the situation, she told her son to hire a horse and buggy and go for Mrs. Mamah, the midwife.

With two rials, equal to about twenty cents, he was

on his way, much happier to go out for a ride than to hang around the house with little children doing their school work or with three women chattering about their problems.

Grandma and Naneh noticed that Madar now needed peace, quiet, and some privacy. (Pedar had gone to Germany on a business trip that would keep him out of town for the next six months.) The ladies gave the children their dinner and sent them to another room.

While the children were walking out of the family room, three sisters-in-law were coming in. As next-door neighbors, as well as relatives, they were aware of the happenings in each other's families. Since they appreciated their husbands' sister Belghace because of her soft voice and listening ear, they came to help in any way possible.

Around 9:00 p.m. the children were fast asleep and never even heard Mrs. Mamah arrive with her 35-year-old daughter who was training to be a midwife like her mother. They came to the door, both wrapped up in their black chadors, holding them tightly under their chins to protect them from the cold.

After examining Belghace, Mrs. Mamah commented that her patient had to wait a few more hours and encouraged her to try to relax. A generous supply of towels sat in readiness on one side of the korsi--a common heating system--while extra bed sheets covered the mattress. To pass the time the eight ladies exchanged gossip and enjoyed the good cooking that was typical of this household. Soon their sentences were interrupted by Belghace's gasps of pain. The contractions were occurring closer and closer.

Grandma sent Jamsheed to the flat rooftop of the two-story house to pray as loud as he could, "*Allah-o-Akbar.*" (God is great.) The news about the soon-to-be-born baby spread throughout the neighborhood. Now at the door appeared Mrs. Bolbol, who had just delivered her own daughter a couple of weeks ago. For Belghace she brought a bowl of *katchi*, a concoction of one part butter to two parts flour--among minuscule amounts of other ingredients, like sugar, saffron, cardamom, water and rose water.

It has been proven that this delicacy provides much needed nourishment and energy after delivery so the new mother can regain her strength. The midwife and her daughter took turns massaging Belghace's shoulders.

After midnight the pain became unbearable.

"Sit up," urged one lady.

"Squat," advised another.

"Push down," directed Mrs. Mamah.

"Take a deep breath," added Mrs. Bolbol.

"Don't worry," they intoned like a chorus.

Around 2:00 a.m. a fuzzy little head poked through--with no help from anyone. Even at this early age he had a mind of his own.

January 1, 1925 the city of Tehran was calm, dark, and insulated with freshly fallen fluffy snow. When Mrs. Mamah held the baby upside down and swatted his behind, he let out one lusty yelp, which announced, "I, Hushang Mofakham Payan, am born." This name and date of birth were written in the back of the Koran which was always kept on a special shelf in the room.

As the screaming newborn objected, everyone, including Mader, smiled. Mrs. Mamah recited a Persian poem from Iraj Mirza, who lived between 1874 and 1924:

> Do you know why a newborn cries and weeps?
> He is so aware of life's griefs to come. He is already worried.

Oceans away, Mark Twain (1835-1910) expressed the same sentiments. "Why is it that we rejoice at a birth and grieve at a funeral?" he wondered. "Because we are not the person involved," he answered.

2
God

According to some psychologists, a normal fetal-oceanic stage of life is said to be a state of continuous, immeasurable tranquility with a feeling of godly-cosmic unity, unlimited wisdom, and power. In such a state of cosmic unity, logic is defied, parts and the whole are the same, and the sense of time and space is nonexistent.

The process of being born, however, teems with stress, pain, and pressure. Because of such trauma, the newborn is stunned and bewildered. With his yelp the child announces that he has arrived. Losing the serenity of his oceanic intra-uterine life, he demands constant motherly love.

Accustomed to the never failing sound of the mother's heart beat, the newborn expects a close physical contact which helps the psychological bonding between mother and child.

Within six weeks the helpless newborn, incapable of even moving his neck, begins to recognize his mother and responds to her with a smile meant only for her.

About this time the baby feels secure in the presence of such an almighty being--his mother. He perceives her as beautiful, caring, kind, loving, forgiving, comforting, omniscient--omnipotent. Thus, the image of God is created.

About the same time that he begins to recognize his mother, he develops a sense of anxiety. With her he is happy and smiling; without her, anxious and crying. The awareness of security vs. anxiety--heaven vs. hell--becomes apparent.

By the time a baby is two months old, he gradually gains control over some of his muscles and body movements. He also begins to recognize a world around him. He further discovers the unfortunate fact that he and his mother are two separate individuals. No longer perceived as an extension of his own physical being, the mother becomes slightly more distant as part of his conception of the world.

By the time he is one year old, the image of Mother-God is gradually transferred into the dark labyrinths of the subconscious. He now sees his mother as another person who cannot always please him.

Looking for the lost image, he focuses on his father, now regarded as the source of power and security--God. Within a few months, this too shall pass.

By the age of two, as the child acquires greater independence by walking and talking, he becomes aware of others--relatives, friends, and health care professionals. Influenced by stories read to him or television programs selected for him, he creates superhumans. With a great capacity of absorbing details, children mix the imaginary with the real. In addition to all these media influences, children are taught to consider God very loving and forgiving. By the time they finish the elementary grades they already have a religion very similar to that of their parents or other care givers.

During teenage years both body and mind change dramatically. Young people become sexually mature. The blood flow of the brain is reduced to almost half. Teenagers begin to establish their own identity with questions like, "Who am I? Where am I going? What am I going to do?" Preoccupied with such introspection, they become very sensitive. The second highest cause of death between the ages of 15 and 19 is suicide. The reason for this appears to be the age-old question, "What is life all about?"

Heroes of teenagers are teachers, politicians (especially presidents), athletes, religious leaders, and screen stars. As young people grow older, some of them become passionately involved with movements and unrealistic ideals. They easily fall into the trap of cults, like the Moonies. The original mother-God image of the newborn and the basic need for security become the basis for the creation of gods and religions.

Unfortunately, some people are erroneously convinced that they represent God and in such a unique position have some sort of divine right to impose their philosophy on everyone else. Religious thoughts which have been partially or totally political have lent themselves to centuries of unquestionable dictatorial powers and abuse of human rights. Superstition, hatred, and ignorance have been promoted for personal gains by some religious leaders.

Because of the emotional need for religion, the seventy-year attempt of the Communist USSR to eradicate God and religion failed. The universal need for security has existed since the beginning of time. Therefore, it should be respected by governments. By the same token, religious leaders, like Khomeini, should stay out of politics and respect the separation of church and state as a basic law in all human societies. Attempts to rule mankind by religious laws that do not recognize change have failed in the past and will fail again. Absolute power always leads to absolute corruption.

3

Visitors

In 1929, when I was about four years old, my mother dressed me in gray pants with red suspenders and told me, "Go say hello to your father's guests. Can you say '*Gooten morgen*'? These men are from Germany. They don't understand Persian. If you want to say 'good morning,' you have to say '*gooten morgen.*' Can you repeat that?"

Dutifully, I repeated, "*Gooten morgen.*"

She was so proud of me. She smiled, pointed me to the guest room, and reminded me, "Tell Mr. Hoschander and his son '*Gooten morgen*'."

I slowly walked toward the guest room. On such a warm summer day, all the doors to the porch facing the courtyard were open. These men were all making funny noises. Since I did not understand what they were saying, they must have been speaking German. As I approached the doorway, shyly I whispered, "Gooten morgen."

Nothing could have made the guests happier or my father more proud. Simultaneously, they both answered, "Gooten morgen" plus many more things that I could not understand. Since they were smiling, I smiled back. "They must like me," I thought.

In an instant Mr. Hoschander's son pulled out his camera. I reached for it, thinking they had brought me a toy.

His smile changed to a frown, obviously worried that I was about to wreck his expensive Agfa box camera.

He said nothing, but sat me on a doorstep. I dared not squirm. No matter what adults asked a child to do, that child obeyed instantly.

Mr. Hoschander then dropped my suspenders over my shoulders and seemed to want to lower my pants. That I did not approve of. I liked my new suspenders right where they were. I made a face, twisted my nose, and glowered at him. When I let out such a yell that blasted his ear drums and poured forth a waterfall of tears, he backed off, but clicked his camera anyway.

The next time these two gentlemen visited my father, they brought candy for the children and a picture for my parents. With tears streaking my face, I was preserved for posterity. Since this was the very first photograph of any member of our family, my mother cherished it as though it were the crown jewels. As the years went by it was copied, it was enlarged, it was framed, it was distributed among the relatives to hang in a prominent place in their homes, especially in our home.

Every time my brothers and sisters looked at it when I was within hearing distance, they would snigger, "Cry baby." And that only made me start crying all over again.

4
Polygamy

Too bad that cameras were not common household items in the latter half of the 19th century. The stories we heard about our ancestors made us wonder what they looked like, especially as they managed their responsibilities, as well as their avocations.

When my great grandmother noticed that her son was starting to itch his chin where whiskers began to sprout, she prodded him to take a wife. His grandfather warned that he would get sick if he did not marry soon. Should the young man show disinterest, the other family members would believe that he was sexually weak. And that would scandalize the family name.

Eventually this son told his mother that Haagee Baba, his boss, talked about his seven daughters, all of whom were available. My grandfather as a young man had his eye on the youngest one.

His mother had other ideas. One day she visited the Haagee Baba family and picked out her own choice. Both sets of parents then met to determine the amount of cash (*naqd*) to be paid to the bride's family before the wedding and the amount to be paid to her in the event of a divorce. Even though divorce was rare, the monetary arrangement was customary. About $50 changed hands.

The night before the wedding a few of the groom's boyfriends took him out to make sure that he was adequately "relaxed" for his wedding day. Together they went to the Shahzadeh Abdolazim Shrine.

Cars were nonexistent. To get from one place to another, people walked. When heavy loads were involved, there was always an available donkey. When the distance was too far to walk, people rented a horse and buggy. Since this shrine was in the southern part of Tehran, the young men rode a train, a brand new train at that, for about a half hour.

Once there they met with a clergyman who found postmenopausal women for them to marry for an hour. Each young man paid a fee of about 50 cents to the clergyman and a similar fee to the lady. After the ceremony, the *seegheh,* the young man suddenly became married and was now able to experiment with marital bliss in a private room and determine whether or not marriage interested him. Furthermore, by engaging in such a practice with an older woman--who was undoubtedly sad, lonely and frustrated--he was working his way to heaven.

Apparently, the clergyman was a pimp for legalized prostitution. By attaching some positive religious significance to the practice, everyone involved felt quite noble.

In 1861 in the United States Abraham Lincoln was inaugurated, in Austria Dr. Semmel Weis discovered the strong correlation between post partum deaths and the lack of sterile conditions on the part of physicians, and in Iran while the British and the Russians were competing to spread their empires, Ali, my grandfather, at the age of 15, married the first of his seven wives, at the age of 13.

During the legal ceremony, the *aqd*, (traditionally in the bride's home) the bride and groom sat next to each other in a room apart from the wedding guests where the clergyman intoned prayers and benediction. The young couple sat on the floor in front of a large mirror, which allowed them to see each other for the very first time. The bride wore a long white dress and a lacy veil that covered her from the top of her head to her waist. The rug in front of this mirror was covered with a new white cloth, like a tablecloth. On top of it was the Koran and an assortment of desserts, breads, fruit and a particularly sweet white candy (*noql*) , the size of raisins.

According to ritual the girl was asked to cherish and obey, for the rest of her life, this man next to her. Also according to prescribed ritual, she did not respond. Such reticence supposedly evinced high morality. The clergyman then repeated his question. Again the bride would not answer. For the third time, the clergyman repeated the question. This time, she answered, "Yes." She was supposed to appear rather reluctant for such a partnership. The groom did not have to say anything. It was assumed that this is what he wanted. Otherwise, he wouldn't even be there. When they both signed the papers, the marriage was legalized. This was the first time that a girl was allowed to wear makeup. The makeup was a symbol like a wedding ring.

Immediately after the ceremony all the guests entered the room, took a handful of the *noql* and a few silver coins, and threw the assortment at the bride and groom. Everyone then proceeded to the groom's home for the traditional reception, most likely on foot. The newlyweds, though, were driven in a white carriage drawn by two white horses.

Since my grandfather had never even seen his wife before, he had nothing to say to her. For that matter, she had nothing to say to him either.

At this reception friends and relatives feasted on an abundance of gourmet delicacies and gossip. Long into the night everyone enjoyed the *roohozi*, music by a live band with dancing girls. The group could be seen from all rooms of this house. During the party the groom sat with the men in one room, while his wife stayed with the women in a different room. At that time in Moslem countries women were allowed to be seen by men only if they were close relatives. Otherwise, they had to remain covered.

As expected, the young couple then lived in the man's parents' house. Within the year Mariam the wife discovered that she was pregnant. Then they just kept on having babies. Every two years they added one more.

* * *

According to Moslem religion a man is permitted more than one wife. When my grandfather was young, a man could have as many wives as he was able to support. Four of those were so-called "permanent," and the rest, "temporary"--temporary for just an hour or for as long as 99 years. Most likely the rationale for such a custom was to assure the parents of enough surviving children. In many parts of the world about 50% of the children died of infectious diseases before the age of 5.

All laws were quite vague. Grandfather never even had a birth certificate, but he thought he was born around 1845. He never even had a surname. People who knew him well simply called him Ali. In business circles he was known as Maahootchi. More than a personal name, it's an identification of one who sells broadcloth, fabric for men's clothing.

He knew this business well. After all, since the age of 10 he had worked in the bazaar, working for a friend of his father's who sold this broadcloth. The bazaar was a collection of shops under one roof. Shop keepers handling the same type of merchandise were located side by side. The shoemakers were all next to each other, the jewelers were all next to each other, the rice sellers were all next to each other, and so on.

To deal with such influential people, a young man had to be presentable at all times. He wore long pants, a long jacket almost to his knees (like Abraham Lincoln's), and a white collarless shirt with long sleeves that his mother made.

At that early age my grandfather was in charge of keeping the place clean-- the sales room as well as the stock room. He was also the errand boy. When his employer entertained other businessmen, he had to bring tea to them from a nearby coffee house. Even though it was called a "coffee" house, the place sold only tea. No one even drank coffee--except at funerals. Sometimes he brought meals to go with the beverage. For such services he earned his lunch with two cups of tea and five *shaahies*, equal to the British ha'penny. He had to relinquish four of these to his mother, but was allowed to keep one for his own pocket money. With this one coin he would stop at the *Ageel-forush* shop and have the owner fill his coat pocket with raisins and chickpeas which he munched on during the day. Besides the business of fabrics, he learned the value of money.

Since he was privileged to learn reading, writing and arithmetic between the ages of 8 and 10, he was qualified to hold a better job at the fabric shop. He handled the correspondence of the business, because his boss did not have such skills, sophisticated at the time.

Within four years my grandfather was promoted again, this time to salesman. He was so good looking, women customers flocked to him. Soon he topped his own sales record.

* * *

After his marriage my grandfather's salary increased and he then earned five tumans per week.

By the time he reached his eighteenth birthday he became responsible for Baby #2 and opened his own shop. This exciting new venture inspired Baby #3. Pregnancies, breast feeding, toddlers running around didn't exactly thrill him. With his friends he went out for more satisfying excitement and entertainment. He soon had enough money to afford another wife.

Soon he married the daughter of another businessman. This time there was less fanfare. This meant that he became the head of another household. For about 100 tumans he bought another house. According to the dictates of religion, he was able to have as many wives as he could afford and divide his time equally. Without all the noise of children Wife #2 was much more satisfying, so he concentrated on her.

It wasn't long, though, before she became pregnant for the third time. After the third child conceived by each wife, he always went looking for a new one.

Every six years or so, the pattern repeated itself until he was married to seven women and produced thirty-nine children. He lost interest in the women in his houses that were noisy with children. When his seventh wife became pregnant for the third time and the house became too lively for him, he was in search of #8. By this time his youngest wife was the same age as his oldest daughter.

At the age of 50 he was really an old man, too old to survive such a hectic lifestyle. One morning the youngest wife discovered his body in a heap, all curled up next to the korsi.

Some think he had a fatal heart attack. Others believe that his seven wives formed a conspiracy and poisoned him.

5
Bibi Joon

As we celebrated Persian New Year as usual on the first day of spring, my mother gathered her children to visit my great-grandmother. To reach her home several miles away we traveled by horse and buggy, as well as on foot.

After about an hour in this buggy and about 20 minutes on foot the air at Bibi Joon's was filled with "*Salaam, Bibi Joon*!" (Good morning, Dear Grandma.) ("Bibi Joon" seemed to be the only name she had.) She in turn wished everyone "Happy New Year." Meanwhile, all the relatives greeted each other with a hug and kisses on both cheeks.

When I was 5 years old, my mother was around 30, my grandmother was around 65, and Bibi Joon was exactly 105. At any reference to my age, I always thought of Bibi Joon, who was exactly one hundred years older than I. By this phenomenal age she had many children, many more grandchildren, many, many more great grandchildren, and a fifth generation of still more children. According to custom on Persian New Year, younger members of a family always visited the older. As the eldest in our family, Bibi Joon had a procession of visitors all day long on this first day of spring, which is also the first day of the Iranian calendar. This little old lady with silky white hair and a pale complexion greeted her guests in the corner of the living room, where she always sat on a thin mattress covered with a white sheet. For some reason, she was unable to walk, not even stand.

Since the concept of a nursing home did not exist in Iran in the 1930's, Bibi Joon's youngest son and daughter-in-law shared their mother's house to take care of her.

When my 13-year-old brother tried to take her picture with his brand new Agfa camera on this festive holiday, he asked me to sit near her and talk to her--to get her into a natural position for a true candid shot.

At the sight of my brother with his box, she admonished "Take pictures of old people from a distance. Otherwise all you will show is a sea of wrinkles."

In spite of her objections, Lotfi clicked the camera while she was trying to figure out who I was. "What's your name?" she asked me. With such a large family of more than 100 relatives she had a hard time remembering who was who. "Whose kid are you?" she continued. After she got my place straight in her line of descendants, she told me that my mother, whom she nicknamed "the little lady," was her favorite granddaughter.

Her reminiscing about my mother's youth was interrupted by a few ants crawling around the Persian rug. On this warm day it was only natural for a few ants to join the party uninvited officially, but encouraged to follow cookie crumbs dropped by the kids who kept running in and out of the house. At the sight of one bug on her mattress, she told me to take it outside.

Instantly I obeyed. I grabbed the ant between my fingers, pressed them firmly together, accidentally squished it, and tossed him out the window.

Bibi Joon was horrified. "Oh heavens, I didn't say to kill him! I said to put him out--outside, not out of his misery. Get a piece of paper, place it in front of the ant, and let him walk on it. When he's in the center of the paper, gently take him on his paper outside and let him walk off into the garden where he belongs."

Then she recited a poem that still floats in my mind:

Don't disturb the working little ant.
His life is as sweet to him as yours to you.

Years later I discovered that those lines came from a poem by Firdausi who lived a thousand years ago. While most Iranians at the time were illiterate, Bibi Joon could read and write classic poetry. As a member of the fifth generation descending from Nader Shah, a king of Iran in the early 1700's, she was privileged to be tutored. Even at the age of 105 she had vision so keen, she could still read without glasses.

Within a few months of that momentous Persian

New Year celebration, all these relatives gathered again--this time for Bibi Joon's memorial service. As a 5-year-old I had no understanding of such goings-on. According to Moslem law, a person must be buried the same day of his death. The ritual service was held three days later. Since we were with all the family again, I naturally kept looking for Bibi Joon.

"Where could she be?" I wondered.

"Gone to heaven," my mother replied.

6
Korsi

When I was a child in the late 1920's in the city of Tehran, Iran, neither electricity, nor gas, nor oil was available for heating rooms in a house.

Since our house was an old one with huge doors, tall windows, and high ceilings, wind blew through the openings freely, making the cold rooms colder. To keep some of this cold out of the room my mother would hang inexpensive rugs on the doorways. But this was only an exercise in futility, as five children and at least seven grownups would traipse in and out all day long, always opening the door that accommodated the heavy traffic--as well as the cold air--and often forgetting to close it.

A good heating system was absolutely necessary. In the center of a metal container was placed a ball of coal, crushed compacted powder, surrounded by ashes from the previous day's fire. This brazier was then placed on a large metal tray and covered by a wooden table about 6' x 6' x 1 ½', "korsi."

This korsi stood in the middle of a square made of four mattresses, each the size of a single bed. A huge comforter then covered the korsi and the mattresses. Encircling these mattresses were large pillows--soft enough for comfort, yet firm enough to support your back while you sat on the mattress with a huge comforter covering you from the toes up as high as it would reach.

This comforter was covered with white sheets which were like bed linens. Over this was another cloth, this one more colorful--like a bedspread. At night at least four adults could sleep under one korsi. With so many people living under one roof, our house had four different rooms, each one having its own korsi. The ball of coal could keep the area warm for 24 hours, costing about two cents.

The top of the korsi served as a table where a

tablecloth was spread at meal time. It also served as a desk for the children to do their homework. At night a kerosene lantern provided light for the children to study or for the adults to read us stories. Some of the stories were so long, it took a whole winter to finish. My mother often spent the evening sewing and mending while sitting under the korsi. The real truth is that this is how she kept her eye on the kids, who weren't always on their best behavior. A little boredom was often relieved with a kick in someone else's leg or a poke in his ribs. Only after schoolwork was there time for games, usually with cards. Even the cats found comfort under this comforter. They often curled up near us to keep us company and to keep themselves warm.

Sitting or sleeping under the korsi was so cozy, especially on a cold night, getting up to leave the room was almost traumatic. A child would often struggle to delay the urges of nature, rather than crawl out of the korsi and brace himself for the cold on the way to the outhouse.

Since World War II the korsi has been replaced by heating systems fueled by gas or oil.

7
Nightmare

It was bitter cold one evening. As we gathered around the korsi, my visiting uncle Jamsheed told us stories (as he often did)--the scarier, the better. Through his imagination and into our gullible minds romped shadowy ghosts, screeching monsters, creeping dragons, or attacking arms--unattached to bodies.

It was so cozy under the comforter of the korsi, my mother had no trouble persuading the children to go to sleep right there. Since my grandmother was visiting at the time and since I was the smallest one, she joined me during the night--as was her custom when she was a house guest.

In the middle of the night the door creaked. It was so old, the least change in its position made a raucous, especially in the dead of night. Immediately my grandmother lifted her head from the pillow and noticed the beam of a flashlight from behind the hanging rug.

By this time she had had enough of her son's silly stories and sillier pranks. The greatest insult she could inflict on any irresponsible boy was to refer to him as a dancer. (Till this day I wonder how she would have reacted to Fred Astair or Gene Kelly.)

"Get in this room and get to bed, you Dancer!" she scolded.

The noise woke me up, but I was so scared, so full of Jamsheed's make-believe, that I couldn't even scream. I scooted under the covers, turning the comforter into a little trembling heap. I was positive that if I didn't see him, he couldn't see me. I was only 4--a small 4-year-old, at that--much too small to take on a giant.

The silly boy continued to hiss funny noises, sillier than ever. The squeak of his shoes became louder . . . and closer.

"Jamsheed," Grandma yelled in a more assertive voice. The threat was suddenly interrupted by the sight of the sleeve of a leather jacket, nothing like any clothing that Jamsheed wore. "This is not my son," she gasped.

Defying the intruder, she jumped from under the covers, called everyone else in the house to wake up, and proceeded to light the kerosene lamp.

The burglar must have been more frightened than I. He was out of the house before anyone else reached our room. He must have escaped through the door that led to the roof of the house. Within seconds the cold air chilled the room, people were running all over the house, the lamps burned brightly, and the night was changed into day.

Soon 14 people were all gathered around the korsi and exchanged accounts of what each had discovered stolen: a watch, a necklace, a pin, a sweater, some money.

Apparently the burglar climbed a wall along a narrow alley, jumped onto our neighbor's roof, and climbed down the huge mulberry tree which grew taller than our two-story house and had sturdy branches that extended over to the neighbor's building. The courtyard was enclosed by the house. Within the house there were no locks on the doors, but the door to the street had a padlock. To reach the roof every house had stairs, at the head of which was a door with a latch. It was through this one and only exit where the thief must have disappeared.

The night became more unusual when loud noises filled the alley. Apparently the burglar repeated his routine in a few other houses and got the entire neighborhood out of bed.

Many years later, I still have this recurring nightmare. A muffled scream and helpless cry awaken my wife, who assures me, "Everything's O.K., Hank. Everything's O.K."

8
Train

On another winter day when frost transformed the bushes and the flower beds into a world of silver, January 1 signaled my fifth birthday, but even I didn't know that this day had any significance. There were no presents, no birthday cake, no candles, or no Happy-Birthday-To-You song to tell me so. On that cold drizzly day in Tehran even the cat wanted nothing to do with me. He curled up on the korsi, ignoring the fact that I wanted someone to play with.

My mother gave me that grin-and-bear-it look and urged me to go with her to the "chest room," a special corner of the house that housed many large wooden, clean leather-covered trunks, where she kept the family's underwear, socks, shirts, towels, linens, and other boring stuff. I could have cared less about these things, but at least it gave me a reason to move away from the korsi. I had no idea why she asked me to go with her.

Some of the chests were locked. When she walked toward one of these with the key angled toward the key hole of the padlock, she simultaneously opened my curiosity. Slowly the lid of the chest went up. An ocean of cloth-covered bundles lay within. In the middle of it all surfaced a box. Ever so carefully she pulled it out.

She took me by the hand, led me to the middle of the floor carpeted with a Persian rug, and gently pushed my shoulders so I would sit down. "This is a train set that your father brought from Germany a few years ago. It is very expensive and very valuable. You cannot take any part of this out of this room. If you promise to be good and stay here, you may play with it. You may not have any other children in this room playing with you. Make sure you do not break anything. If you do, your father will get angry and holler at you."

With every condition I nodded my head, touching

my chin to my chest, indicating, "Yes, I understand. Yes, I will obey. Yes, I will be careful. Yes, I will play alone." I couldn't wait to see this precious train. My eyes got bigger and bigger with every word she said. Bouncing up and down on my toes, I was so excited. I couldn't wait to see what was in that box that had to be locked in the big chest. Carefully my mother sat down on the rug next to me. She looked at me without saying a word. I knew that she was reminding me to be a good boy. Then she opened the box.

"Wow!" I exclaimed in utter wonder. At least one hundred pieces of trains, tracks, and statues of people paraded through her soft hands. Each piece seemed shinier than the other. Everything sparkled like gold. It was the most beautiful thing in the whole world. "How do I play with this?" I asked.

"I will show you," she answered. One by one, she took the tracks and attached them to each other till they formed circles. Ever so meticulously she placed the cars on the tracks and slid them along, warning me to make sure none bump into each other or fall off the track.

"Is this mine?" I asked, completely bewildered.

"No, this belongs to your father. You may play with it, but you must make sure that you do not lose any piece or break anything. Let me know when you are tired playing. I will come to put everything away."

With these words of caution, she left me to my world of enchantment.

A few minutes after she had gone there was an accident. Boom! Two trains collided and fell off the track. A wheel from one of the cars rolled around the floor. Nervously I got everything back on the track, but that wheel refused to sit properly. I realized that I had broken my father's precious toy. I could hear him yelling as his face turned red. He will be so mad. I just knew it. He will probably scream so loud, the Sohrabs will hear him next door. My eyes began to burn with tears ready to erupt.

I called my mother. I didn't want to play any more. "I'm tired," I lied.

She put the box away without noticing the wobbly wheel. I kept visualizing my father as he would take that box of precious toys, start assembling the parts, making the trains go round and round and round, and then discover the broken wheel.

How would he announce this discovery, I wondered. Since he had his own private room, he seldom mingled with his family. My mother spent some time with him, but most of the time with the children. That night he called for her. Instantly she went to his room. With bated breath I expected both of them to come out yelling at me. My lungs were like balloons, ready to pop. I imagined both of them playing with the trains. They must have had a lot of fun because it was a couple hours later when my mother finally joined us, fixing her hair as though she got all excited over the toys.

During the next few days my mother praised me for being such a good boy and asked if I would like to play with the trains again.

With no hesitation, I jerked my head up, meaning "No."

By the following day I could keep my secret no longer. I confessed my sin to my older brother. After all, five years older than I, he was a very experienced man. He certainly would know how I should go about admitting my carelessness.

"Many of the wheels are loose, Stupid," he flatly explained. "When one falls off, you shove it back on."

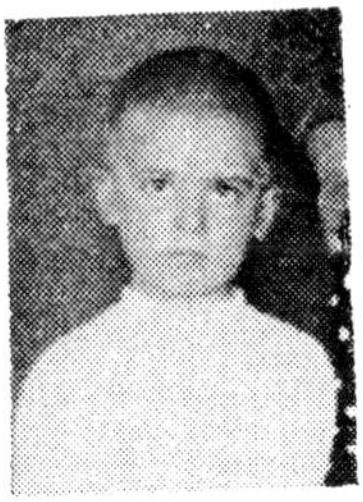

9

Money

"Ice cream, I-I-I-ce cre-e-e-e-m," yelled the ice-cream man, walking down the street where my grandmother lived. He would carry his supply in a kind of ice-cream bucket on top of his head, his mass of thick black hair protected by a cushioned ring, which also helped balance the weight. Probably because of this man's round in grandmother's neighborhood, more than any other reason, my cousin Johan and I loved visiting her, especially on hot summer days. Before this middle aged man even reached the first syllable in "ice cream," all the children ran to their houses to get the penny needed for a big ice-cream sandwich.

Johan and I weren't any different. We ran inside to ask Grandma for money, but it looked as though she were sleeping. "Sh, sh," whispered Johan. "We better not wake her up. She'll only get mad and then won't give us anything."

"But how are we going to get our pennies?" I worried. "If she's asleep, we can't talk to her."

"Look," pointed Johan. "She always leaves change in that fancy bowl on her dresser. We'll just borrow some."

Being five years old, we were too short to see inside the bowl, but tall enough for our little agile fingers to reach into it. We stood on our left toes as high as we could and stretched our right arms up into the fancy dish. Before we took any money, we took another look at Grandma. We made sure she was really sound asleep. It would be wrong to bother her. Apparently, she was rich--very rich. Neither one of us could reach the bottom of this deep treasure trove. We each took a penny. Holding our breath, we tiptoed out of the room, almost in slow motion.

The next day when the ice-cream man came down the street, we again went back into the house to ask Grandma for a penny. This time we couldn't find her. This time we didn't even have to be quiet as we stretched to reach into the bowl and "borrow" a couple more pennies.

The third day when the ice-cream man made his rounds, we again ran into the house to ask for the pennies. Grandma was sleeping again. "Why does she always have to sleep when we need the pennies?" I asked Johan. After all, he was six months older than I and was supposed to know everything.

He shrugged his shoulders and pushed me toward the dresser. Once again we tiptoed past her bed and reached for the pennies, praying that we wouldn't fall off balance and bump into the furniture. "Boy," Johan whispered, "Grandma is so rich, that bowl is still full of money. There's so much money there, she won't even know that we're taking her pennies."

On the fourth day when the ice-cream man came, we did not even bother looking for Grandma. We went straight for the bowl which had been overflowing. We were both in such a hurry that we simultaneously reached for the money.

Once again we stood on our tiptoes and stretched stealthily to poke our fingers into the bowl, only to feel something sticky and slimy. We didn't dare make any noise to show our surprise--or guilt. Slowly we pulled our fingers out--coated with thick black stuff, dirt, and India ink.

In a flash we ran out to wash our hands. In spite of the soap and water, the black stain remained. Since Grandma always came to our rescue, no matter what the problem was, we innocently marched into the kitchen and sought advice about cleaning our fingers.

Without even turning to look at our black fingers, she said, "That is what happens to children who take money without asking."

We were surprised that we were caught, so we apologized. We tried to impress her with how noble and considerate we were by explaining that we did not want to disturb her sleep.

She wasn't impressed. "No excuses. For taking money, people go to jail. This time you are lucky. Instead of a jail sentence, you get only black fingers."

She did help us clean our hands with some kind of oil, but she also made us clean that fancy bowl.

10

God's Daughter

Mrs. Leila Parsi was the second wife of a rich businessman who did not have any children but kept getting married to younger women with the hopes of having them. It never occurred to him that he himself could be at fault. After he married his third wife, he spent less time with the other wives. Leila, for all practical purposes, lived alone in a house with a married couple as her servants, both older than she.

One day Leila had routine errands to run in town, yet she wore a very stylish black chador and black shoes, indicating her wealth. Along the way a beggar lady attracted her attention--not because she was old, gray haired and unkempt like all the others who squatted on the sidewalks with a bowl of coins in front of them--but because she had a little girl sitting next to her. The little one was just as unkempt as the older one, with hair matted like dirty ropes and her dress draping her skinny frame like a torn curtain. Her unusually large sparkling brown eyes gave Leila the idea of the possibility of a very bright future for the child.

The girl was naturally curious of what was going on. As soon as Leila stopped to drop a few coins into the bowl, the girl stopped playing with her stones that she chose from the gutter that ran down the center of the street. She stood up, wiggled her bare toes free of the dirt, and peered into the bowl.

"There was an unusual grace in the way she moved," thought Leila. "You have a beautiful daughter," she commented. "What's her name?"

"Oh, she is not my daughter. She is God's daughter. Reza Shah's soldiers killed her father and her mother died with typhoid. She keeps following me around wherever I go. No one else seems to care what happens to her." Noticing how fascinated Leila was with the little girl, the beggar lady suggested, "If you like her, take her with you. She is quite healthy."

Now Leila studied the girl more closely and asked her, "What's your name?"

Looking down at the ground, she said, "Parvin."

The beggar looked at Leila again and somewhat forcefully, suggested, "Just give me a couple of tumans for what I have spent on her and take her with you. She is a good girl. You won't be disappointed."

Leila, who had been living alone, thought many times of adopting a child. Suddenly the idea of it all excited every pore of her body. She gave the money, equivalent to about two dollars, to the beggar and gently held the dirt encrusted hand of the girl. "OK, Parvin. Let's go."

Without saying a word Parvin obliged, but turned around to take one last look at her shabby friend.

The beggar clutched the money, slipped it between her bosoms, and took one long look at the girl, repeating, "Go, go, go, go on. This is your lucky day."

Leila suddenly stopped and pulled two tumans out of her expensive leather purse, dropped them in front of the beggar, and threatened, "I do not want to see you in this neighborhood anymore. If I ever see you around, I will have the police arrest you and take you to jail."

The beggar took the money, made a face showing disdain for the rich lady, and added this money to the rest next to her body. "Yes, Ma'am," she mumbled, struggling to unknot her arthritic legs. "I am leaving right now. I promise you will never see me again." She knew that such a rich lady could influence the police very easily.

Impeccably dressed Leila and shabby little Parvin walked hand in hand down the middle of the narrow street. At the entrance to the women's public bathhouse, Leila left the urchin with Mrs. Dallak, one of the attendants. "Give her a good bath and throw her clothes away. In half an hour I will be back with clean clothes."

The only way to have new clothes was to have them tailor made. In this emergency Leila hurried to the home of her cousin Belghace to borrow a few for her new daughter. With excitement and happiness Leila related the entire incident.

As years went by, Parvin grew even more beautiful.

11
Mitra

When Mitra turned 13, she noticed blood on her underwear. Since no one had ever told her about menstruation, she was very frightened, almost hysterical. Wondering how she could have become victim of some shameful disease, she dared not confide in her mother. Regardless of consequences, she had to keep her distress secret. While she was able to find rags to protect her clothing somewhat, she had no place to discard the evidence of her plight. She decided to hide the soiled items in her mother's chest room, where anyone seldom went.

One day when the mother went for some clothing kept in storage, she was taken aback by a putrid odor and the sight of dark red wrinkled cloth.

Since Mitra was the only young lady in the house, the mother solved the mystery immediately. She became furious. She called her daughter every name under the sun and accused her of flaunting her womanhood to the world.

The daughter became more confused than ever. First she had no idea what her health problem was. Now she had no idea what her moral problem was. The only thing she knew was what her mother had told her: she was the worst example of humanity in the entire world. Her sobbing continued as her frustration intensified. Without any conversation, not even "Good night," Mitra went to her room for the night.

The following morning when the mother called to wake her for school, Mitra did not stir. The mother spouted another volley of insults, positive that her daughter refused to obey.

After her anger had her head throbbing, the mother stormed into the bedroom, screaming for Mitra to get out of that bed and get dressed for school. At the bedside the mother shook her daughter with force she never realized she had.

Mitra offered no resistance. Mitra was dead.

After a few chaotic hours the doctor informed the family that Mitra had taken an overdose of opium pills which were kept in the medicine cabinet to alleviate occasional discomfort, like a headache.

12
Love

When I was still in grade school, I thoroughly enjoyed going to cousin Meena's house when the figs on the tree were at their ripest. Since Cousin Meena was much older than I, I hardly ever said more to her than *Salaam.* During these visits the children spent the time climbing the tree and gorging themselves on the fruit, while the adults gossiped.

Almost as unusual as that fig tree was the bickering between Meena and her husband. Even when they had guests, they would nitpick. Between bits of news shared with the relatives, they would find something about each other to argue about. For instance, when one asked for salt during a meal, the other would interrupt whatever was going on, ask why, and wait for an answer.

As superintendent of a girls' high school in Tehran, Meena naturally ordered everyone around all day long, including her husband. As a colonel in the army, her husband was also used to giving orders all day long. In spite of the fact that they did live together, they seemed to have disregarded each other their entire lives.

A while after Meena had retired, she was hospitalized for cardiovascular disease and gangrene of the foot. Rather than undergo the necessary amputation of her leg, she swore at the doctors and signed herself out of the hospital--in spite of the fact that her husband advised her to listen to the doctor.

To avoid confrontation at home her husband continued to disregard her as much as possible and kept his distance. Two weeks later, she died, probably because of septicemia, infection of the blood. Over and over again the husband told everyone how much he missed her.

A year later he too died.

Too bad they did not listen to my grandmother, who used to say, "In marriage, you should look for a friend, not for a lover. Love disappears; friendship lasts."

13
Cyrus

People marry for innumerable reasons. After suffering the anguish of gonorrhea, Uncle Cyrus decided to get married.

By 1917, Cyrus had already been employed for four years and saved a considerable amount of his wages. An enterprising young man about 18 years old, he decided to manage a business for himself. On Lalehzar Avenue he rented a shop for three tumans (about $3.00) a month and invested his savings in equipment to roll cigarettes and pack them 10 to a box ready for sale.

Soon his business flourished to a point that he needed an assistant. He hired Morteza, a gentleman five years younger than he. They each had two years of schooling which equipped them with the skills of reading, writing, and keeping records of their accounts.

By the time Cyrus was 22 years old his business thrived. Morteza, his first employee, by now was 17 and in charge of about 10 people mostly teenage boys, who rolled cigarettes by hand. Cyrus and Morteza became good friends by now and spent much of their free time together. They often went out to drink and patronize Sharhr-No, the red-light district of Tehran.

A few days after one of these escapades Cyrus noticed purulent discharge from his urethra. At the time, other than the burning sensation, his only discomfort was the discharge, which hardly disturbed him. In a few weeks, however, his pain became unbearable. With every attack he screamed and cursed God for creating the gonococcus, the bacteria which cause gonorrhea.

When he eventually consulted a physician for relief, his problem was diagnosed as gonorrhea and bilateral orchitis, or inflammation of the testicles. Treatment of gonorrhea at the time was worse than the disease. Disinfectants which were used to irrigate the urinary tract caused even more pain. Several weeks later Cyrus returned to work feeling better.

As he entertained the thoughts of marriage, his mother was ecstatic. She spent much of her time going around in search of a "decent" girl from a "good" family.

Eventually she narrowed her choice to Yasaman, the 18-year-old daughter of a religious businessman. Because Yasaman never attended school, but prayed every day, the girl was an excellent candidate. After both sets of parents agreed to the marriage, the young people were allowed to see each other for the first time, but only in the presence of others.

Two years after they were married, the wife of Morteza (Cyrus's friend) was glowing as she nursed her first child.

Yasaman still was not pregnant. This siutation disturbed Yasaman, as well as her mother. Together they consulted a clergyman who suggested certain daily prayers and visits to a shrine not far from Tehran. At the shrine they devoutly decorated the carved woodwork with delicate ribbons. They lit candles near the grave of the entombed saint, threw money on his sarcophagus, and prayed for pregnancy.

After a few such visits Yasaman revealed her plight to the mullah. Her predicament became worse, she confided, when her husband began to spend more time than ever with his friend Morteza. "Could he be homosexual?" she wondered.

The clergyman suggested she prepare a meal from the mullah's special recipe and feed it to her husband without telling him what it was.

Yasaman could not wait to attend the circumcision of her 6-year-old nephew.

When the operation was done, she helped her sister clean up. She picked up the stained clothes and sheets, as well as the foreskin which she wrapped in leftover gauze and tucked into the pocket of her skirt.

That evening Yasamen served *kofteh*, ground meat. For her husband she added something special--one that had the foreskin mixed in--according to the mullah's recipe.

In spite of all the effort, Yasamen never enjoyed motherhood.

Uncle Cyrus, who had become increasingly wealthy, became less and less interested in his relatives. Socially he preferred his friends.

The women in our family delighted in gossiping about this man. For years I heard so many snippets of these incidents I really never knew what to believe. Generations of women seemed to delight in repeating any version of Cyrus's misery, adding or editing details simply for the titillating effect. I hardly knew the man. Since he was much older than I, our relationship was practically nonexistent. By the time I was old enough to be curious about sexual functions, Cyrus had already become somewhat of a legendary character.

14

Circumcision

One morning I was taken to the public bath by my mother for the last time. "After this, circumcision, you will go to the men's public bath with your father or uncles."

"What is circumcision?" I asked my mother apprehensively.

"Nothing, dear. Don't worry. Nobody is going to hurt you. You will be all right."

I was only 5 years old, but I sensed something not true about my mother's words. Even at this early age, I had heard about little boys getting their penises cut off in a procedure called "circumcision."

As the guests arrived that warm afternoon, a huge Persian rug was spread out in the yard. A mattress was placed in the corner of the rug along with clean white sheets and a short clean wrap around cloth, previously measured to my size, made by my mother. Since circumcision makes a boy's lower body rather sensitive, I was to wear this loose garment around my body like a sarong crisscrossed in front with the corners tied around my neck. All preparations made, my mother served cookies and tea from the samovar.

When Mr. Reza, the barber from Shahabad Avenue, arrived with a little bag like a doctor's, I knew that something strange was definitely going to happen. I hid in the basement.

In the courtyard the barber had tea and cookies with the other men--my father, two uncles, and an elderly cousin. Women, including my mother, a few aunts and female cousins stayed inside the living room, enjoying more tea.

Soon my father called me, but I did not answer. Uncle Nasser knew where I was, so he came down to the basement, only to find me in tears.

"Oh, come on. Don't cry. The whole thing takes only a few seconds. Tomorrow you'll have forgotten about whatever happened. Let's go. Everyone's waiting for you."

Even though I felt sure that something terrible was about to happen, I took my uncle's hand and followed obediently, still sobbing.

The men in the yard and the ladies in the room, all stopped talking to give me their undivided attention. Only my mother felt a twinge of remorse, as tears filled her eyes. To the rest the event was quite exciting, certainly one of the more interesting diversions of the year.

When Mr. Reza and Uncle Nasser forced my pants off, I was more reluctant than ever to be in this courtyard. I kicked and squirmed, but the men towered over me, ignoring my tears. "Lie down," they commanded and turned me upright on my back, exposing the most private part of my body to the entire world. Uncle Nasser knelt at my head, while Mr. Reza sat at my feet. To keep me immobile, my uncle took my hands, placed each one under each of my knees firmly, all the while pulling my legs apart and upward. The position alone with Uncle Nasser almost lying on top of my head made me more frightened than ever.

Mr. Reza, the barber, burned some cotton and ran his sharp shiny shaving razor blade over the cotton to sterilize it. Each time the barber brandished the blade, I screamed louder and louder. With neither warning nor anesthesia Mr. Reza grabbed the foreskin and cut it from the penis. I screamed, wiggled, screamed, and wiggled till utter exhaustion made me feel that I was about to die. Blood poured all over me, as well as the sheets. The agony became more and more unbearable with every millisecond of the immolation.

In the eyes of the adults, the ritual may have lasted less than a minute, but in the mind of the victimized child, the procedure was endless torture that I would never forget. Uncle Nasser and Mr. Reza immediately stood up, finding the blood somewhat messy, but they just left me sob in my pain and humiliation. My mother ran from the living room to the courtyard to comfort me as best as she could, wrapping the specially made cloth around my limp body.

When I awoke, the guests were gone.

15

Mutilation

Surgery is always coupled with risk. Performance of circumcision is no different. Inadequate facilities or equipment, lack of technical skill, fragile condition of the person, and complications of the procedure may endanger the individual.

As early as the Stone Age circumcision was practiced--undoubtedly with extremely primitive equipment, like knives made of sharpened stone. The surgery must have been excruciatingly painful. The pain, however, was stoically tolerated for the observance of a sacrificial act to unite man with his god. Such self-imposed obligations blinded the religious person of the torture imposed on his victim before sacrificing him to the gods.

At the dawn of civilization man was commanded, "Thou shalt not kill." (Deuteronomy 5:17) Still unable to forgo sacrificial practices, man had to satisfy his desire to spill some blood in the name of God by cutting his own flesh or preferably that of someone younger. Clearly, circumcision of one's child was much better than death or torture. In Genesis 22:1-13 God told Abraham, "Take now thy son . . . for a burnt offering." After Abraham unquestioningly followed God's orders, an angel called to him to release his son from the pile of twigs, "Lay not thy hand upon the lad." God rewarded Abraham for his obeisance.

Throughout history no one ever questioned the practice of circumcision, just as Abraham did not question the orders from God. The oldest and most prevalent surgical procedure done throughout the world, circumcision was practiced long before organized monotheistic religions and definitely before organized medicine. References in the Bible to circumcision occur often, fifteen times alone in Genesis.

According to Genesis 17:13, God demands that it be done. "He that is born in thy house and he that is bought by thy money, must need be circumcised: and my covenant shall be in your flesh for everlasting covenant."

About a hundred years ago in England female circumcision was recommended as a treatment for masturbation. Now, however, the procedure is illegal in England, as well as Canada. In the United States, in hopes of curtailing the horrendous practice of female circumcision, there's a bill pending in the United States Congress to make it illegal. There is, unfortunately, no such move anywhere in the world to stop the medically unnecessary act of circumcision in boys.

In the October 1995 issue of The Atlantic Monthly Linda Burstyn tells how the custom of female circumcision, infibulation, recently noticed in Egypt and Ethiopia, is slowly creeping into the United States. A 1993 issue of American Journal of Obstetric and Gynecology reports consequences of the practice ranging from acute infection to hemorrhage and occasional death. Long term complications vary from psychological problems to sexual dysfunctions.

Fortunately, female or pharaonic circumcision (excision of the clitoris) afflicts a very small number of women today. Since the name 'pharaonic' describes the operation, it obviously existed during the time of the pharaohs and before the time of Moses. Likewise, male circumcision goes back to prehistoric times, but today it is still a common practice prescribed by some religions and even doctors.

My parents were no different. For the sake of religion, they had me, as well as my brothers, circumcised without anesthesia when we were five years old.

My medical career, along with my personal observations, convinces me that Nature should not be tampered with, unless an anomaly needs correction.

Years ago circumcision, like many other surgical procedures, was performed by barbers. It was no different in Iran in 1930 when I was circumcised. By the time I was in medical school, only licensed physicians were legally permitted to do this procedure only in hospitals under sterile conditions.

One day in 1948 in Tehran an experienced physician, performing circumcision on twin 5-year-old boys, injected a local anesthetic. Both boys gradually became very quiet and sleepy. Pretty soon it was obvious that they were comatose. Hypotension, shallow breathing and a weak pulse were followed by cyanosis and pinpoint pupils. In less than two hours the boys were dead. Investigation proved that what the surgeon thought was novocain was in reality morphine.

In 1953 during my internship in New York City I admitted a very unusual case of a 22-year-old man who suffered a mild chronic inflammation and severe pruritus (itching) of the prepuce. To alleviate the condition, a private physician, a urologist, performed circumcision. During his 48-hour stay in the hospital the patient was naturally sore. Aside from receiving antibiotics, he was under observation for possible hemorrhage. Every time a certain young nurse wearing a short skirt worked in his room, he would wince, scream, and complain of jolts of pain. After I analyzed the situation, I had no choice but to write this order in his chart:

1. Young nurses with short skirts must stay out of Room 321.

2. The patient needs an ice bag.

16

Char Chappy

On a warm summer afternoon when grownups were sleeping, my 10-year-old brother, a cousin and I got 10 cents from my mother to go to the movies. Squealing with delight, we ran from the house to the theater four blocks down the street. Our mood changed abruptly when the man selling tickets told us, "You each need 10 cents."

"We don't have 30 cents," my brother said. "This is all we have--10 cents."

"I can't let you in for that money."

So we waited and from the corner of our eyes kept looking at this man in the booth as he busily exchanged tickets for coins.

A minute before one o'clock just as the movie was about to start, he looked at us and said, "Oh, all right. Give me the *rial.* Go ahead. Go in."

My brother gave him the money, but the man didn't give us any ticket. As we filed past him, he yelled to the usher, "Let them go. They're O.K."

As we walked in, we found the place half empty. As usual, we sat in the very first row. We were just in time for the silent movie to start.

My brother cheered, "Oh, Char Choppy!"

"Oh, he is good," my cousin said, clapping his hands as loud as he could.

A man stood to the left of the screen and explained the details of the story, The Gold Rush. We paid little attention to the man. Just the sight of Char Choppy's baggy pants, twirling cane, and wiggly little black mustache made us laugh and laugh and laugh. When he almost tripped over his oversized shoes and split his undersized jacket we laughed so much more till we rocked in our seats.

What was even more exciting was to tell the boys with whom we played in the street about the movie. We lorded over them the fact that we had seen a movie and they had not.

Two weeks later six of us went to the theater. Once again we stood in the same spot and stared at the same man who sold tickets in the same booth.

"What do you kids want?" he growled.

"We want to see the movie," said my brother as he worked his way in front of the rest of us, face to face with the man--only it was more like face to stomach.

"Ten cents apiece," he demanded without even looking at us.

"We have only 20 cents."

"So, only two of you can go in."

All six of us walked around the entrance, looked at the posters about the movie featuring Laurel and Hardy, and stared jealously at the people who were entering the theater with tickets in their hands. Every other minute we turned our heads to give the ticket seller one of our woeful looks.

Just before the movie started, he said, "O.K. kids, give me the money. Next time you come make sure you each bring 10 cents. Understand? Otherwise, I won't let you in. Did you get that?"

"Yeah," we each giggled, pushing each other to move faster.

Once again as we filed past him, he yelled to the usher, "Let them go. They're O.K."

17
School

Two weeks before the beginning of the school year my mother took me to the tailor's to select the traditional gray fabric for my school uniform. The material plus the fee for making the suit totaled $2.00. We proceeded to buy a pair of shoes for me for 80 cents, a backpack for 50 cents, and the usual school supplies of pencil, notebook, and the prescribed textbook which all came to less than a dollar.

That particular year we moved from the city to the outskirts, where bus service was infrequent (not to mention expensive with fares of two or three cents) and horse and carriage transportation was more prohibitive. School buses were unheard of. Obviously, the average person did not have a car, even though the King had a Rolls Royce. Rumor had it that the gold front bumper alone cost $2,000.00, the price of a house.

When the first day of school arrived, I wore my new suit, shoes, and backpack. My mother handed me my standard two-level aluminum lunch container. The bottom part held leftovers from the previous night's dinner, while the upper part had my bread and apple. My spoon hung from special hooks alongside the handle.

My brother was told to take care of me. As a young man of 15, he was more interested in his friends and the girls who walked by than in a kid brother. As soon as we were beyond seeing-distance of our house, he unloaded his food container on me. Apparently, carrying a lunch bucket did not present a very good image. All my baggage became more and more cumbersome as we walked and walked and walked for at least an hour and a half. The closer we got to the school, the greater distance my brother walked between us. A kid brother did not fit into his image of a dashing young man either. Trying to catch up with him, I kept walking faster and faster, sometimes even running a few yards. My new shoes pinched so badly, I had to stop a few times to readjust my toes. When I started to cry, he really wanted nothing to do with me. Instead of sympathy, I got a scolding, "You're going to make me late for school. If you can't walk, you should stay home."

Eventually we reached my school, just a little before his. In disgust he took his lunch and told me to wait for him on that very spot until he came after school.

By now I was already in tears. And I didn't even enter the building! I had no idea where my classroom could be. Finally one of the teachers helped me join a group of kids. "Your classmates," he said. I was directed to take my lunch to a place called "lunch room." This was very small. Since most of the children lived near enough to go home for lunch, there were very few lunches that needed storage.

The school itself was huge. At one time it probably belonged to some rich man. The many rooms were built around three courtyards, each room having a bare one-hundred watt bulb dangling from the ceiling. Twelve of these rooms were converted into classrooms, two rooms for each grade. There was neither running water nor indoor bathroom facilities.

As I joined my classmates (all boys), we formed a line. We were assigned to one room or the other by size. The taller children went in one group; the smaller, in another. I fell into the latter. First of all, we were instructed to pray. Like a few others, I did not know the words. They were in Arabic, not the language spoken in Iran.

After the prayer session, a bell rang which signaled us to enter our classroom, where we were welcomed by a very old man--stooped, bearded, wrinkled, and bald--who seemed about 90 years old. He probably had very little formal education, but he was kind and he did know how to teach the alphabet.

At odd moments throughout the day I cried. Heaven only knows what triggered my tears. Stress of the unfamiliar situation? Separation from my mother? The stiffness of the new shoes? The school personnel had no concern about my psychological welfare. They probably never even heard of psychology or any of the great men like Freud. For that matter, no one else in my world knew or cared either. And I had absolutely no idea why I had to go to school anyway.

At noon I was crying again. The teacher at least came to me to see why. He suggested that I go home for lunch, like most of the other kids. Through sobs I explained that I lived so far away, I had to bring my lunch.

"Then go get your lunch," he said.

"I don't know where the lunch room is." The mere thought of this problem only increased my misery.

He took my hand, led me to the room, and left. Everyone else there was bigger than I. At the sight of me, two of the oldest boys stopped talking, looked at each other, and then started laughing. All I cared about was my lunch.

When I opened my container, it was empty. My food was gone. The discovery inspired more tears. This time a janitor wondered why I was so upset. Luckily, it was the janitor, whose apartment was part of the school complex. Immediately he went for some bread, cheese, and a glass of water. We then agreed that from now on I would give him my lunch for safe keeping every day.

In Iran it was customary to enjoy a two-hour lunch time. For me it was a lonely two hours. I can't remember how many more times I cried. I was never happier to see 2:00 p.m.. At the sound of a bell, we all lined up. At the sound of another bell, we marched quietly into the classroom.

The boy who sat next to me in the morning was missing. I was more distressed when I realized that now I lost a partner. He soon appeared, however, and explained to the teacher that he lives far from the school. The teacher suggested that he bring his lunch.

Later on I told him that I too live so far that I have to bring my lunch. I invited him to join me and suggested that he give his food container to the janitor to make sure that the wise guys don't eat his food. This pact sealed our friendship which lasted throughout high school. That day he even stayed with me after school till my brother came. Together we walked behind my brother, once again I was laden with my backpack and two food containers, mine and my brother's.

When we got home, I couldn't wait to go to school again to see and have lunch with my new friend.

18

Drowning

While everyone was inside the house, enjoying a summer siesta, a blood curdling scream shortened this customary pleasure. Three-year-old Azar was crying and screaming--all alone in the courtyard--in spite of the fact that children were constantly warned about the danger of going near the pond unaccompanied by an adult. With the fear of death imprinted on our minds, we were constantly advised to scream for help, should a need for help ever arise.

Within seconds every member of our large family spilled out of every room of the house. Azar just kept crying and screaming, louder and louder, standing about three feet from the edge of the manmade pond. Whatever caused this panic was hardly placated by the hovering of the adults, all questioning Azar. The uncustomary disarray of bare feet, unbuttoned clothing, disheveled hair was enough to create worse panic.

"What's wrong?" pleaded my mother, bending down in front of her.

The reminder of something being wrong just made the crying and screaming increase a few decibels.

Being five years older than Azar, I assumed the big-brother role and edged my way between the legs of these relatives. "What's wrong?" I whispered, bravely controlling my own fear of whatever danger was lurking.

Azar still sobbed uncontrollably, but she did point toward the pond.

All I saw were the pretty little fish that wiggled around all year round.

With a shrill of one more scream, she wailed, "Rescue it, rescue it. It's going to drown and die!"

Staring at the pond, no one saw any evidence of any drowning. The frisky fish just kept swimming. Even the broom that floated in the water didn't disturb them.

For that matter, the broom floating in the water

didn't disturb anyone else either, because this pond provided what we needed to do the dishes or water the flowers.

"Who's drowning?" pleaded my mother.

"The broom," sobbed Azar, "the broom."

19

Bee

No one was happier to move back to our old house in the city than I, because now I was only two blocks away from Asquar. Every day we walked back and forth to school together, sat next to each other in the classroom, and after school hours played together--always careful not to get dust on our uniform, the only clothes we had. We had a mutual understanding to check each other's gray Bermuda shorts, white shirt, and gray Nehru jacket to make sure that every inch of our clothing made us as presentable as seven-year-olds could be. By the end of the second grade, we were very good pals.

At the beginning of our second year, a fall day was so pleasant that all the doors and windows were wide open. The children were taking turns reading out loud a story about Rostam, a legendary powerful warrior. My attention shifted to a bee on my right leg. I grabbed it with my hand, threw it on the floor, and stomped on it--as hard as I could. Without a doubt Mr. Khavary, our teacher, wondered who was hammering away at the floor and why a very quiet boy like me was doing a noisy jig in his classroom which was always as silent as a tomb.

Within a minute I passed out and fell on top of Asquar. He was so frightened, he screamed. All the other children stared toward our desk and whispered to each other in wonder.

Mr. Khavary probably never had such a disruptive experience in his entire life. He must have become excited, trying to calm the other children as best he could in this pandemonium, and immediately carried me to the office of the principal, Mr. Modeer. While there was telephone service in the school, there wasn't any at our home.

Mr. Tameez, the janitor, was told to take me home and to let Asquar lead the way. For the entire twenty minutes that it took to reach my house, Mr. Tameez carried me over his shoulder, while I remained unconscious.

"*Vai, vai!*" gasped my mother. She was sure that I was dead. Hearing the commotion, her brother who lived across the courtyard came to help. After she thanked the janitor and my very best friend, she gave the older man some money for his trouble. Mr. Tameez and Asquar returned to school.

Then it was Uncle Nasser's turn to carry me as he and my mother walked through the narrow street toward the busy intersection where the horse and buggy waited for passengers. At the address of the doctor's office my mother paid the driver and left the buggy.

Once we were inside, Dr. Rastegar's nurse covered my red swollen leg with an ice bag. Gradually, I regained consciousness. In my delirium I noticed the nurse mixing some white powder from a paper package with water till it bubbled like alka seltzer. She held the glass to my mouth till I drank the last salty drop.

The drink was given to me probably for my mother's peace of mind, rather than for my trauma of the bee attack. (At that time there was no treatment for anaphylactic shock resulting from an insect sting.)

That evening at home my leg was still hard, swollen, and red, but I felt better. Instead of playing with the other children after school as we usually did, Asquar spent a few hours with me and showed me the homework that I was expected to do for the next day. Sprawled on the floor, propped on one elbow, we practiced penmanship by copying from pages of the textbook designed to give us practice of every letter of the alphabet.

The next day at school Mr. Khavary lectured about bees and cautioned everyone to stay away from them. We had to be extremely alert because without central air conditioning (unheard of at the time), the windows had to remain opened. There were no screens either.

Years later, as a physician, I learned that every year bee stings cause twice as many deaths as snake bites do. Most people stung by hymenoptera--bees, wasps, hornets, and yellow jackets--develop local swelling, itching, and redness. One percent of those, however, are so sensitive to the venom that they have an allergic reaction. Such anaphylactic shock causes respiratory distress and vascular collapse, followed by urticaria (hives), skin pruritus (itching) and angioedema (swelling of the skin). Nowadays epinephrin, antihistamine and corticosteroid are used very effectively to counteract such a reaction. Not one of these, however, was available in 1932.

20

Shashoo

Occasionally I did not get out of bed at the expected time in the morning. Aunt Moheeb, on the other hand, always was up and around before everyone else in the household.

With the first note of the muezzin's chant from the minaret, she was wide awake, intoning with him, "God is great." She immediately performed *payab*, the ritual of cleansing, and devoutly said her morning prayers.

The other part of her morning ritual was to supervise the children as they prepared for school.

Whenever she noticed that I was not in step with the other children, she quietly inched her way toward my bed. She knew very well why I was not getting up. In a flash she pulled off my comforter and scolded, "Did you wet your bed again, you miserable *shashoo*? Get up and change your god damn underwear." (In the 1920's and 1930's in Iran pajamas as sleeping attire were not common. Everyone slept in underwear.) In front of her I was frightened. In front of my brothers and sisters I was ashamed. Seven-year-olds were not supposed to wet the bed.

Reluctantly I raised my head from the pillow, swiveled to the edge of the bed, but remained sitting. My brothers and sisters who shared the room sniggered. Aunt Moheeb towered over me like an angry giant. When she decided that I was not moving fast enough to please her, she thrust her massive hands under my bony armpits with a huff, lifted me off the bed, and hurled me across the room like a javelin. For a few seconds there I lay, wondering what more she could do to ruin my day.

As I cowered in the corner, she pulled off my wet pants in front of everybody. Now with my buttocks exposed, she kept me flat on the rug with her left hand on my neck while she used her right hand to beat me with a wooden stick. As I cried and screamed, she too screamed, angrier than before. Her adrenalin gave her the strength to beat my bottom only so much harder. Red lines immediately surfaced. My bottom soon became swollen. When she finally let up, I got dressed, picked up my bookbag and headed for school without even eating breakfast.

So much confusion made me late for school. Noticing my red swollen eyes, Mr. Khavary, the kind, young teacher, asked, "What happened? Why are you late?"

The mere reference to the turmoil of the morning produced more tears. "I'm sorry I'm late," I sobbed.

"O.K.," Mr. Khavary said. "Go ahead and sit down."

As tears still came down my face, I confessed, "I'm sorry. I don't think I can sit down." The welts on my body still smarted.

Mr. Khavary, who apparently had seen such an incident before, whispered, "Oh, O.K. You can stand next to your desk until you feel better. Then you can sit down."

When I looked around and noticed another boy sitting on his jacket to cushion the wooden seat, I felt better. I realized that I was not the only one who wet his bed. Immediately I too sat on my jacket.

That evening I kept my distance from Aunt Moheeb as much as I could. When I noticed her anywhere near me, I kept my eyes down. When I eventually glanced at her, she was standing, facing Mecca, praying again.

21
CockFight

When I was a kid in Iran, my brother and I--like any other kids anywhere--enjoyed excitement and thrillers, as long as we were the spectators, not participants. I as a second grader and Mohsen as a seventh-grader played with toys that were clever inventions of our own or copied versions of someone else's product. Out of rags we made balls. From two pieces of wood (a long one to hit with, like a bat, and a short one to be hit, like a ball) we enjoyed *alack-doelack*. Only pet cats were allowed indoors. Pet dogs were kept outdoors. The only other animals we ever saw were those sparsely pictured in our textbooks. Other than the apes in the Tarzan movies or the lion at the end of an MGM production, we never had any idea of the sounds that animals made. After a movie, all the kids left the theater either lumbering like the apes or roaring like lions.

Once my brother Mohsen and I were allowed to keep a few chickens. At the end of the courtyard we built a coop for them. Before long, they grew bigger and didn't tolerate our handling them. Hens laid eggs and roosters made noise.

One day I noticed a hen sleeping right on top of her fragile eggs. I ran into the house and begged my mother to keep the other chickens away from the hen. To keep me happy and probably quiet, my mother piled some shredded newspapers in a corner of the basement and let the hen rest comfortably. To announce her hunger the hen would run out and cackle loud enough to wake up the dead until we fed her some bits of bread or leftover cooked rice. Completely ignoring us, the hen gobbled it and strutted back to her new bed in the basement. She never minded our watching her, but violently objected if we even tried to touch her or her eggs.

Three weeks later magic permeated our lives. As we

casually walked by the roost in the basement, something seemed different. A closer look proved that it was an egg that was different. It had thin crooked lines on it. As I stared at these lines, they began to crack open--wider and wider. A baby chick poked her head through the shell to greet me. It came out all wet, but in a blink it fluffed itself dry.

"Chirp," said my new pet.

"Good morning," I answered excitedly.

"Chirp," he repeated.

"Chirp," I repeated, hoping it would understand my accent in chicken language.

I was so excited, I didn't know whether to run back to the house to tell everyone else or to stay and watch the baby chick. One quick call on the top of my lungs soon brought the rest of my family to stand in awe next to me. I think the chicks liked us. As soon as all of us gathered around the nest, the first hatched chick pushed himself out of the shell and shook himself loose to fluff its silken feathers. I leaned over to pick him up, but its mother stretched her neck to peck at me.

"Here, chick chick," I whispered. Believe it or not, he came!

"Here, chick chick," my brother echoed and about 10 more fuzz balls answered his call.

Cottony fluff made a halo around chick chick's whole body. All of them were like some teeny tiny yellow clouds on webbed orange feet. He and his 10 brothers followed the mother hen everywhere, as though they were held together by an invisible string. At the sight of Pashmy, our cat, Mother Hen spread her wings to rein in the little ones close to her body. Her cackling announced her displeasure to the entire world.

The cat understood this much chicken language and stayed away. Pashmy seemed afraid of the hen. By the end of the day they returned to the basement where my mother made sure they had enough food, especially some millet for the babies.

Eventually they grew strong enough to join the rest of the chickens. On the sly, Mohsen and I fed the two young roosters bits of meat that we saved from our own meals. We were hoping that this diet would turn them into fighters. Mohsen even did some research about cock fighting.

Pitting trained cocks against each other was an old sport, common in Persia, Greece and Rome. Recently in Latin America, Asia, and parts of the United States, this sport has grown in popularity. The cock is considered defeated when it refuses to fight. Apparently those who had serious cock fights knew that these fights had to be done on neutral ground as the cock who fought in his own nest ground always fought better as if it were defending his territory against a foreign intruder.

In about a year, it was Mohsen and I who had to do the fighting. My mother mentioned taking our new pets to the butcher's. We cried. Mother insisted. We cried. Mother got mad. We cried. Finally she allowed us to keep two roosters and two hens.

We soon became very proud of one of the roosters. He became so cantankerous, he would attack anyone in sight and chase Pashmy till the cat almost went crazy. It was most fun to see this rooster jump on any little girl's head and try to peck her skull through a bushy head of hair. He also considered it quite a challenge to greet adult guests with a lusty peck or scratch on their legs. Somehow, visitors did not share our glee.

One day Uncle Abdy came over with his wife Irandokht and their 3-year-old daughter Fahimeh. They were hardly at our doorstep when Mr. Rooster flew on Fahimeh's head. She screamed in terror and the rooster jumped to the ground. Uncle Abdy became furious. He was angry with my parents for letting this monster loose. My father would not tolerate to be reprimanded, so he yelled back. Within a half hour or so, everyone calmed down and enjoyed the hot tea from the Samovar and idle conversation about the antics of government officials ripping the chador off the ladies in the streets. Mother and Aunty Iran agreed that people should be allowed to dress as they wish, provided they remain decent. Fahimeh left her daddy's side to join the kids outside in the courtyard.

One second later Fahimeh let out a blood curdling scream. Mr. Rooster flew back on her head, parting her shiny blond hair again. And again she ran inside the house.

I was disappointed that she didn't even want to play with us.

Inside the house the same scenario repeated itself. Fahimeh sobbed uncontrollably, Uncle Abdy huffed at my father (thinking insults that he dared not express verbally). My father expressed his displeasure (likewise with his facial gestures, rather than words). Twenty minutes later all calmed down.

Fahimeh much preferred the conversation about toys outside to the debates about politics inside. Once again she hardly had one foot out of the door when the rooster attacked her again. Fahimeh screamed louder than ever. Uncle Abdy yelled louder than ever. He was so infuriated, he insisted that my father "kill the damn rooster right on the spot."

His wife then told my mother how he had recently bought a gun and practiced his aim by shooting chickens in the head. Uncle Abdy offered to bring his gun to our house to kill Mr. Rooster.

My father neither agreed nor disagreed. He simply listened, showing no reaction. He knew that Mohsen and I would never allow anyone to harm Mr. Rooster, let alone kill it.

Now it was Mohsen's and my turn to cry. Every time anyone used the word "kill," we increased our screaming one decibel. Father was not accustomed to such a disorganized house. Any other time, the split second anyone noticed him approaching the entrance, the children would run to the opposite end of the house and stay out of sight. Mother insisted that nothing, absolutely nothing, disturb father--not even the breeze. This day Father had gusty breezes from too many directions. If Mr. Rooster had not been so feisty and hard to catch, my father would have probably wrung its neck right then and there.

Two days later we came home from school, hopping with the news of the day and greetings to our roosters and hens. But we exchanged the news of the day with only one rooster and two hens. Where's Mr. Rooster? Bookbags in tow, we immediately ran to the chicken coop to see if our feisty friend were sick. Along the way we found feathers, exactly the same brownish red of Mr. Rooster's, lying near the pool.

22

Corruption

Third graders in Iran always had a lot of homework. For Friday, the only day we had off after six straight days of school, we were tortured with a double dose. This particular Friday we had 10 pages to copy for the sake of practicing penmanship.

In the absence of Mr. Lankarani, our teacher, a sixth grade student was placed in charge of the class. Row by row the children, all boys, filed out of their benches to line up in front of the room. This "substitute teacher" inspected every third grader's homework in turn one at a time, making sure that each kid had 10 pages completed. To prevent a child from presenting the same work for another assignment, it was customary for the teacher to draw a red line diagonally across the entire page as a symbol of work done satisfactorily.

When it was my turn to reach the head of the line next to the teacher's elevated desk, he counted and marked, "one, two, three, four, five, six, seven, eight, nine. One is missing," he yelled at me.

"No, it's not. There are 10."

"Don't lie to me," he stood up, shouted, and slapped me across the face.

I started to cry. I was not only physically hurt and angry, I was humiliated. "Count them again," I asserted myself in a slow, low voice, refusing to move on.

He did so. There were 10. "I'm sorry," he apologized, patting me on the head, as he sat down in the teacher's chair.

I returned to my bench next to four other boys and kept crying.

Even though corporal punishment was fairly common in school, I never had reason to be victimized by such inhumane behavior. None of my teachers ever punished me the whole year. Now this boy who is only a few years older than I decided to hit me. Since this sixth grader became the authority figure, I could not retaliate. Furthermore, there was no sense complaining to anyone, because he was the son of the principal.

Even among children, power corrupts.

23
King of Kings

It was not unusual for my mother to be able to prepare a meal for unannounced guests at a moment's notice.

One warm summer day in Tehran my father brought Mr. Malek home for lunch. As mayor of Babol in northern Iran, he was in Tehran on business with officials of the Ministry of Interior. As a graduate of the University of Tehran with a major in political science, he was an intelligent man with whom my father enjoyed discussing politics.

That very same day my older brother brought another guest, a distant relative by the name of Abbas Afshaar. As a descendant of Nadir Shah (1736-1747) it was only natural for this young man to have a regal bearing. He was tall, handsome, and impeccably dressed.

In spite of his royal lineage, his intellectual perspicacity was so limited that he was unable to graduate from high school. Thanks to an influential relative, however, Abbas spent his time in a government office doing insignificant work just to pass the time of day and earn a small monthly salary. In spite of such personal attention, he could not assume even these minimal responsibilities. As a consequence, he lost his job. Since he had nothing in particular to do, he readily accepted my brother's invitation to lunch.

That day my mother served *abdugh-khiar*, a mixture of yogurt, cucumber, chopped mint, ground walnuts, raisins and onions, seasoned with salt and pepper. To keep it cool and dilute the yogurt she added large pieces of ice. Into this mixture she dropped *nan e-khoshkeh*, a kind of flat bread, broken into bite sized pieces. After she welcomed the men, she simply added more yogurt which was always on hand.

For these two illustrious guests, my mother sent our elderly maid Naneh and me to the kaboby for servings of lamb kabob that came with tomatoes, onions and an assortment of herbs--like tarragon, mint, chives and basil.

Since the shop was only five minutes away, the food was still warm when it was placed on the *sofreh*, a white tablecloth spread over the Persian rug. (Chairs were not used during a meal. Everyone sat around the tablecloth.)

Such a heavy meal made everyone feel groggy, especially on a hot summer day. It was only natural for everyone to take a siesta, the men in one room and the women in another. Before resting, however, my mother and the maids cleared the *sofreh* and removed it.

Later in the afternoon around 5:00 p.m., when the yard was mostly in shade, the boys unrolled a Persian rug in the courtyard, where everyone gathered again to enjoy my mother's serving of assorted fruit, cookies, and darjeeling tea from the shiny brass samovar. My father and Mr. Malek continued to discuss politics, as though they had never stopped talking to take a nap. Abbas interjected, "Royalty in this country really belongs to our family. I, not Reza Kahn, should be *Shahanshah*, King of Kings."

Somewhat horrified, Mr. Malek tactfully suggested, "Young man, be careful how you talk outside. You can go to jail for such ideas--even get killed! Reza Shah's secret police can be anywhere and everywhere."

Such advice did not faze Abbas in the least, but he did remain quiet, only because he had nothing further to contribute.

As evening approached, Mr. Malek, whose obesity made walking difficult, invited Abbas to stroll with him along Lalehzar Avenue, a popular gathering place for the young and the restless to talk, window shop, or do real shopping. The stores were open between 6:00 and 11:00 p.m.; restaurants and theaters, till midnight.

Along the way Abbas suggested that he and Mr. Malek have dinner at Shemshad Restaurant to see what this new business establishment had to offer. They feasted on *dolmeh-ye barg-e mo* (stuffed grape leaves), *shirin polo* (rice with candied orange peel), *borani-e karafse* (chopped celery in yogurt), and *nan-e sangak* (flat crisp bread).

As they emptied the last drop of *sharab-e Shiraz* (red wine from Shiraz), Abbas shoved the check across the table to Mr. Malek. "Sorry, Sir," he apologized soulfully, "I don't have any money on me, but I'm sure that an important person like you, the Mayor of Babol, has enough to treat everyone in this restaurant."

Unfortunately, Mr. Malek had no money either. The embarrassment made him rather irritated and extremely nervous. "Abbas, why didn't you tell me before we walked into this place? Have you any idea of what we have to do now?"

Abbas stared at him nonchalantly, smiling, "Don't worry, Mr. Mayor. Just follow me."

Abbas stood up, adjusted his coat lapels, took a deep breath, and shrugged his shoulders. Mr. Malek stood up, staring at Abbas.

Abbas swept his eyes around this enormous dining area, turning full circle. Mr. Malek continued to stare at him, doubting the young man's sanity.

Slowly, confidently, Abbas walked toward the door, almost on a run in slow motion. Mr. Malek had no choice but to follow him, bouncing along at a much slower pace. Two hundred and fifty pounds did not make one's body a lithe frame like that of an Olympic sprinter's.

Outside the restaurant they headed toward a group of noisy young people and soon got lost among the crowd. When Mr. Malek finally caught up to Abbas and took a moment to catch his breath, Abbas began to laugh uncontrollably. Mr. Malek was the funniest person he had seen in a long time. "And wasn't it fun to run out without paying?" he asked Mr. Malek.

Without a word, the elderly gentleman turned on his heels and left Abbas with the crowd.

Within a few days all the relatives heard about the incident. My grandmother mentioned that for the past few months she had heard about the crazy things Abbas was saying. From the time that he lost his job, he became more and more roiled about his conviction that he is the one that should be on the throne.

Abbas's mother was convinced that her neighbor Marzi, a woman 10 years older than Abbas, was at fault. Marzi was so infatuated with Abbas, she cast a spell on him and altered his food by witchcraft. Abbas's mother was sure that Marzi was a witch.

Two weeks later, Abbas was still gloating over his

success of feasting free. This day he walked toward a jitney stand in Toopkhaneh Square. At the sight of a large shiny black American convertible, he ordered the young driver to get behind the wheel and take him to Saadabad Castle, which happened to be Reza Shah's summer home. Abbas was so well dressed and so handsome, the chauffeur dared not question such a request. Besides, Abbas slipped him a twenty-tuman bill (about $20.00)--four times the usual fare for this forty-minute ride.

Nearing the castle, the driver asked, "Sir, where would you like me to stop?"

"Go through the gate," answered Abbas. "Go inside."

As the car pulled up to the 25-foot iron gate, military guards pointed their guns at the head of the driver, who naturally did not proceed as directed. Within minutes more soldiers and then a commanding officer appeared. They had no trouble detecting the fraud. Instantly they beat Abbas and the driver, pummeling them unmercifully with their hardened fists. Before Abbas could think of something clever to say, he and the driver were on their way to jail.

After a few days in prison the driver was released, but Abbas was sent to the State Mental Hospital and diagnosed as schizophrenic.

Two weeks later he was discharged into the care of his parents.

No one ever saw this driver at the jitney stand anymore.

Abbas, likewise, was seldom seen. Since the parents owned a large house, Abbas busied himself quietly with weeding and arranging the flower beds. Every time the mother saw her son in such a pitiable state, through tears she blamed Marzi's witchcraft.

Two years later Abbas's mother died. Only he and his aged father occupied the building.

Marzi had been in love with Abbas as long as she could remember. Now that Abbas was in need of care, she felt that he would definitely want to marry her. She suggested the possibility to Abbas's great-aunt, pointing out that once she lived with him, she could take care of the entire house, including the father.

The mullahs frowned upon such a union. After all, Abbas had been declared schizophrenic and did spend time in an institution. It is illegal to marry someone who cannot swear to any responsibility. The clergyman proposed another idea, "Marry Abbas's 70-year-old father. He's too old to even bother with you and actually you are 10 years older than Abbas, but you will be able to take care of the son." Within a few weeks she became Abbas's stepmother.

People wondered with whom Marzi consummated the marriage--if ever. Most doubted that she would be able to cuddle up to either man. A few years later the father passed away, leaving Marzi and Abbas together till their old age and deaths.

24
Projector

The neighborhood kids patronized Mr. Tahreer's stationery store when they needed pens, pencils, notebooks, ink and inkpots. In addition to such necessities he sold strips of motion picture films no longer needed by the theaters. For a few pennies one could buy a single frame of a star--like Charlie Chaplin, Laurel and Hardy or Greta Garbo. For the same price one could get a whole strip of developed movie film showing lesser known stars or exotic animals.

On our days off from school when we were all finished with our fourth grade homework, my friends and I admired the movie stars by holding the pictures against the sun. Just the sight of Char Choppy made us laugh. We could care less that his name was really spelled C-h-a-r-l-i-e C-h-a-p-l-i-n.

One day in the store I overheard Mr. Tahreer and a customer discussing a way of looking at these pictures when the sun was not out. They devised a system of projecting their film in a dark place by using a magnifying glass, a box and a light.

I decided to adopt their brilliant idea. One afternoon, when everyone else was too busy to play with me, I went to our basement to find my own entertainment. I took a shoe box and made one small hole on each of the opposite ends to let the light shine through the length from one end to the other. On each of the wider sides I made a vertical slit through which I threaded the film directly in front of the path of the light. To thread the strip from left to right I used two pencils, like reels, one on each side of the box. Inside the box in front of the film I placed the magnifying glass, just right to enlarge the picture as it was to shine on the wall.

Since we did not have electricity and since I was not allowed to play with the oil lamps, I lighted a candle and placed it near the opening of the box, opposite the end that housed my film. That was my light source. While I attempted to adjust the film, a ball of fire rolled in front of me. The film blew up into dust. My hands were burning red. My face was stinging. I was lucky that the flame lasted less than a second and nothing flammable was around. In spite of my fright, I blew the candle out immediately.

As fast as I could, I ran to the pond in the courtyard to splash water on my hands and face. Just then my mother took one look at me and gasped in horror.

"What happened to you? Look at you. No eyelashes. No eyebrows. The hair on top of your head is singed."

After a closer look, she decided that the damage was minimal. She led me to the mirror and advised me to water my hands and face often as though I were a plant.

25
Moses

When school finally let out for summer vacation, there was big to-do at our house. One day we all had to pack our things: clothing, towels, etc., because we were going to Affjeh, a village in the mountains that was really just a summer resort.

Seldom did we travel anywhere. Something unusual was happening. My 18-year-old brother wanted my mother and the family to meet the 17-year-old sister of his friend.

It cost 20 cents to hire a horse and buggy to take my mother, two brothers, two sisters and me from our house to the bus terminal. After traveling by bus about 60 miles from Tehran, we rode donkeys along tortuous roads for almost the same distance but more time. My little sister sat in front of my mother, while I, like all the others, had a donkey all to myself. I was so excited. I felt like a cowboy on a horse in American movies. By nightfall we reached the village, laden with suitcases--my father's discards, worn from his European trips. We were all tired and ready for bed.

In the morning we met my brother's friend's family. As formal introductions were being made, my brother and this girl were allowed to look at each other and get red in the face. Sixty years ago it was customary for young people interested in each other to be chaperoned at all times. No matter where they turned, the family followed.

For my other brother and me, chaperoning was rather dull. We decided to go for a walk and explore. He was anxious to try out his new camera that he bought for $1.50. The 20-exposure roll of film cost another 10 cents. After making such an investment, he would allow no one, not even me, to touch his camera. He took pictures of everything. Many times I served as his human subject.

Today it was the donkey who was picture worthy and I was supposed to sit on it. First we had to ask permission from an old man about twice our age. That would be about 18. He not only consented, but helped me climb the donkey. This was so much fun, my smile must have reached my ears, until . . .

The donkey took off like a bullet and the bushes were reduced to a blur as we sped along the dirt road. Within minutes my face was all scratched from the extending twigs and I was pale from fright. Now it was the man's turn to smile and laugh hysterically. Obviously, the man touched the donkey on a sensitive spot that meant, "Go." Go he did. The man probably thought he was going to show these city kids how stupid they were.

For the next few days we were forbidden to go near the donkeys. My brother had to find other ways to explode his enthusiasm for photography. All our hosts and our family did was talk. They always looked so serious, even unhappy at times. By late afternoon we were very disgusted, waiting for them to become models for award winning pictures. Even though they looked nothing like the people we saw in the American movies, my brother took pictures of everybody and hoped for miracles.

One late afternoon, my brother and I were back to exploring, but nowhere near those donkeys. Around sunset we climbed a hill. Once again my brother had ideas of how I was to be his subject. On the horizon I had to hold a stick in one hand and raise my other hand toward the sky. He was determined to duplicate a picture he saw of Moses silhouetted against the sky, only this time I was Moses.

"Talk to God," he yelled, "and don't move."

With my arms stretched stiff I yelled back, "What should I tell God?"

"You don't tell God anything. You pray."

"What do I pray for?" My arms were getting stiffer.

"Pray for anything, anything you like--anything." For some reason he seemed upset, even though I was the one standing like a statue. This was hardly my idea of fun.

So I prayed. "Dear God, please make these people finish their monkey business soon. I want to go home and play with my friends. I don't want to be with donkeys and I don't want to be Moses."

Apparently God heard my prayer. The next morning we returned home.

My brother never got the girl, but I still have the Moses picture. After sixty years it's just as clear as it was after my brother had developed it.

26

Song

The following summer signaled another vacation from school and another trip with the family. In Iran men always traveled and hung around with other men. Women and children associated with other women and children. Segregation of the sexes was common.

Badry, Iran, and Soosun--three of my aunts--often came to visit my mother. One afternoon they decided to escape the heat of Tehran and enjoy the refreshing breezes of the mountains. As an excuse they planned a pilgrimage with their children to the shrine of a saint by the name of Emam-zadeh Davood.

My mother was not interested, but suggested that I go. Joining my six cousins between the ages of 6 and 10, about my age, for a bus ride and a donkey ride sounded like fun. That evening my mother packed my socks, underwear, shirts, soap, towel, tooth brush, tooth powder, and blankets for camping.

Early the next morning seven children and three old ladies met at Aunt Badry's house. Each person was prepared to carry his own bag. In addition to her personal needs, Aunt Iran had a box filled with a few cooking utensils, a samovar and charcoal, plus enough tea and sugar to last the week of our trip.

The children could not reach the bus stop fast enough. After the driver's assistant stacked our gear on the roof of the bus, we all boarded. While the aunts leaned back in their seats and visited, the children sat at the edge of theirs and stared through the windows, bouncing up and down as though they were telling a horse, "Gitty up." As the bus started to move, the excitement intensified.

While the bus bounced along and hit every hole in the dirt road outside of town, the children giggled and the women gossiped. Every dip in the road was high adventure. The sight of sheep and goats in the villages along the way convinced the children that they were passing through another world.

After one hour they had enough of this. "Are we there yet?" asked Jamsheed, turning around to his mother three seats behind him.

"Shut up!" Soosun scolded.

Ten minutes later Bahman yelled back to his mother, "Mohsen has to pee."

"Later," consoled Aunt Badry.

Meanwhile Mohsen sat in agony with his legs crossed up as high as he could.

So about an eternity later Maheen looked back at her mother and asked, "Are we there yet?"

"Shut up!" yelled Aunt Soosun.

The cousins were tired of the bus ride, tired of each other, and tired of being told to shut up.

Each child was so restless, just one little poke, even the slightest touch, from his seat partner created a scream of annoyance that inspired a complaint of abuse. Soon they were all crying and arguing. Amir changed seats to join me. Monir decided to sit next to Maheen. Bahman slid next to Jamsheed and demanded the window. "I sit here," grumbled Jamsheed, so Bahman hit him on the head.

"Is it time to get off?" I asked. I was lonesome for my mother.

"No," answered Aunt Badry, adding, "Shut up! We just had a rest stop."

That took my mind off my misery for a while, because I wondered if I somehow missed seeing my mother at the rest stop.

About 70 miles and five hours later, which seemed like five years later as far as the kids were concerned, the bus lurched to a stop. As each passenger filed out of the bus, the kids complained about everything and anything louder than before. Now they were hungry.

What a relief to get off at Farahzad! At this stop they all hurried to a park. The aunts found a spot under a tree where they spread the rug on the ground and doled out the lunch. As each child had something to whine about, the aunts corked their mouths with cucumber and cheese sandwiches. Since there was no time to brew tea, they drank water from the outside faucet. The icy cold well water was most refreshing. Everyone attacked the lunch with pleasure.

They ate quickly and worked their way to the donkey stand. Aunt Soosun hired six donkeys. Each of the aunts had one of the youngest sit in front of her. While Jamsheed and Bahman shared one donkey, I shared mine with Amir. The last donkey carried our baggage. Like this we paraded through the village on our way to the mountains. What fun--at first, probably the first fifteen minutes. The youngsters squealed with delight. They had so much to see, so much to say. Naturally, they could not share their observations with their donkey mate. Anything they had to say was meant for someone at least one donkey away. So they yelled. The narrow paths presented no challenge to the surefooted animals, but the sight of the steep drop along the mountain side soon quieted the passengers. Besides, the slow ride became boring.

"I don't like this donkey," cried Jamsheed. "He doesn't move fast enough."

"I don't like mine either. He shakes too much," said Mohsen.

"Maman," cried Amir, "I'm tired."

Maheen yelled, "So am I."

Not to be outdone, Monir yelled louder, "Not as tired as I am."

After four tortuous hours on the donkeys, we finally reached the village of Emam-zadeh Davood. By this time the aunts were in no mood to start cooking. Aunt Badry found an area at the edge of the camp ground under the trees away from the other tourists. This was our place for the next few days. Each person spread out his own things. The aunts decided that Aunt Soosun would stay to watch over the children, while the other two walked to the *keboby* for a kind of take-out meal of lamb kebobs, fresh mint, fresh tarragon and flat bread. Everyone was so exhausted, no one had trouble falling asleep after the meal. Each one curled up in his own blanket and fell asleep under the stars.

Early in the morning we got up. The place was so jammed it looked as though no one stayed home. Other than vendors, clergy, and businessmen these visitors included mostly women and children. After breakfast the aunts lined up the cousins to go to the shrine. For one whole hour we walked in a single file--children grumbling and adults arguing. The sight of the golden dome of the shrine and the minarets silenced everyone--for a few moments.

At the open doorway, everyone removed his shoes and checked them with the *kafshdar* for about a penny a pair. Aunt Badry walked at the head of our line. Slowly, reverently, everyone circled the tomb of Emam-zadeh Davood. Many of the people gently touched the intricately ornate wooden grill that surrounded the tomb. This fancy wood was at least 10 feet tall and 10 feet long on each side. Many people in this procession kept whispering strange sounds as they circled this sarcophagus. Aunt Iran explained that they were praying in Arabic.

Once outside the shrine, the quibbling among my aunts resumed at unbearable decibels.

These three women, who normally lived in separate houses, were now crammed next to each other, each with her own children, who normally played outside. Pretty soon friction, irritation, screaming and yelling escalated. I thought I had left all that at home, where my father yelled constantly. Now I had my aunts, three of them yet, yelling all the time, either at the kids or at each other. And I was supposed to be on vacation. My cousins didn't like this any more than I did.

Every day we mechanically repeated our visit to the shrine and blindly paid our respects to Emam-zadeh Davood.

By the third day the situation became intolerable. I suggested a solution to the kids.

Jamsheed doubted that anything could control these women.

"I think," I said, "we should all sing as soon as the ladies start yelling."

"What?" asked Jamsheed.

"That new song about a pretty girl, '*Gol Pary Joon*'."

So we practiced a few times and were soon ready.

From then on as soon as the aunts started arguing, the children started singing,

"Gol Pari, Joon. . . . Baleh.
In ja ee Joon. . . . Baleh."

This was so effective that even the yelling adults would stop and smile. Then we would stop singing and just look back at them. The split second they started yelling, we started singing again,

> ***"Gol Pari, Joon. . . . Baleh.***
> ***In ja ee Joon. . . . Baleh."***

On the way home on the bus, even when no one was arguing, all 10 of us had fun singing,

> ***"Gol Pari, Joon. . . . Baleh.***
> ***In ja ee Joon. . . . Baleh."***

27
Velvet

Traveling at the time was a rare experience for most Iranians. Very few people were able to go out of town for any reason. Fewer yet traveled out of the country.

Yousef, a friend of my brother's, attended the University of Geneva in Switzerland. On his days off from school he enjoyed going to the movies. At one theater it was customary for the person at the ticket booth to alternate odd numbered and even numbered tickets to boys and girls respectively, who came alone. Quite often, before the movie was over, a boy and a girl became friends, sometimes very good friends--just from sitting next to each other. It was a way for out-of-town students to enjoy not only a movie, but a new acquaintance.

Yousef was no different. One day after entering the dark theater directly from the bright sunny outdoors, he became momentarily blind. Since the movie was already in progress, the theater was very dark, darker than a thousand midnights. He had to feel his way to his seat in a row already partially occupied. As he stumbled and stepped on feet, he was greeted by grunts and foul language. Nevertheless, he poked along. He felt his way to the left. He felt his way to the right. As soon as his approach was met without rejection, he sat down.

As he kept his eyes on the screen, he placed his hand on the lap of the person in the next seat, enjoying the touch just as much as the movie. As the movie stars enjoyed expressions of love, Yousef enjoyed stroking the velvet-covered knee. He often flirted like this during a movie, but never before had his advances been so easily accepted. He was in ecstasy. This flirting escalated throughout the movie.

He hardly paid attention to the plot of the excitement on the screen. He agonized, waiting for the movie to end--not to find the solution to the mystery, but to learn the identity of his mysterious neighbor in velvet.

"She's probably rich," he surmised.

After what seemed like a century, Greta Garbo and her lover kissed and made up. The credits rolled down the screen and the house lights turned up. Yousef's neighbor was wearing a grin from ear to ear and the cassock of a stately, bearded Orthodox priest.

28
Encounter

All the schools in Iran resumed classes after summer vacation on the first day of fall. It was a pleasure to walk with my friends, kick the fallen leaves, and tell stories about our summer fun.

For some strange reason I walked home from school alone, rather than with a few other third-grade classmates, as I usually did. I walked slowly, because I was tired.

As I turned into the alley near our home, a middle-aged man appeared out of nowhere. I saw his shabby clothing before I noticed him.

"Don't I know you?" he asked. He wrinkled his eyebrows quizzically. "What's your name?"

"Hushang," I answered obediently.

"No. Your last name. Your father's name."

"Mofakham Payan."

"Of course, I recognized you. You're the son of man who lent me some money. I have it now. If you come with me, I will give it to you to give to him."

I hesitated, but considering this detour as something I should do for my father, I agreed.

"Follow me," he continued. "I live in the alley on the other side of the street."

He then went ahead of me, while I followed. None of my father's acquaintances ever looked so poorly dressed. Anyone with whom he associated was always the epitome of decorum, dressed in a suit, formal shirt and tie. I had trouble visualizing him among this group. By the time we reached the main street, I was sure that I should not have been where I was, definitely not with this man. What I was sure of was my mother's warning: "Never talk to strangers and don't accept money from people you do not know."

As soon as we approached the crowded area of the street, I told him I would come back another time--soon. Luckily I recognized a grocery store owned by one of my father's friends and ran in. I often shopped there for my mother when she needed things, like rice or cooking oil. Mr. Razaz recognized me immediately. He also noticed immediately that I was frightened.

"Hushang, what's wrong?"

I blurted out the whole story, so much in a hurry to get the incident out of my mind, the words got all mixed up coming out of my mouth. He quickly ran to the door, hoping to see this stranger, but the man was nowhere in sight.

Naturally, by this time I was getting home later than usual. Once again I related the incident. My mother assured me that I was right not to follow this man. "Never talk to anyone you do not know," she again warned me.

My mother repeated all the details to her sister-in-law Iran, who then repeated all the details to her husband Farhang. Since Farhang worked for the police department, he became most concerned. A little later that evening he came to our house to get more specific information from me. Again I described the man and the street where we walked together. Now that everyone was reminding me about the possible danger of the situation, I became more frightened than I had been while talking to this stranger.

The next evening when the newspaper man made the rounds of the neighborhood, my father gave me the required penny to get the daily paper. It consisted of only four pages--mostly news, an occasional story, and very few ads. The headlines reported a missing boy. He was the sixth victim in about four months.

At that time, such kidnaping in a city of 250,000 was extremely rare. The Shah, who was a military dictator, ordered the chief of police to find this man guilty of kidnaping and killing children. If the police failed to do so within two weeks, the Shah would have the Chief hanged. The entire department was put on alert to get this alleged serial killer.

In about a week the man was caught, his picture covering the front page of the newspaper. I had no doubts about the identity of "Asghar, the Killer." "He's the one who approached me," I showed my mother.

Couple of weeks later in the city square at sunrise, this man was hanged. I was not allowed to go and watch.

29

Accident

While no one was looking, 3-year-old Mohsen crawled up the brick circular staircase outside that led to the third floor. While proud of his accomplishment to get around by himself, he did realize that he was not supposed to venture anywhere on his own. Three steps from the very top he looked back to see who, if anyone, was watching.

He lost his footing and tumbled down 30 feet, bumping each edge of the brick steps. He lay there on the brick courtyard--quiet and stunned. When he tried to move to get up, he writhed in pain, screaming.

Mother, Grandmother, Aunt Iran, her two children, and the two maids--all ran out from the house to see what had happened. As Mohsen's mother leaned over to pick him up, he only cried so much harder, unable to cooperate. His legs were limp.

Utterly devastated, his mother quickly took him to a doctor at the American hospital, which had the reputation of providing excellent health care. After examining the boy as thoroughly as possible, the doctor diagnosed the problem as a broken thoracic spine. To prevent his back from moving, Mohsen was fitted with a body cast. The only advice the doctor gave the mother was that the boy should rest and the family should pray.

After a year Mohsen was able to feel sensation. Six months later he began to move his legs and a few months after that he actually was able to stand and eventually walk.

As the years went by, Mohsen's back never did grow straight. As a result of his hunched-back he always appeared short. At age 15 he was as tall as the boys five years younger, like me. Consequently, he developed friendships among boys his own size, not age.

Even if his physical development were normal, he would not become close to his older brother anyway. In a paternalistic society, like Iran, people seldom became friends with an older sibling. His elder brother, three years his senior, not only commanded, but demanded, respect--whether he deserved it or not. Even though the younger children always admired the eldest brother they were always aware of that invisible wall between them. Such an attitude of feigned respect and definite detachment was even more pronounced between a child and his father.

Because of Mohsen's back problems, he was unable to attend the public school. Since he was quite bright, at home he readily learned how to read, write and cipher. He was so intelligent that his reading ability led him to study the greatest Persian poets--like Omar Khayam, Sadi, Hafez and Rumi. He even composed poetry of his own. Intellectually he performed wonders. Physically there was neither hope nor help for his back.

When he was a teenager, he still suffered from an abscess on his back. Once again he visited a chain of physicians and hospitals. On the basis of clinical judgment alone, without any bacteriologic examination, the condition was diagnosed as Pott's Disease or tuberculosis of the spine. Treatment was limited to superficial antiseptic dressings changed daily, cod liver oil served with each of his three meals, and Mohsen placed outside to sunbathe as often as possible.

At that time I was 12 years old. In spite of my age, I was given the responsibility of changing Mohsen's dressings and bandages. No one ever considered the possibility of my contracting tuberculosis.

When I was in high school, penicillin was discovered and extolled as a panacea. With that hope Mohsen and I visited our neighborhood doctor to get some of this magic medicine. The doctor doubted its efficacy in regard to tuberculosis of the spine, but decided, "At least it won't hurt you."

With that, he showed me how to mix penicillin powder with saline and inject Mohsen every three hours.

After three days of this treatment the abscess drained completely. After a week the wound was closed and covered with thin skin.

Apparently, Mohsen had osteomyelitis, an infection of the fractured bone, not tuberculosis.

30

Deep Pockets

At age 12 our neighbor Taymour was already employed full time, working at Economy Photo Shop. Spending 10-12 hours in the basement darkroom deprived him of daylight much of the year. For all his work in a 60-hour work week he earned $3.00 a month.

When the owners of the Durbin Photo Shop, Economy's competitors, learned how efficiently he developed and printed pictures, they offered him $6.00 a month. That much money for a 16-year-old was most welcome.

At the end of each day an old lady, the wife of the owner at Durbin's, detained every employee before each left the shop. Slowly she would reach into every pocket of every person and thoroughly wiggle her fingers around to make sure that no one stole anything. When she found nothing that belonged to the shop, she stepped aside from the door and bade each one "good night."

Day after day the routine continued, much to the disgust of everyone but the owners.

One evening her search of Taymour's pockets lasted less than a second. She pulled her hand out of his pants pocket faster than she put it in. This time there was no end to this teenager's pockets. He had cut open the seam of the bottom of each one. Furthermore, that day he did not wear underpants.

31
Prince

No matter what the profession is, no matter what the project is, experience is always the best teacher. As a new intern in Razi Hospital in Tehran in 1939 Dr. Cyrus was excited to be able to shadow experienced physicians. In addition to learning by observation he read extensively about the disorders of the patients he had seen.

One late Friday afternoon when he was on call, the phone interrupted his concentration. He was needed in the operating room for an emergency.

As he entered the surgical suite, he was surprised to see Dr. Handjan, professor of surgery. On such a holy day of the week, late in the afternoon yet, it was rare to see anyone at work. It was even more rare to see the chairman of the department scrub for an emergency. Furthermore, never was surgery performed late in the day.

"Good afternoon, Dr. Handjan," said Dr. Cyrus, hoping to learn the reason for such a break from normal schedules.

"Hello, Cyrus," responded the eminent physician. "Wash your hands and get dressed. We have a case of gun shot wound of the face." No one offered any explanation why such a renowned surgeon had to be called for this particular case.

The patient was a 40-year-old woman with a large wound of the lower part of the left jaw. Since no X-ray could be taken because the radiology department was closed on Fridays, Dr. Handjan could only surmise that a fracture of the body of the mandible complicated the situation. The bleeding was easily controlled; the wound, cleaned of debris; and the gaping hole, covered by dressing.

Outside the operating room a police colonel and

another gentleman sat and waited, explaining their presence to no one.

As the patient then spent six weeks in the hospital, Dr. Cyrus had many occasions to talk with her. According to what she told him, she was the nanny of 17-year-old Prince Ali Reza, the second son of the Shah. The afternoon of her admission she and the prince were enjoying the brisk fresh autumn air in the royal gardens. He was toying with a gun. On an impulse he put the gun under her chin and insolently asked, "Do you want me to shoot you?"

Going along with this kind of playful mood, she answered, "My life belongs to you, your Highness. You can do with me as you like."

Prince Ali Reza arrogantly sneered and pulled the trigger. The sight of blood terrorized him. She was immediately taken to the hospital. At the same time telephone calls went to the police department and a chauffeur was sent to drive Dr. Handjan to the hospital.

Ever since that moment the city police, as well as secret police, hovered around her room to make sure that she said nothing to ruin the reputation of the royal family.

No account of the incident was ever publicized in the media. The hospital chart simply stated, "Accident."

32
Childbed Fever

As my Aunt Kimia's pregnancy with her fourth child progressed, she moved around more and more awkwardly. The women around her gossiped, "She's awfully big. I bet she's having twins." She was so enormous, she used both hands to hold up her stomach when she walked. It was no wonder that she had difficulty getting around. In spite of her discomfort she never complained. In fact, she had such an infectious smile and positive attitude, everyone felt good in her presence.

One day when I went over to play with her children, the older daughter Mondana ran to me, holding her finger up to her lips, warning me to be quiet. There was a lot of commotion in that house. Old ladies were swishing in and out of Aunt Kimia's bedroom, carrying towels, bed sheets, and pans of water. I soon went back home. There was no sense staying here; nobody wanted to play.

Aunt Kimia's husband, who seemed old enough to be her father, always treated her like a baby, but this week he was more solicitous than ever. Without the presence of a physician, Aunt Kimia gave birth to triplets. Uncle Fazel was really relieved when the ordeal was over.

She would never even consider having a physician at her side, because it was not customary to do so. Even in a dire emergency she would not call a physician unless the doctor was female. Women agreed to gynecologic examination only when performed by other women.

Three days later all the people who were busy and excited now were silent and solemn. The triplets died. When Aunt Kimia developed a fever and hemorrhagic vaginal discharge, the midwife suggested that a doctor be called. Uncle Fazel did just that. After diagnosing the problem as puerperal or childbed fever, the doctor prescribed prontosil, aspirin, soft diet, and ice bags. In spite of the treatment, she gradually felt weaker and her general condition worsened. She was so weary, nothing interested her--not even her own children. Gone was her infectious smile. A few days later she too passed away.

Her death was so devastating for her husband, one year later he too died. These deaths affected the entire family. For years all the relatives talked about the tragedies.

* * * * *

In 1935 facilities to take care of such fragile premature babies or such sick mothers were limited, especially in Iran. Until a century ago, infections were rampant (even in hospitals) not only because of the lack of sterile conditions, but maybe even more so because of the lack of knowledge. Around the world research led to gradual control of puerperal fever brought on by bacterial infection.

At the beginning of the 1800's, Friedreich Henle suspected germs to be the cause of some infectious diseases. In the second half of the century Louis Pasteur proved the association of microorganisms and certain diseases. In 1867 Joseph Lister further noticed that since infections in surgical patients are caused by bacteria, they could be prevented. By doing so he confirmed Pasteur's antiseptic theory.

As early as 1844 Semmelweis noticed a 25% mortality in maternity wards in Vienna hospitals. He attributed the deaths to puerperal fever. Comparing child births assisted by physicians with those assisted by midwives, Semmelweis noticed the dramatic difference. He was convinced that "invisible cadaveric particles" were transmitted by physicians from the autopsy room to the delivery room. He then insisted that all doctors wash their hands in a chlorine solution before examining pregnant women or delivering babies. The mortality rate dropped to 1.2%.

While the results were astounding, Semmelweis's influence was not. Since he was a Hungarian in a foreign country, he did not speak German fluently. His colleagues equated his language skill with his medical expertise and had the chairman of the department dismiss him. In 1849 he returned to Budapest. It took decades before his theory was proven credible and still more decades before it was universally practiced.

33

Neema Yusheedge

After an entrance examination I was accepted at Iranian-German School, a prestigious high school in Tehran, which focused on the training of engineers. During the first three years German as a foreign language was a required course. After that the science classes were taught in German.

Among the teachers was Ali Esfandiary, a man who preferred to be called by his pseudonym, Neema Yusheedge. Never realizing that this man was a published poet, the seventh-grade students thought he was an eccentric individualist. As our teacher of Persian literature, he encouraged us to write creatively--poetry and prose of all kinds. With a total disregard for tradition and grammar, he expounded on content, meaning, symbolism, and style.

His appearance was just as bizarre as his teaching methods. In winter under his jacket he wore a vest covering his chest and neck, like something from the closet of a rural person, not like the other teachers. In the summer his tie would hang crooked around his neck or dangle out of his pants pocket. He wore shiny black leather shoes, but no socks.

He may have created negative impressions by his dress, but he impressed everyone most powerfully with his poetry. Considered "modern" at the time, his work startled most teachers of Persian poetry. When he read poetry out loud, he would savor every word and almost go into a trance over a phrase. He would bow his head in thought till his bald head shone like the sun.

In contrast, Mr. Muhammad Dayheem, who taught grammar, was dressed as formally according to tradition as were the fixed rules of writing and homework. In spite of his rigid rules, most students appreciated neither the content of his course, nor his demeanor.

One day a very noisy discussion was coming from the teachers' lounge. Mr. Neema and Mr. Dayheem locked the proverbial horns about each other's specialty in the realm of language. "What you write, Mr. Neema, is no poetry. It's nothing but rot, pure garbage. You disregard grammar and totally ignore the noble tradition of famous poets--like Hafez, Sadi, Rumi, and Khayam." His criticism became so intense, his face became beet red.

"What is important," calmly replied Mr. Neema as he inhaled and made his pointy nose even pointier, "is content. The idea must be expressed in the most effective words possible."

"Without form," continued Mr. Dayheem, "there is no poetry. Poetry is tradition."

After such repartee for almost 10 minutes with comments, insults, and slurs growing louder and louder, Mr. Neema screamed, "You know what else I think, my dear Mr. Dayheem. YOU are an ass."

"Are you insulting me?" screamed Dayheem as he pounded something, probably the table.

"No, my dear colleague, I am telling you the truth."

Mr. Dayheem refused to listen to another word. He came out of that room, breathing hard as though he had run a marathon. As he went down the hall, he took heavy, almost marching, strides toward the dean's office.

Rumors still persist about this interview, as well as the one between the dean and the teacher of modern poetry. When the dean saw Mr. Neema to hear his side of the story, he asked, "Did you call Mr. Dayheem an ass."

"Yes, I did."

"Why?"

"Because he is."

"But you can't go around calling people names, no matter what you think."

"If you wish, I will no longer refer to him as an ass, but that doesn't mean that I will no longer regard him as such. Whether I say it publicly or not, he is still what I called him: an ass."

Rumors may add questionable titillating details as the years go by, but beyond the shadow of any doubt, Neema Yusheedge is Iran's most profound poet of this century and the best teacher I ever had.

34

German School

When the scholastic year began in 1939, the German school was no longer in existence. Rumor had it that the reason for closing that school by government was political, now that England and Germany were at war. Since the British had a great influence in Iran, they orchestrated the departure of all native Germans from the country. This included the excellent teachers who taught their language. Anything German was *verboten.*

The students had to attend other schools, most of which offered French and/or English as the foreign language. Since those children suddenly found themselves among others already familiar with the course, they were forced to repeat the entire seventh grade--even though they had passed every other subject.

Lucky for me that my brother had a friend who was an English teacher willing to tutor me during the summer. I invited my friend Asquar to join me twice a week when Mr. Goodarz came to our home. He gave us enough homework to keep us busy the rest of the week. By the end of the summer we were both so good in English, we were accepted at our new school in the regular grade where we belonged. Since 80% of the students had chosen French to fulfill their language requirement, we weren't even sure that we would be able to continue our study of English. But lucky again, there were enough young people interested in English to hold the class.

As the school year progressed, so did my interest in English. My only regret was that since the German school closed I was never able to see Mr. Neema. No one could ever forget this fascinating man. Not only was he a motivating teacher, he was a sensitive and compassionate gentleman. Nowadays I see his poetry in the most respected Persian literary publications.

35
Camphor

When I ejaculated for the first time at the age of 13, I was positive that I had gonorrhea, even though I had no idea what that was. A pus-like discharge from my penis coupled with an unusual feeling had me so worried I could hardly sleep. I was afraid to even mention it to anyone, particularly my parents. When my mother questioned my sudden moodiness, I dismissed the question by saying that I was just tired.

My being tired for days in a row only made my mother worry. She decided that I see old Dr. Shahrdar.

Reluctantly I described my symptoms.

"Have you had intercourse with a woman?" the doctor asked. He had no trouble leaning over me, because he was so naturally hunched from old age.

"No, no. Of course not," I sputtered, almost jumped out of my chair, shocked at the insinuation.

"So what makes you think you have gonorrhea?" he continued, glancing at me from the corner of his eye.

"This discharge is thick and sticky." I whispered, so no one else would hear.

"When does it happen?"

"Mostly at night when I am asleep."

"That is not pus, young man. It is semen. Your experience is part of growing up, part of sexual maturity."

"Is there a way of preventing it? It is disturbing. Sometimes it happens during the day when I am excited about an examination or things like that."

The old man looked at me, smiling for some strange reason and mumbled, "Some day you will be very happy to be sexually mature. No way will you want to stop the process." Nevertheless, Dr. Shahrdar wrote a prescription. "This is camphor," he explained. "Take one capsule a day. It will reduce the frequency but you cannot stop it completely. Eventually, however, after a few years perhaps, it will slow down by itself."

For a week I took one capsule every day, but it did not do any good. For the next few days I took two. Nothing changed. Then I decided to take five capsules--all at once.

That next morning my mother found me unconscious. Instantly she sent for our neighbor, young Dr. Andalibi, who lived next door.

Gradually I came to. When I tried to stand up though, I was ready to throw up as the room spun round and round and round. With every attempt to stand, my knees turned to *shole zard*, a rice pudding as unstable as jello. When I glanced out the window, the trees, as well as the buildings, were swaying.

Dr. Andalibi suggested rest, no school for a few days, and absolutely no more camphor capsules.

36
Leila

Just as my mother was about to prepare *khoresh-ghormeh sabzi*--an Iranian delicacy of fresh herbs, like fenugreek leaves, parsley, and Persian limes--she discovered that she had run out of turmeric. For some reason I was always the one who did such last-minute or spur-of-the-moment grocery shopping. She gave me some money and sent me off to Mr. Attar's shop, a veritable haven of spices, herbs, dried vegetables, and seasonings. Saffron, almonds, pistachios, poppy seeds, table salt, pepper and dill decorated the shelves and filled the air.

Apparently, he was not very impressed with the treasures of his surroundings. He seldom smiled. Since he must have been at least 100 years old, he had lived long enough to know every person in the neighborhood.

Just as I walked in, so did Leila--the 14-year-old daughter of a neighbor of ours. Her mother had run out of sugar. With her golden hair and porcelain complexion she was absolutely beautiful. I was expected to keep my eyes down and be very shy, but I could not help but notice her. If I were allowed to describe her, I would run out of superlatives.

"What can I do for you, Leila?" asked Mr. Attar. He almost smiled, but not exactly.

"Madar needs ½ kilo of sugar."

Mr. Attar weighed the sugar, poured the sparkling crystals into a cone shaped bag rolled from newspaper, and priced it at 2 ½ rials. "Do you need anything else?"

"What I need," she answered, "is a good-looking husband. Someone like him," she added and pointed at me.

I felt like jumping into one of his 50-pound bags of jasmine rice. I too was about her age, but definitely--very definitely--not as mature as she, socially or physically. My face turned the same color as the dried red peppers in the bin at my side. I gasped. I could not believe what I heard--first from Leila, then from Mr. Attar. It was the very first time

I had ever heard him laugh.

I heard that Leila had been kicked in the head by a horse when she was 8 years old. Now I believed it. This girl suffered from delusions. She was demented.

Quickly I told Mr. Attar what my mother needed, I paid him, and ran home--praying that Leila was as slow in using her legs as she was in using her head.

Everything else about her, though, must have been quite normal. About a year later she delivered a baby, supposedly fathered by Mash-Ghorboon, the butcher.

37

Word from God

"Where is your mother?" my father yelled, as I carefully balanced his tray, carrying dinner to him in his room.

"She doesn't feel well," I meekly answered. "She has a headache."

"Nonsense." He yelled so loudly, I almost dropped the tray. "Tell her to get up and come here. Now!"

As I moved slowly out of his room--my chin, as well as my eyes, lowered--he roared, "Move!"

I ran to the children's room, where my mother was trying to rest while the kids played backgammon. "He wants to see you."

"I know, I know," she said. "I heard."

Reluctantly she pulled herself up from the floor, slowly uncurling her legs from sitting against the huge bolster. Her face became beet red. She mumbled something about hot flushes, while she wiped her brow.

My father, 10 years her senior, seemed to be in a mood worse than usual. "Bellghace, are you coming?" he growled.

As he screamed for her again, this time he added his favorite quotation from the Koran after her name, "*Azvajakom va oladekom addovvon lakom* (Your wives and your children are your enemies)."

My mother swallowed two aspirins that moment, then laboriously walked toward my father's room.

The volume of their discussion changed from loud to louder as they argued about my older sister, who at the age of 27 was trying to get a divorce. Gradually the volume of their voice changed from quiet to quieter. Soon the door slapped closed. The light that shone through the glass in the upper half of the door disappeared.

My grandmother was the only one brave enough to mutter under her breath, "It is the male hormone building up in him again. It makes him wild. He definitely needs a second wife. One is not enough for him. His father was never like this. That man had seven wives. Now, that was a happy man. In fact, so were his families."

I dared not breathe a word. For that matter, I never dared speak to my father either. I avoided him as much as possible. Anything he represented was everything that I wanted no part of.

The following day everything was calmer and everyone was at peace. I decided to check my new Koran that had the Persian translation to see if Muhammad really did say, "Your wives and children are your enemies." I thumbed through the pages of my Koran and soon found 64:14:

> O ye who believe!
> Truly, among your wives
> And your children are
> enemies to
> yourselves: so beware
> of them! But if ye
> forgive and overlook,
> And cover up,
> Verily Allah is
> oft-forgiving, most merciful.

I recalled reading in a history book that when Muhammad migrated from Mecca to Medina, many Moslem men followed him, leaving their families behind. After a while some of the families missed their husbands and their fathers. They soon complained by letters and messages, requesting their return. Muhammad, on the other hand, had no such concerns. Several of his young wives were always with him in Medina. When he became aware of these complaints, he somehow heard this revelation from his God.

Just as I was about to close the book, my mother remarked, "I knew you would find it, but it should really be:

> O ye who believe!
> Truly, among your husbands
> are enemies to
> yourselves."

38

Escape of the Soul

According to the Bible, Genesis 2-7, "the Lord God formed man of the dust of the ground and breathed into his nostrils the breath of life and man became a living soul." According to the Holy Koran, Al-Hijr 15-29, "When I [God] have fashioned him (in due proportion) and breathed into him of My spirit." According to my observation, all living things breathe.

Once a year, on Ashura, the death date of Hussein (the grandson of Mohammed), a day prescribed by religion to be extra kind to the needy, my mother made halvah. She took pains to prepare this very sweet delicacy. It was so rich, no one could eat very much of it. The summer that I was about fourteen years old, my mother gave me a dish of it to take to the youngest of my grandfather's seven wives. As a widow at this time my grandmother shared her home with another widow at least 20 years older.

As I walked into their courtyard, where the door to the street was always left open during a summer day, Mrs. Omead, the daughter of the older lady, was right behind me.

"Hello," she greeted me.

"Hello, Mrs. Omead."

"And what is in the bag you are carrying so carefully?"

"My mother sent some halvah for the ladies."

"Oh, good. How thoughtful! Tell her, 'Thank you'."

Together we continued across the courtyard. Mrs. Omead lived quite close to us with her husband and several children. Always distinguished and well dressed, Mr. Omead worked for the government. He and his wife seemed quite educated and sophisticated.

Standing at the window, my grandmother was very happy to see us.

"Good morning, Mrs. Mofakham Payan. How's my

mother today?"

"I think she is still asleep," whispered Grandmother.

My grandmother and Mrs. Omead exchanged a few routine pleasantries (*taroff*). Then Grandma smiled at me and took the dish of halvah while Mrs. Omead worked her way to her mother's room. Outside I waited for my grandmother to empty the halvah into one of her own dishes and return my mother's to me. Through the open windows I could see both ladies move about.

Within a minute or two Mrs. Omead started calling my grandmother, asking her to go to her mother's room. Her voice carried a tone of urgency. My grandma ran over while I remained in the courtyard, watching and hearing everything.

Mrs. Omead stammered, "Mother . . . apparently . . . died . . . in her sleep."

"God bless her soul," commiserated Grandma.

"Please help me turn her toward Mecca," begged Mrs. Omead.

As one lady lifted the shoulders of Mrs. Omead's mother and the other lady, her legs, the movement caused a noisy discharge from the corpse. Suddenly Mrs. Omead dropped the body, got on her knees, and raised her arms in supplication, "Oh, God, my mother's soul just departed. Please find a place for her in heaven." Then the daughter sobbed uncontrollably.

Finding this unexpected reaction to the flatulence quite humorous, my grandmother dropped her end of the body, put her hands to her face and stifled her laughter, equally uncontrollable.

Then they hugged each other, each body quivering, each shaking for a different reason.

When I finally got their attention, I could only smile politely and say Good Bye.

The Good Books talk about how a soul is breathed into the body, but never mention how it leaves. Now I know.

39

Stomach Ulcer

For a teenager nothing is more stressful than studying for a test, taking examinations, and then waiting for the results. When I was 17, the tension was so disturbing, I began having stomach aches after each meal.

Once again my mother sent me to see Dr. Shahrdar, the old family physician. As he examined my abdomen, every time he applied pressure, I flinched. He was positive that I had an ulcer. X-ray examinations were not common those days, especially when a physician was an old general practitioner and the tests were expensive.

His solution to my problem was a liquid diet. I was to eat only soup for at least three months.

Three months later I still had mild discomfort after each meal. His advice was to continue the same diet: nothing but soup for another three months. He did not even give me supplemental vitamins, as he thought pills would aggravate the ulcer and the stomach.

Since I was young and growing I was always hungry. The amount of soup I consumed was monumental, phenomenal. In spite of all the eating, I was losing weight. By the end of six months I had lost at least 15 pounds, more than 1/10 of my usual weight. My cheek bones became quite prominent and I could count my ribs. The situation made me depressed. Instead of playing soccer with my friends, I preferred to be alone, to be quiet. Sad stories, like Victor Hugo's *Les Misérables*, seemed even more sad.

As I contemplated suicide one day, I admired the children of a distant relative, two brothers, 16 and 18 years old, who had taken an excessive amount of opium and died. When I mentioned this to my mother she calmly replied, "We are all going to die sooner or later. No need to rush it." My mother was not exposed to any great formal education, yet she was intelligent. She decided that I should change doctors.

This doctor changed my diet. Gradually I began to feel better. Gradually I seemed normal. I even played soccer again.

Years later in medical school I learned how puberty can be a stormy and traumatic stage of a person's life, affecting not only him, but those around him. Riding emotional waves creates anxiety and depression. The radical physical and emotional changes in teenagers demand the loving care and utmost patience in others of the family.

Unfortunately, all young people do not bask in love. Suicide is the second most common cause of death among those 15 to 19 years of age.

40

Koran

When I was a youngster, my immediate family consisted of three households--my parents and their five children, my mother's brother, his wife and their three children, and my father's sister with her two children. My earliest recollections of my widowed Aunt Moheeb portray her as more religious than most of the other people around me. Before the first wisp of sunrise, hearing the faint chant of the muezzin from a Mosque minaret in the distance, she would jump out of bed and begin her day with the ritual of *payab* and *namaz*. As a symbol of cleansing her soul, she would go to the pool in our courtyard, rinse her face, her hands up to her elbows, and her feet as far as the ankles, thus complying with *payab*. Returning to the house, she would wear her chador which covered every part of her body but her face. She then opened her prayer napkin which held a piece of smooth, hard, cream-colored clay from Mecca. Alongside this holy stone measuring about ½" x 1" x 2" was a string of prayer beads. Facing Mecca she began her prayers--*namaz*. She repeated the ritual of *payab-namaz* five times a day: before dawn, before noon, afternoon, before sunset and after sunset. The words she intoned as prayer were in Arabic, a language neither she, nor anyone else in our family, understood.

During the month of Ramadan she would fast during the daylight hours, but eat and drink after dark. During this religious season she added another ritual to her prayer routine. After *eftar*, the first meal right after sunset, she would read and chant passages from the Koran.

Most solemnly she would approach the high shelf that held the Koran out of reach of the children. She lowered the holy book gently, pressed it to her lips devoutly, and pressed it lightly against her forehead. Koran in hand, she sat on the floor covered with Persian rugs. All the people in the room, especially the eleven children, were expected to come and sit around her--exactly as she did--kneeling down and sitting on their hunkers. Throughout these directions the word "respectfully" came along several times.

When everyone was settled according to her wishes, she would read excerpts from the Koran out loud in her melodious voice. If anyone wiggled or made the least noise, she would interrupt the reading and scold in a solemn tone, "You are disrespectful to Koran. These are the words of God. You must remain quiet and pay attention." While the culprit settled down, she would hold her index finger to her closed lips, looking at every single person around her to make sure that they got the message.

Once when I was about six years old I inched a little closer to her in the middle of her chant and asked, "Aunt Moheeb, what are you saying? I cannot understand a word."

"She stared down at me and didn't even seem to breathe for a moment. "It does not matter. I don't understand it either. These are the words of God and you just repeat them." Her stare spoke louder than her words. "It's a sin to talk like that." Out loud she answered, "You must try to read the Koran as it is written."

Later I learned that not only was the Koran written in Arabic, but people in Iran prayed in Arabic. Hardly anyone had any idea of what was being read or said. I could not understand why the God of Persians had to be an Arab. God is supposed to know everything. Why not Persian?

By the time I was 16, God really piqued my curiosity. He expressed his revelations in Arabic and imposed it on believers who did not know the language. I wondered why no one ever translated the Holy Book and how people could pray with words that were mere sounds. Could it be that the mullahs, the religious leaders, did not want people to read a translation of Koran so they would never know its contents?

By this time I was self-disciplined enough to save my hard-to-come-by money and independent enough to browse around the stores. Along Shahabad Avenue, not far from our home, I walked into Eqbal's bookstore. "May I help you?" asked the salesman.

"Yes. I'm looking for a copy of the Koran."

With no trouble he reached for one on the shelf

behind him, held it up for a moment in a gesture of respect, pressed it to his lips and lightly against his forehead. He then turned toward me, Koran in hand, held above the counter between us, and said, "That will cost you one tuman (about a dollar)."

"Not this kind," I told him. "I want one with a Persian translation."

"Oh," he stared at me in surprise. "That is much more expensive. Right now I don't even have one. I can order one for you, though."

"How much?"

"Four tumans," he replied.

"I don't have that much money," I confessed.

"Would you take one slightly used--for two tumans, perhaps?"

"That's much better," I smiled. "I still have to go home and get more money from my mother."

When I relayed the experience of the day to my mother, she seemed just as curious about a Persian version as I was. Immediately she gave me money to make up the difference, but suggested that I take my schoolbag for carrying it home. "This way no one will misinterpret your handling of Koran."

I don't remember in which direction I walked faster: to Eqbal's to get the Koran or to my house to sit and read it. All I wanted to do was read, read, and read to finally learn what were these words of God. My mother, however, insisted that before I read it, I go through the ritual of *payab.*

With my clean feet under me, I began, "*Be name Khodavandeh Bakhshandehe mehraban.* (In the name of God, most gracious, most merciful)." I continued,

> "Praise be to God
> The Cherisher and Sustainer of the Worlds:
> . . .
> Thee do we worship . . .
> Show us the straight way,
> The way of those you favor,
> Not those on whom you incur your wrath,
> And not those who go astray."

By habit from being a diligent student, I underlined salient points and wrote notes in the margins. "Arabic God likes praise.. . . Vain . . . my God needs no praise. He also wants to be worshiped.. . . Self-centered, like people. . . Likes some people, but not others. Why create people you don't like."

I could not lay the book aside. I read on . . .

2:5 Those who believe . . . will prosper.
2:6 Those who reject faith will not believe.
2:7 God has set a seal
On their hearts and ears.
On their eyes is a veil.
They incur great chastisement."

In the margin I wrote, "Why did God put a seal on their hearts and ears and then promise chastisement? This does not sound like a logical person, let alone a God. I don't believe my God would do anything like this."

As I read more, I was soon convinced that these were all human thoughts, many of which were not even logical, but emotional, in response to day-to-day problems of life. I was more relaxed now, stretching my legs out in front of me (not exactly the respectful position prescribed by Aunt Moheeb), reading, underlining, and jotting notes in the margins. When my mother came to the room, her face showed mixed emotions of surprise and anger. "What are you doing?" she asked, her voice getting louder and louder with each word. "That book is sacred. It is the words of God. It is a sin to write on it. What is wrong with you?"

I pulled my legs under me again, assuming the respectful position. I certainly did not want to upset my mother or hurt her feelings. "Mother," I began, "I am writing on the Persian translation. I did not touch the Arabic part, the words of God. I assure you I will not touch that part."

She was not satisfied with such a lame excuse. In her anger she reprimanded, "Make sure you hide that book so no one else will see it. That is blasphemy. If that Koran in that condition ever falls in the wrong hands, you may get killed."

Later I read:

5:102 People before you, asked questions and lost their faith.
4:91 Seize those who turn away from religion and slay them.

Then I understood why my mother was worried when she noticed my reaction to the Koran. She knew of the violent fanatics and troubled people who just waited to make life difficult for others, to use them as a public example of some infraction of any religious law.

About 10 years later, as I was about to board the plane at the Mehrabad Airport for my eventual arrival in the United States, she reminded me that my Koran is in my suitcase. In no uncertain terms she told me to leave it there, as it cannot be disposed of any other way.

41

Whirling Dervish

In Iran a dervish is a proponent of meditation, mysticism, and hypnotic practices of chanting and whirling that lead to ecstatic trances, a state of nirvana absorbing one's soul into the supreme spirit of Godliness. As such mystics denounce worldly pleasures, they limit their clothing to basic essentials usually made of wool, like that of St. Francis of Assisi. Because the word "wool" in Arabic is *"suf,"* dervishes are called Sufi. Sufis emphasize love of God for the sake of innate goodness, rather than fear of hell or promise of heaven.

Whirling dervishes achieve a state of ecstasy as a result of music, poetry, dancing and twirling. This trance-like state is tantamount to serenity, exultation and cosmic unity free of time and space. This philosophy transcends the bounds of formal religion, encompassing the positive attitude of "Love thy neighbor." Even though the word *Sufi* is Arabic, the philosophy intrinsically is Indo-Iranian. Sufiism developed as a reaction against the worldliness, loose morals, and government oppression.

Mr. Morshed, a devout Sufi mystic, devoted his life to physical simplicity while attaining spiritual sublimity. In fear of being ridiculed or possibly harmed, he spent his days in hiding. Because he was old and feeble, a young man and his family lived in his house to take care of maintenance. The dervish spent part of his day discussing the philosophy with his followers, including a 22-year-old college student named Mateen.

Mateen had a friend, a fellow college student, who played the violin quite well. One day he invited his friend Lotfi to accompany him not only to hear the elderly gentleman, but to play for him.

As Lotfi had never seen a true dervish, he accepted the invitation to go one Friday morning, the Moslem Sabbath, when they were both off from school.

As soon as they knocked, the housekeeper opened

the door and directed them through the long courtyard to the dervish's quarters. They entered a long reception room with a Persian rug covering the floor and draperies serving as a dividing wall. Realizing that the dervish was behind this divider, Mateen said, "Good morning, Sir."

A weak voice from behind the curtain answered, "Good morning to you, Mateen."

"I brought my friend Lotfi. He would like to play violin for you."

"Oh, good morning to you too, Lotfi."

"Good morning," Lotfi responded to the voice, all the while wondering what was going on, why this man was hiding.

"Please go ahead and play whenever you like. I would like very much to hear your music."

Disappointed that he was not able to see the dervish, Lotfi almost lost his enthusiasm for playing. In spite of being somewhat miffed, he began to play. Actually he was somewhat irritated. He could be doing something better than fingering his violin in front of an enormous piece of fabric.

After he played about twenty minutes of classical Persian music, the curtain was suddenly pushed aside. Wearing a long flowing robe and no shoes, a 75-year-old man with long white hair and a long white beard stepped into the huge room and began spinning and chanting in tune with Lotfi's playing. Lotfi was speechless. He wondered whether or not to continue. Noticing the hesitation, Mateen nudged him to go on. For more than half an hour the dervish danced and danced and danced until he collapsed. Once again Lotfi looked at Mateen, wondering what to do. Mateen urged him to play for another 15 minutes.

When Lotfi finally stopped playing, the dervish gradually sat up, wiped the perspiration off his brow, and slowly walked toward Lotfi. Lotfi extended his hand. Mr. Morshed reached for it and kissed it. In return Lotfi was about to kiss the man's hand, but the dervish said, "No, you only kiss the hand of an artist. Those hands that could produce such beautiful music are truly gifts of God to all people." Then he hugged Lotfi and said, "Thank you for coming." Turning to Mateen, he then hugged this young man and said, "Thank you for bringing your friend."

Lotfi, who was upset a while ago, was suddenly elated. He sensed a peculiar energy racing through his body as he was hugged by the dervish. "The room seemed brighter," Lotfi commented later. "A warmth and glow went through me as though I had a large glass of wine." Before the college students left that reception room, the dervish talked to them for a long time and recited poetry from Rumi and other Sufis.

With penetrating eyes, Morshed added in a whisper, "When music touches one's heart, God Himself dwells within one's soul."

42
Immolation

Mystics, like the Sufis, accept and respect all religions. Religious fanatics, on the other hand, not only believe themselves to be better than others, but often go to any extreme to try to change anyone who appears different. Some fanatics simply harm themselves. Japanese committed *hara-kiri*, the cutting of the stomach, to please the gods, thus earning eternal happiness. Many fanatics dwell on the misfortune of others as though they suffer vicariously and believe that this will earn them spiritual rewards. A preoccupation with the ills of the world somehow supposedly cleanses one's soul. For such believers, negative activity seems to produce positive psychological satisfactions.

Even before the days of the Old Testament, for the sake of religion, self-righteous people practiced immolation, the mutilation of one's body. Millenniums ago such activity must have been quite prevalent, since there was an awareness to prohibit it. According to Leviticus 19:28, "Ye shall not do any cutting in your flesh for the dead, nor print any marks upon you."

Too often fanaticism for any cause overrules one's common sense. Cruelty, like such mutilation, reverts man to a state worse than his uncivilized days. According to Nigel Davies in his book Human Sacrifice cannibalism often went hand in hand with infanticide. In Israel burning merely symbolized the eating of the victim by the god. Greek mythology overflows with tales of infants who were slain and often eaten. Sacrificial suicide was also quite common. The early Christians often thought suicide was retribution for a sinful life.

When I was a child in Iran, weeping and moaning (as an accompaniment to prayer and/or meditation) in mosques and even at times in private homes were not uncommon. Once a month a mullah came to our house. While he sat on a chair, the women and children of the family gathered around him, sitting on the floor. Half talking, half chanting, he was difficult to understand. He seemed to be telling the story of Emam Hossein, the grandson of Muhammad who was unjustly killed in 680 A.D. by Yazid, an enemy who then declared himself a future caliph.

As I grew older, I realized that for the sake of religious ritual, mere appearance, people would weep bitter tears and sob dramatically. With the departure of the mullah came the departure of the gloom. Within an instant, everyone was joking and laughing.

Such morbid behavior intensified during Moharram, a month of the lunar Arabic calendar. Ashura, the tenth day of this month, commemorates the death and martyrdom of Hossein. All businesses were closed. Listening to music, reading for pleasure, and even laughing on this holy day are considered sinful. Around noon the Dasteh, a group of men, marched in procession around town. To flaunt their piety these young fanatics beat their naked chests and flagellated their naked backs to the point of bleeding. Some even cut their heads with sharp blades. Some even subjected their children to this mutilation. These naive men were extremely proud to chant and beat their chests, especially when women would gather around and watch them. Unfortunately, the mullahs encouraged such irrational behavior.

According to the rules of the elementary school which I attended all boys had very short hair, almost stubble. When Asquar complied with school policy, his nearly shaved head revealed several longitudinal scar lines. Every time I glanced at Asquar's head, I wondered how those marks got there. I dared not ask such a good friend such a personal question.

Other children rumored that Asquar's religious father had made a covenant with God. When this man learned that his wife was pregnant, he wanted a son very badly. Upon the suggestion of a fanatic mullah he promised to cut lines in the baby's scalp if that baby should be a son. This practice was supposed to be a sign of piety. Fortunately, in the upper grades, boys were permitted to wear longer hair. Therefore, by the time Asquar reached high school his scalp was covered, although scarred for life.

Years later, a surgeon friend of mine talked about

his practice in a small religious community in western Iran. When he was called to the Emergency Room one day, the mutilated scalp of a year-old boy required more than a hundred sutures to repair the wounds. The 22-year-old father had slashed the baby's head down to the skull. The child even needed a transfusion to save his life.

On holidays like Ashura most people stayed home, being afraid of friction with the fanatics and the mullahs. Even though people remained indoors, it was considered wrong to engage in pleasures of any kind, especially sexual intercourse. On such a holy day anything to do with sex became a grievous sin. Some believed that for such an offence a man and a woman (be they husband and wife) would stick to each other forever.

When I was 13 years old, it was on such a day that I went to visit my friend who lived about 10 minutes away. Along the way two stray dogs were busy mating. About 10 feet from them two sanctimonious boys, each about 10 years old, were throwing stones at them.

"Why are you doing that?" I asked.

"They are sinners," one of them declared. "Today is Ashura. Nobody should do such things, especially today. They must be stoned to death."

Historical records give endless accounts of people killing each other over differences of ideology. Under the guise of doing good, they could not have done anything worse. These boys were no different. As a way to impose their religious beliefs on others, they chose violence--even against innocent animals.

Such insane fanaticism exists everywhere, even in today's world. The war between Moslems and Jews in the Middle East, the war between Christians and Moslems in Bosnia, the hostility between Catholics and Protestants in Ireland jeopardize not only world peace, but every individual's peace of mind. On a smaller scale, in April, 1997, 29 disciples of Marshall Applewhite from "Heaven's Gate" committed suicide with the hope of joining the Hale-Bopp comet and reaching happiness "above human level."

Apparently, extreme religiousness is associated with the oldest part of the brain, the limbic system, which is the seat of basic emotions. The cortex, on the other hand, which controls the emotion is brand new, a hundred thousand years old. Perhaps since the cortex is new, we still don't know how to use it.

Fanaticism could be laudatory. It's the interference with others' lives--physical, spiritual, or psychological--that denounces such zealots. I pray that I may develop their enthusiasm for learning which leads to understanding which leads to appreciation which leads to positive interaction which leads to learning . . .

43

Children and Religion

Sometimes in matters of religion, some people develop a warped mind. They smother themselves in the external manifestations dictated by their beliefs till they cannot sense the true spirit intended by the tenets of their faith.

Akbar Ordookhany, a classmate of mine who lived a few doors down the street from us, loved to wrestle with other kids, especially when they were smaller than he. He would push a kid on the shoulder, knock him down, sit on him, and then say, "I am Rostam. I can kill you now, but I prefer to let you free." Rostam was the "hero of Iranians." It sounded as though he were giving a slave his freedom.

One day he ran into Serkis, an Armenian classmate and neighbor, with his customary push on the shoulder. While the two boys were as tall as each other, Akbar was more muscular and stronger. In about two seconds Akbar was sitting on Serkis' stomach, commanding, "Repeat after me:

Ash-hado an la elahe el Allah .
Ash-hado anna Muhammadan Rasul Allah.
Ash hudo anna Alion valy Allah."*

Neither Serkis nor Akbar understood the words they blurted out. While Serkis gasped for breath and tried to push 100 pounds of boy off his stomach, Akbar solemnly pronounced, "Good, now you are a Moslem. Now you can go."

Akbar performed this routine with Serkis so many times, Serkis knew those three sentences better than Akbar did. After a while just the sight of Akbar had Serkis repeating these Arabic words. Just like Pavlov's dog, he was giving a conditioned response.

Years later in Marquette, Michigan, Mahmood, the only 10-year-old son of a Moslem family was very friendly with the other children of the neighborhood.

On a bitter cold winter day some children, all Christians, decided to play "church." They walked around the yard as though in procession, then stopped at the birdbath. Mahmood was chosen to lean over the birdbath and look for cracks. Patrick then reached for the hose and turned on the nozzle. Icy cold water filled the bowl and drenched Mahmood.

Shivering from cold, Mahmood ran home. He had enough of this game.

For one brief moment his mother seemed frozen into shock. "Oh, my God, what happened to you? I told you to stay away from the lake."

"I never even went near the lake," Mahmood defended himself. "I was baptized."

* I observe that there is no God other than God.
I observe that Muhammad is a prophet of God.
I observe that Ali is a slave of God.

44

Mahroo

Seventeen-year-old Mahroo, who had been married to 25-year-old Seeavash for three years, was upset because she was not getting pregnant. They lived quite a distance from Malayer, far from Tehran.

In the late 1800's, in the absence of physicians (especially in small towns and villages) her last resort for help was the clergy. One day when she was utterly distraught, she walked a few hours to a mosque in Malayer to consult a mullah.

After hearing the details of her predicament, the clergyman, who seemed to be about the same age as her husband, advised her to say her prayers daily and follow all the other dictates of her Moslem religion. He too promised to pray for her.

Before they parted, he wrote a prayer on a piece of paper and advised her to drop it into a bottle of water as soon as she got home. Every night before bedtime, she was to sip some of the water made sacred by the ink of the prayer on the paper. As expected, the ink disappeared almost immediately and after a few days so did the water.

After a few months, when Mahroo was still not pregnant, she retraced her long walk to the mosque to confer with the same mullah. He urged her to pray so much more fervently and return with a progress report.

Several months later she did just that. And he repeated what he had suggested: pray.

Back and forth she went, only to hear the same advice. The mullah truly felt sorry for Mahroo. After all, she was pretty and pleasant. She should not be denied the joys of motherhood.

After exhausting all possible ideas of helping her, he told her about the prophet Elias, known to Iranians by his name in Arabic "Khezr." One of the 124,000 prophets of God, Elias apparently found the fountain of youth in the land of darkness (most likely the Arctic Circle) during the time of Alexander. As one who has drunk from this miraculous spring, he lives forever and is omnipresent. Since he is able to help all kinds of people with all kinds of problems, he is able to appear as different as circumstances demand. As the mullah expounded on Elias's miracles, he urged her to follow those prescribed rituals. For 40 consecutive days before dawn she was to clean the entrance in front of her home most diligently. During the day she was to say the prescribed set of five prayers most devoutly. He assured her that she would know whether or not she is pleasing God. If she accomplished this task to God's satisfaction, Elias would visit her very early in the morning of Day 41.

She wondered how she was to recognize this holy prophet. She couldn't ask her husband for help, because as a baker he would have left for work at 2:00 a.m.

Looking most soulfully into her eyes, the mullah warned her not to discuss this plan with anyone, not even her husband. As he comforted her and calmed her doubts, he assured her that she would have no trouble identifying Elias. Since he is able to look like any ordinary person, for the faithful he will assume a familiar face. He added that Elias may even resemble him.

On the forty-first day, immediately after the baker left for work, Mahroo heard a knock on the door. Thinking her husband had forgotten his apron or something, she jumped out of bed to see what he needed.

Instead of Seeavash, she saw Elias. The mullah was right. He did look just like him. He even knew all about her troubles and her wishes. Mahroo was beside herself with excitement. If the miracle happened so far, surely more miracles would come. With absolutely no hesitation she agreed that they go inside the house together. Not only did they walk hand in hand into the house, they continued into the bedroom onto the bed. Mahroo never experienced such excitement sizzling through her every pore.

Three months later she was returning (almost running) to the mosque. She could hardly wait to tell the mullah the good news about her pregnancy. Along the way she told everyone she met about the miracle Elias performed. The news spread like wildfire. When it eventually reached her husband, he was not exactly excited and definitely not happy.

When he came home from the bakery, he was furious. Like Elias he led her into the house. Unlike Elias, he was not very gentle as he pushed her into their bedroom. More violently he shoved her down onto the bed. With every epithet that he screamed at her he hit her on the head with a hammer. In a pool of blood she soon lay there dead.

Since he really loved her, he could not understand how she could be unfaithful to him. Maybe he did feel guilty for some failing he had. That same afternoon he was found next to her body, just as still as she. He had committed suicide, most likely by overdosing opium, a popular pain remedy (analgesic) when taken in small amounts.

The mullah disappeared.

45

Wisom of Age

Mr. Manuchehr was the *arbab* of an agriculture enterprise, similar to the overseer of a feudal state. Among the 100 farmers and their families who worked under him, many seemed older than he. As their father figure, everyone--regardless of age--respected him and followed his orders. He was their boss, their judge, their jury, and their representative. On their behalf he dealt with clergymen, as well as government agents -- including the gendarmery, who likewise knew him and respected him. Since there were no doctors within 50 miles of the farm complex, he even assumed the role of doctor for them, obtaining drugs through one of his brothers who was a physician in Tehran. On his personal property Manuchehr relegated to some of his servants the responsibility of his big house and swimming pool--an uncommon luxury in Iran at the time.

With so many employees, Manuchehr had time to socialize. Every morning Mr. Peer, who was 90 years old, came with his assistant Mr. Javan, who was 30 years old, to enjoy breakfast with Manuchehr, their employer, who was also 30 years old. Mr. Peer was the *kadkhuda*, the oldest inhabitant of the compound, and as such was a most venerable gentleman. During these pleasant morning gatherings, the men philosophized and solved the problems of the world. More seriously, they discussed the specific welfare of the 100 families who worked the farms in Ghaderabad about 150 kilometers north of Shiraz.

One day Mr. Peer leaned forward, holding the top of his cane with both hands and asked, "Manuchehr, why don't you get married? People need a little excitement around here. It's definitely time for a party."

In return Manuchehr asked, "Why don't you ask your assistant Javan to get married?"

"Oh, you know he can't. He is supporting a widowed mother and a sister in Shiraz. Since he had earned his high school diploma and I needed someone to do my bookkeeping, I gave him the job. Because he is a nice boy, I have sort of adopted him as my son. He even lives in my house."

Manuchehr laughed, "Could that be why all your children look like him, rather than you?" To himself he thought about the Moslem laws directed toward husbands and wives. If a husband noticed his wife's slightest indiscretion of infidelity or even casual interest in another man, he would have every right in the world to kill her.

The 90-year-old smiled with a faraway look in his eyes. Most likely, he too had the same thought twirling in his mind. "Well," he mused, "everyone deserves some pleasure in this life. When I was young, I worked for an old rich man who had a wife my age. When he died, I married this woman and shared her inheritance. After fifty years she died. Then I married my present wife who was 20 years old at the time. At night she still keeps me warm in my bed. She is there when I need her. If the children look like Javan, it is OK. When I die, Javan will probably marry my wife and share her inheritance. It is better for my money to go to people I love, rather than to the government or *ankhunde moftkhor* (useless clergyman)."

"All that aside," Mr. Peer said to Manuchehr, "since you are the father figure for all the villagers and since they look up to you, you already do assume the responsibilities of a married man. Why not be one? Wouldn't that make everyone happy?"

Manuchehr, who at times considered marrying a distant relative chosen by his mother in Tehran, said, "If you promise to dance at my wedding, I will get married."

As though in meditation, Mr. Peer smiled from ear to ear. As his face radiated, he stretched his bony hand out to Manuchehr, "That, my good man, is a promise."

One month later Manuchehr drove his brand new, shiny, 1940 V-8 Pontiac to Tehran with Mr. and Mrs. Peer as his passengers. His parents were hosting his wedding reception with a few hundred guests. Everyone they knew, including our family, was invited.

At the Tehran reception people of all ages and all walks of life came to share the happiness of the young couple.

They sat around the huge court yard covered by Persian rugs. In the center of it all was a small pool surrounded by a stone wall about 18 inches high. During such gatherings this *hoze*, the pool, was covered by planks to serve as a stage. Here professional entertainers presented their production, their *roohozi*--like one-act plays related to legends or national epics. The tone was usually humorous, even satirical with barbs attacking the foibles of society, politicians or international dignitaries. Between skits appeared male musicians with female singers and female dancers.

Mr. Peer was so captivated by the spirit of the occasion and the rhythm of the music, he asked the musicians to play one of his favorite songs. As soon as they complied with his request, he started to dance on the stage. Encouraged by the rhythmic clapping of the onlookers, including Manuchehr, Mr. Peer's wrinkled arms and skinny legs gyrated in all directions. When it almost reached a frenzy, my friend Ahmad (brother of the groom) whispered to me, "He may fall and break something. He seems a little drunk."

Right then and there, exactly as feared, Mr. Peer dropped to the wooden floor with a thud. Manuchehr jumped onto the stage to see what had happened. Mr. Peer seemed to have a hard time breathing. He looked up at Manuchehr and smiled. Immediately the old man's face became pale and expressionless. Manuchehr's older brother, a physician, also jumped up onto the stage, directing everyone to clear the area and help put Mr. Peer into his car so he could drive the man to the hospital.

Manuchehr and his bride could do nothing else but remain with their guests. Observing the customs of the occasion, they waited until midnight to be excused and sent to one of the interior rooms prepared for them. As they departed, the entertainers sang the special song, "How beautiful the bride, how handsome the groom." Throughout the ritual Manuchehr was quite ambivalent.

The following morning everyone woke up to the news of Mr. Peer's death.

A year later another wedding was celebrated, that of Mr. Javan and Mrs. Peer.

46

BP--Benzine Pars

When Parvis, one of Manuchehr's friends, decided to continue his education, he went to oil engineering school. One day at the Anglo-Iranian Oil Company (AIOC) in southern Iran, he heard about a contest. The British managers of his company were offering 100 £ to anyone suggesting a new name for the company. They wanted to eliminate the word *Iran* without disturbing the Iranians. Since the source of the oil was Iran, the British had to be most diplomatic to be able to sustain their financial interests. Since they were British, they had to be most tactful to maintain the interests of their own country. Somehow the name had to be acceptable to both countries.

Parvis thought and thought. After scribbling many names to see how they looked and repeating them to hear how they sounded, he decided on simple initials: B.P. For those who spoke English, *B.P.* would represent *British Petroleum.* For those who spoke Farsi, *B.P.* would mean *benzine Pars.*

Parvis won the prize.

47
WW II

On August 25, 1941, it was so warm, my father came home around noon. As usual, two rapid hard knocks that almost split the door announced his arrival. Like everyone else in the household, I knew that it was he. I ran to let him in--ran because I did not want to be a victim of his usual foul temper.

"Go to Mr. Razaz's shop on Shahabad Avenue. I just bought 50 kilos of rice and 20 kilos of shortening and paid for the delivery of both. Go show the delivery man how to get to our house." He pushed me out onto the street without even saying hello.

Sheer inertia had me half-running and half-walking. Fifteen minutes later when I reached the shop, I was able to relax somewhat because Mr. Razaz was not very busy. His pleasant smile and calm voice also helped release my tension. As my father said, he already knew why I had appeared.

"Get the rice and shortening for the lad," he ordered two of the delivery men, handing them two rials apiece (about 20 cents). With these items on their special backpacks the men followed me home. They were so hunched over by the weight of the sack of rice and the can of shortening, their backs formed the letter C.

Radio news seemed to be blaring from every household that we passed. "The Russian and British armed forces have attacked Iran from the north and the south. Both armies are moving gradually toward Tehran."

No sooner had I walked into the house, my father gave me money to return to Mr. Razaz's shop for one more sack of rice and one more can of shortening.

By the time I reached the store for the second time, only 40 or so minutes later, people were pushing their way to the door of the shop, shouting and shoving to be ahead of one another. Chaos ruled as the mob panicked. I was so bewildered, I ran home without buying a thing.

Naturally, my initiative to do the opposite of what

my father told me to do did not sit well with him. Staring at me with angry eyes as big as soup bowls, he sputtered, "Where are the delivery men?"

"They did not come," I meekly answered.

Before I had a chance to explain, he railed at me more violently than ever. After a few minutes that seemed like an eternity he finally stopped shouting and let me describe the situation at the store. For no apparent reason he began yelling again, even louder than before, and ordered my older brother to go with me.

By the time I reached the store for the third time, now about 2:00 p.m., the street was empty. This time there was no crowd. There wasn't a single person in sight. The deserted street was eerie. I kept recalling the behavior of the mob and rattled on as I described every second of the chaos to my brother.

He seemed to ignore me until we reached the entrance to the shop. The windows were all boarded haphazardly and a big sign pasted across the door. "Sold Out" it said.

Every day someone from the family returned in hopes of replenishing my mother's supply of staples. About a week later we finally succeeded, only to find the prices quadrupled.

48

Tehran Conference

I turned the knob on the radio in hopes of listening to the news, but got nothing, not even static. When I mentioned my frustration to the neighbors, they too were having the same problem. This definitely was not an electrical malfunction. After all, all the lights in the house were on.

Along Toopkhaneh Square the usual busy telegraph-telephone office was suspiciously dark. "CLOSED," the sign on the door said. Apparently all communication systems--mass media, as well as telephones--were inoperative, most likely "out of order" by order of the government. This was November 28. 1943.

As usual, the people attributed the inconvenience to the British and/or Russians. When the wind blew in one direction it was the fault of the British. When it blew in the opposite direction, it was the fault of the Russians. This time their suspicions contained some element of truth.

That evening, some people talked about seeing Mr. Winston Churchill being chauffeured from Mehrabad Airport to the British Embassy in Tehran. Along Pahlavi Avenue he greeted many onlookers with his index and middle fingers separated to signal V for Victory. He was sure that the gesture created positive reactions and excellent rapport with the Iranians. When some people went very close to his limousine, however, he had moments of apprehension that his physical well being was endangered. Apparently, until that incident Churchill was unaware of the animosity many Iranians felt against him and the British government.

Roosevelt and Stalin, on the other hand, shunned the crowds when they arrived for the Tehran conference.

These three government officials met for three days to discuss primarily the opening of a second front in western Europe. Stalin had been proposing this operation for about a year. Churchill was definitely against it, because he had visions of emerging as the winner of the war after the

Russians and Germans would have suffered military weakness. The Americans, on the other hand, were in favor of such a front. To prevent Stalin of imagining a conspiracy against Russia, President Roosevelt stayed in the Russian Embassy and refused to have a private conference with Mr. Churchill. By so doing, he asserted himself as independent. This was to dispel the rumor, even among Americans, that he was influenced by Churchill.

In an attempt to become friendlier with Stalin, Roosevelt called him "Uncle Joe." Not understanding American culture, Stalin construed the expression demeaning.

November 20, the last day of this conference, was also Churchill's birthday. That evening he hosted a dinner at the British Embassy. At the dinner table Stalin was nervous about the etiquette, especially in regard to using all the silverware. After a few drinks, however, he relaxed.

In spite of the fact that the young shah and the old prime minister of Iran were both Anglophiles, neither was invited. The only Iranians present at the party were servants. As conversation and gourmet delicacies flowed, Stalin called one of the Iranians, poured him a glass of champagne, and toasted him and his countrymen.

When the Tehran Conference came to an end on December 1, 1943, normal communication resumed throughout the country.

49

Interview

On May 8, 1945, the war in Europe ended. People in Iran were happy and hopeful that life would soon return to normal. As I finished my last year in high school, I had to decide how I would earn a living for the rest of my life.

The educational system in Iran consisted of six years of elementary and six years of secondary schools. After each division the students were subjected to a grueling national examination which brought most of them physical distress. About 50% of them suffered further distress after they had learned that they did not pass the examination. For these low achievers there was no possibility of entering the university. In this government system technical schools were very few and no other talents were nurtured.

Like the educational system for children, the university was also patterned after the French. Dr. Charles Oberling, the dean of the medical school who was formerly a professor of pathology at the University of Paris, maintained an enrollment of 150 students per year. In 1945, 1500 candidates vied for acceptance. The ultimate selection depended on the results of the *concours*, a competitive entrance examination. It took a month for the university to score the tests and post the results.

While waiting for the results, one hot summer day I met Ahmad, who had taken the exam to enter the school of law. As we walked together down Lalehzar Avenue, we noticed a sign at the entrance to Cinema Iran, a movie theater:

> "WANTED: Talented young men who speak English. Mrs. Cook, an American film producer, will conduct interviews between 10:00 a.m. and 12 noon."

We decided to investigate the possibilities of exhibiting our latent talents.

I was the first one to be called to Mrs. Cook's office, so Ahmad remained in a waiting room. A rather large, but pleasant lady, she sat behind a desk in a plush office decorated with autographed photographs of movie stars.

"Good morning," I said.

"Good morning," she replied with a smile, brushing her gray hair over her left ear. "Have a seat. And what is your name?" she asked.

"Hushang Mofakham Payan."

"Repeat that please, each syllable separately. Then spell it."

I did.

"Your age, please."

"Nineteen," I proudly answered.

"What education have you had?"

"I just finished high school."

"Have you ever acted?"

"No, not yet."

"Do you play any instrument?"

"Yes, the violin and the santur."

"European or Persian music?"

"Only Persian."

To my surprise she reached to the floor and produced a violin. "Here, play."

I took the violin, placed it under my chin, and sighed with self-confidence. "Chahar Mezrab-Dashti" soon filled the air. I wondered whether she was familiar enough with Persian music to appreciate it. In my mind's ear I heard my mother complain about the noise when I tuned to European classical music on the radio. As I fingered the strings, Mrs. Cook took notes.

"Come back in two weeks," she advised, never offering any reason for my return.

Then it was Ahmad's turn to be interviewed and mine to wait. Afterwards, we both left the theater. He too was instructed to return in two weeks. We may not have been too confident with our performances, but we were delighted that Mrs. Cook from Hollywood understood our English.

The following week the results of the *concours* were posted. Of the 150 successful applicants I was placed #133. I was accepted into the school of medicine and Ahmad into the school of law. We never did check on the possibility of an acting career. Somehow, medicine and law seemed to be more reputable professions.

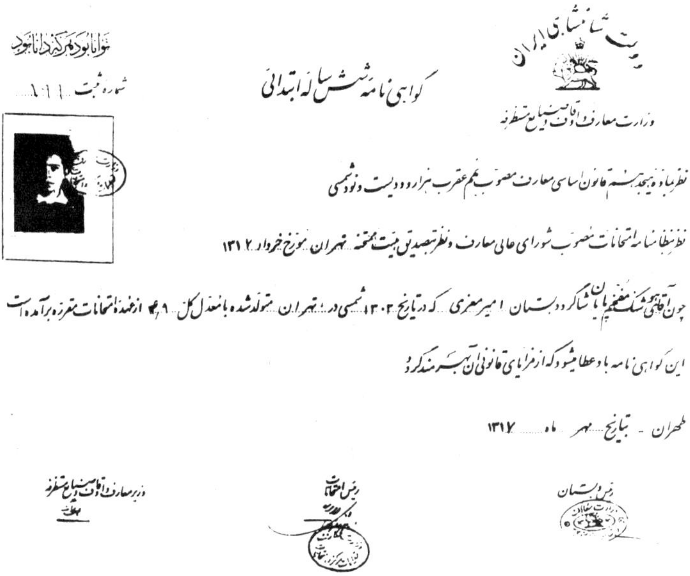

دولت شاهنشاهی ایران

وزارت معارف و اوقاف و صنایع مستظرفه

توانا بود هر که دانا بود

شماره ثبت ۱۰۱۱

گواهی نامه شش ساله ابتدائی

نظر بماده هیجدهم قانون اساسی معارف مصوب نهم عقرب هزار و دویست و نود شمسی

نظر بنظامنامه امتحانات مصوب شورای عالی معارف و نظر بتصدیق هیئت ممتحنه تهران مورخ خرداد ۱۳۱۷

چون آقای هوشنگ معظم پایان شاگرد دبستان امیر معزی که در تاریخ ۱۳۰۲ شمسی در تهران متولد شده با معدل کل ۴٫۹ از عهده امتحانات مقرره برآمده است

این گواهی نامه باو عطا میشود که از مزایای قانونی آن بهره مند گردد

طهران - بتاریخ مهر ماه ۱۳۱۷

رئیس دبستان

رئیس امتحانات

وزیر معارف و اوقاف و صنایع مستظرفه

50

Professor of Botany

One of the most motivating professors of my first year of medical school was Dr. Golgolab. He was always approachable, no matter how trivial a student's concern may have been. This teacher's mission in life was to have his students understand and appreciate botany. In addition to science he was keenly interested in poetry, music, and foreign languages--especially Russian.

His fluency in this language enabled him to attend international gatherings. In 1930 when he was a young man in his 30's, he participated in a physiology conference in Moscow. Arriving a little late, he was ushered to one of the last seats available--right in front of the speaker's podium. As he waited for the speaker--somewhat nervous since he came alone--he found himself sitting next to a white bearded Russian who soon put him at ease.

Very politely, the gentleman greeted him, "Hello. Where do you come from?"

"Iran," Dr. Golgolab answered, hoping that the Russian understood his accent.

"Welcome to Russia," beamed the elderly man.

"Thank you. I can't wait to see and hear Professor Pavlov."

"You won't have to wait too long," assured the man. "According to this program, he's about to speak soon."

Their conversation came to an abrupt ending as a man at the podium began to speak, first introducing himself as the coordinator of the conference, Dr. Cherkofsky. After the usual preliminary remarks he recounted the many accomplishments of the next speaker--Dr. Ivan Petrovich Pavlov. "Dr. Ivan Petrovich Pavlov received his MD degree from the University of St. Petersburg in 1883. The following two years he studied physiology in Germany, after which he was appointed the director of physiology at St. Petersburg Institute for experimental medicine and has been there ever since. In 1904 Dr. Pavlov was awarded a Nobel Prize in physiology and medicine. His discovery of conditioned reflexes is known around the world. Today he is going to talk to us about the interaction between physiology and psychology. It is with great pleasure that I introduce to you Dr. Ivan Petrovich Pavlov."

Amidst thundering applause of the audience, another stately gentleman approached the podium--the very same one that sat next to Golgolab just a few minutes ago. Dr. Golgolab was so absorbed in the remarks of the coordinator that he never even noticed the departure of the man with whom he was chitchatting.

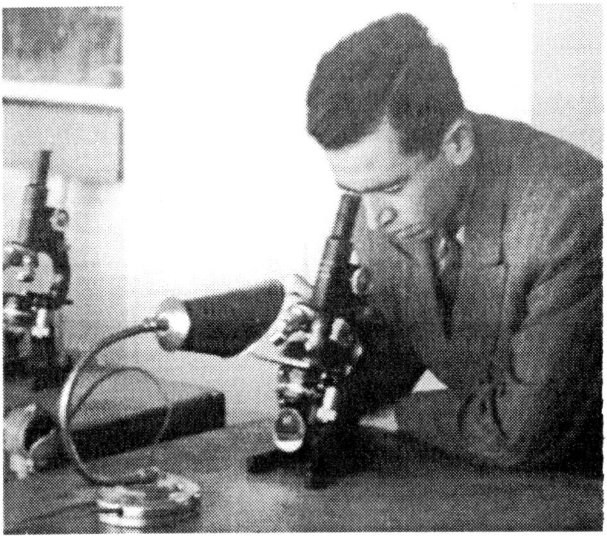

51
Gen. Razmara

After World War II the economy in Iran, as in many other countries in the Middle East, was depressed. Fewer opportunities for employment decreased per capita income and increased everyday needs. Many families could hardly afford substantial meals, let alone expenses related to higher education.

Such financial difficulties troubled even medical students. The only educational institution that solved the financial dilemma was the Military Academy. The Iranian Army was able to support the burden of such expenses because of the United States military aid. For many young men, the only way to continue medical school was to enlist in an army program (similar to R.O.T.C. in the United States after World War II). From the many who applied, only 10 were accepted. The year that the Army offered to double the enrollment, the applicants tripled. I was among them.

As soon as this announcement was published, thirty medical school students appeared in the lobby of the infirmary of the military academy. It was so crowded, many of us had to stand.

As we waited to be interviewed by Colonel Bahramy, the physician in charge of the military medical students, a young officer opened the door to the main entrance and commanded loudly, "Attention!"

Naturally, we all stood up in our nonmilitary haphazard fashion and looked around. Someone whispered, "General Razmara" just as he walked in. Almost immediately Colonel Bahramy appeared from his office at the rear of the building. The two men greeted each other and shook hands.

The general gave the crowd a cursory glance and asked, "Who are these civilians?"

"Medical students, Sir," the colonel responded. "Thirty men are requesting admission to the new program that can accommodate only 10 more. Most of them will have to be rejected."

"No, no. Accept them all. We need doctors in the army--all we can get."

General Razmara, who was Chairman Joint Chief-of-Staff, had a reputation of being an honest officer and a diehard military man. According to rumors, he stayed abreast of international events and kept a dossier on all Iranian politicians, even the Shah.

The general and the colonel walked into the office at the rear of the building and closed the door behind them.

The medical students submitted their applications to the clerk, delighted at the speed and ease of their acceptance.

The next week when they reported for duty, they were issued uniforms and orders. About a third of the second-year medical students were now in The Imperial Iranian Army. As military personnel they were housed at the base, receiving room, board, and a stipend. While they were subjected to the disciplines of military life, they pursued their medical courses at the university full time. In return, these students were obligated to devote two years as army physicians for every year they benefited from the military program.

52

Anatomy Hall

From the beginning of time the dead conjure elements of mystery, which always seem to evoke fear, uncertainty, and negativism toward a corpse. According to the Bible "He that toucheth the dead body of any man shall be unclean for seven days." (Numbers 19:11) Moslems also believe that anyone who touches a corpse must observe *Qosl*, a ceremonial bathing. Zoroastrians who come in contact with the dead are labeled extremely unclean. They would also grievously sin should they bring the dead in contact with anything that could be polluted, like water. In Egypt embalmers rank among the dregs of society. Even most renowned physicians refrained from touching a corpse. Aristotle and Hippocrates never looked inside a human body; Galen learned anatomy as a result of dissecting animals. Aware of the danger of infectious diseases and epidemics, leaders promulgated rules more for the physical, rather than spiritual, welfare of their followers. Such fear of the Lord forced the distance between the living and the dead.

Current awareness of anatomy had its inception in Europe in the 16th century. Only in 1832, however, did the British Parliament pass an anatomy bill that allowed anatomists to use the unclaimed bodies for dissections for learning purposes.

About the same time in Iran the first European type institution with a medical school opened its door to students in Dar-al-Fonun, founded by Prime Minister Amir Kabir. This polytechnical school evolved into the University of Tehran in 1934. Dr. Charles Oberling, professor of pathology at the University of Paris, was appointed dean of the medical school and remained in that position until 1945.

Under the direction of Dr. Oberling a separate building was used to house the anatomy facilities. Unclaimed bodies were donated to the school by government hospitals. When a body was not claimed within 48 hours, it was transferred to the dissection hall to be prepared for the students. Several months after the cadavers were prepared and preserved, they were transferred to the dissection hall for the students to work on. By the same process bones were prepared and made available for students to borrow, study and return.

A pungent odor of chemicals--mostly formaldehyde--identified the activity in the building. Aside from the unpleasant odor, medical students faced unpleasant sights. Preserved cadavers had brownish-black leathery skin, sunken eyes, and gaping mouths. Even today, most students need time to become acclimated to a dissection hall. When I was in medical school, first-year students dissected the musculo-skeletal system and extremities. Second-year students concentrated on the rest of the cadaver. Anatomy labs met from 2:00 till 6:00 p.m. twice a week.

One afternoon in late spring as a few friends and I were enjoying a few moments of conversation while waiting for the class to meet, two elderly men approached us. Their baggy pants, collarless shirts, dark suits, dirty boots and hats interrupted our train of thought. One of them seemed to be crying and repeating, "I want his body back. I don't care what shape it is in."

As they approached us, the crying man asked, "Are you doctors?"

"No, we are students, but some day we will be," my friend answered proudly.

"Is this building the Dissection Hall?"

He obviously could not read. High above the door huge letters against a mosaic background measuring 5' x 10' identified the building as "Dissection Hall."

"Yes," I answered.

"I would like to talk to someone responsible for getting the body of my son back."

My friend and I looked at each other and wondered what the man was talking about, but told him, "There is no one in the office until two o'clock. You could sit here and wait till then."

After the men sat down next to us, I asked, "What happened to your son?"

"About a year ago he fell ill and died in Razi

Hospital. His body apparently was sent here. People at the hospital told me so. I want to see if I can get it back to give it a proper burial in our village near Damavand." He continued his story with incidents surrounding his son's enlistment in the army at age eighteen. "He was a good boy, hard working, until he went into the army. There he learned many things including how to drink, smoke and gamble. Occasionally he wrote us letters, but seldom visited. Once a year his mother and I left the village to come to Teheran to visit him. That's how we became aware of his bad habits. Even though there were many nice girls in Damavand, he never married. He preferred the life style of the sinful city. Now I came to town to see him, only to be told that he died. When I went to the hospital to see his body at least, I was told that it's too late. He was a patient over a year ago and the body had been sent to Dissection Hall."

"At the hospital, did anyone tell you how he died?"

"One of the doctors mentioned that he died of a bleeding stomach ulcer and a liver disease brought on by excessive drinking. I just want his body back. I don't care how he died."

The cadaver to which my lab partners and I had been assigned could easily have been this man's son. Mr. Innominate, as we called the corpse, seemed to be about 40 years old. The good condition of the heart and arteries led us to that conclusion. The problem was early cirrhosis of the liver and a large duodenal ulcer which could have been associated with bleeding, typical of a person following the life style that we just heard about.

When the clock struck 2:00, we escorted the man to the office. All the while he moaned and cried, his friend tried to console him. Of course we knew that his request could not be granted. He was too late.

53
Accident

My medical school classmates, like medical school students anywhere else in the world, devoted their time to professional courses. In Iran, though, those in the military were exposed to two summer months of rigorous training, which consisted of marching, horse back riding, exercising, and quite a bit of target shooting.

In 1946 many of us wondered when, if ever, we would use our new learned skills. At the firing range 10 students at a time would line up in a designated position for target practice, all under the supervision of Capt. Farazi. The split second that he shouted "Fire!" gunfire echoed throughout the woods fifty miles around. After this group tried their skill, another 10--who were on the sidelines observing--had their turn.

After each round of shooting, the papers from the target stands were removed, examined and graded by the Commander, who kept them as records of improvement. Bahman was always among the volunteers to run the hundred feet to get the papers.

One day as the second group of students lined up, now more confident after having noticed what to imitate and what to avoid from the performance of the preceding group, they simultaneously discharged their guns when Farazi shouted, "Fire!"

Above the volley of gunfire, they heard a piercing scream. From behind the targets came Bahman, falling to the ground. For some reason he did not return with the two others who had just collected the target sheets.

Now Captain Farazi yelled, "Stop shooting. Put the guns down." To Shafa and Afshar, he ordered, "Run to the infirmary for the ambulance."

Everyone else ran out onto the field. Bahman's khaki shirt was drenched with blood over the abdomen.

Very frightened, he moaned and pleaded for help. By the time he was carried to the road, the ambulance was waiting to take him to the Army Hospital. During the two-hour drive Bahman grew steadily weaker, paler, and quieter.

At the hospital, he was pronounced DOA.

54
Cavalier

When I was a child trying to walk and run, I fell every few feet and whimpered almost as often. My mother would go behind me, support me under my arms, and gently set me on my feet again. "When you fall, pick yourself up. Dust your clothes off and keep going."

When I was 20, I spent a summer in officers' training school. Part of the training to be an officer in the Iranian Army was knowing how to ride a horse.

During the one short introductory lecture in a classroom, we were given all the tips on becoming successful horsemen. Effective communication with the horse seemed to be the most important lesson. We relied on natural aids or "cues"--like our legs, our hands, our body weight, and our voice. Artificial aids included the rein, whip and spurs. If we wanted to control the horse's direction, gait, and speed, these aids had to be properly executed. "To be able to handle and control the horse, you have to be smarter than he, or at least make him believe that you are," emphasized the teacher.

With so many warnings twirling in my brain, I went outside with my classmates and met my horse, Thunder. Exactly as I was told, I faced the horse first, touched him, even smiled at him to be nice to him, and whispered "sweet nothings" as I stroked his face and neck which seemed four times the size of mine. So far so good. I knew we were going to be friends, even though he showed absolutely no reaction to my memorized greetings. After I put the reins over his head, I walked to his side and put my left foot on the stirrup. Up I went--what seemed about one hundred feet with only the horse and air between me and the ground.

Walking and trotting the horses around on a level field presented no problem for any of the twenty novice riders. Satisfied with our progress, the commander decided that we ride on uneven fields around the camp.

As we continued on flat land before reaching the hilly terrain, all went well. As we started downhill, Thunder sparkled with enthusiasm and sent me flying through the air, over his head and down on the ground. Fortunately, the ground was soft and I was young. Just as my mother told me, I bounced back up and dusted off my clothes. At the same time a voice much sterner and much louder than my mother's bellowed, "Get up, dust off your clothes, and get that horse. Walk in front of him. Don't show any fear. You must show him that you are in charge."

Cautiously, I walked toward the horse and repeated our get-acquainted maneuvers. As I caressed his face and neck, I begged him not to do that anymore. We had a man-to-horse talk, eyeball to eyeball. Reluctantly, I got on his back again, pulled the reins, and directed him to follow the other horses walking so perfectly in line.

Two minutes later, I went flying again. I was beginning to believe that I was in training to be an acrobat, not an officer.

Again, I followed the directions on how to mount a horse, only this time I pleaded with Thunder to take it easy. "Please, Thunder, please, please, please, take it easy. I've never been on a horse before. You are my very first one."

Most likely my horse was deaf. For the third time, he took another unexpected, fancy step. He began to kick and fling and send me waving at the trees.

A classmate, who handled horses all his life on his father's farm, ridiculed me. "You city boys are all sissies. You will never make a horseman."

I was never so glad to see lunch time for Thunder and me. He went to the stable and I went to the cafeteria.

Two days later we were to practice our newly learned skills again. This time my experienced "Country Boy" friend was assigned to Thunder. I knew that he would show me up. I was mortified just at the thought of his handling that horse with insolent skill.

Nevertheless, I followed the commander's orders and tried not to look at Country Boy. My determination to do well obviously got to my second horse. He understood every syllable I uttered and obeyed perfectly. I was actually beginning to enjoy trotting along. Somewhat relaxed now, I even glanced in the distance to enjoy the scenery. I took a deep breath of self-satisfaction.

At the head of our line of horses clopping along rhythmically, something went out of rhythm. Something went flying into the air. “Something” was Country Boy.

At the end of the day we also had to learn how to lead our horse to the stable. As the stable boys relieved us of our horses and removed the saddles, they noticed a sore on Thunder’s back, just in front of the place where the saddle rested. Every time the horse went down a hill, the saddle slipped forward--rubbing this sore spot. To tell his rider a thing or two, the horse simply flung his hind legs up and sent the rider flying.

As we left the stable, Country Boy and I just happened to be side by side. “How is the Cavalier today?”I asked.

55
Strike

The third year of medical school changed the rank of the student from cadet to officer. Although we were under the jurisdiction of the Military Academy, we now lived at home and participated in medical school activities as other students did. Unlike the nonmilitary student, we were expected to join other officers for ceremonial duties and those exercises that prepared us for them.

That year, General Baharmast was appointed Commander of the Military Academy. As a new director, he had new ideas. He decided that military medical students, regardless of their rank, exercise every morning between 6:00 a.m. and 7:00 a.m. In order to meet this schedule I had to get up at 4:00 a.m., leave the house by 5:00 a.m. before public buses resumed operation, then walk an hour to reach the base by 6:00 a.m. in order to exercise for at least an hour. After that session, I had to walk another hour to reach the hospital. By 6:00 p.m. when classes at the medical school were dismissed, the military students were lucky to be awake, let alone be able to study.

General Baharmast also had the habit of concluding our morning exercise session with a lecture. He always talked longer than time allowed and made everyone late for the first class in the hospital.

The general apparently knew a lot of history, including history of medicine. He delighted in telling us stories of the doctors of long time ago. As a St. Cyr graduate, he also had a treasury of experiences of his own. The general's stories were indeed interesting, but not for busy medical students who hardly had time for their required courses.

After two months of Gen. Baharmast's morning exercises and lectures the medical students reached their saturation point. One afternoon Ali Koocheck, an aggressive individual, invited all the military-medical students to collect in one of the classrooms after 6:00 p.m. to discuss the situation.

After a brief discussion they unanimously agreed that a "strike" was in order. "Tomorrow no one should show up for exercise."

The following day I joined 15 other students at the hospital, rather than at the Military Academy. Fifteen others did report for exercise. The remainder called in sick. The news of the strike reached the general, who was infuriated. Since the Army could not interfere with our education, General Baharmast could not retaliate. His idea of a punishment was to keep the striking students at the base for the following three weekends, thus depriving them of the usual free holiday time on Friday.

As a result of the strike, exercise at 6:00 a.m. at the base was no longer a requirement for military medical students. Had students pursued this line of action a few years earlier during the reign of Reza Shah, they probably would have been imprisoned.

56

Patient's Dignity

With unbridled energy and explosive enthusiasm I spent the mornings of my third-year of medical school in the hospital. One morning Dr. Zeshtgoo, assistant professor of surgery, explained the pain and topographic anatomy of the abdomen. "In order to identify the source of abdominal pain, a doctor must be familiar with the nine areas of the abdomen and the associated organs." Escorting a group of 10 students to the female surgical ward, he said, "We are going to look at a patient now. Here is a case of hyperthyroidism, but we can study her because the abdomen is perfectly normal."

She seemed young, probably about 16 years old, but she looked insecure and helpless. Most likely she felt uneasy at the approach of 11 men. Her eyes bulged slightly, possibly because of exopthalmus or because of sheer distress and lack of sleep. As 10 young male medical students circled her bed, she stared at us apprehensively.

Dr. Zeshtgoo grabbed her bed sheet to expose her body covered only by a hospital gown. As he held one corner of it, she clutched the other, pulling it back. She became so nervous, she trembled. When Dr. Zeshtgoo succeeded in ripping the sheet away from her, he tugged at her hospital gown to expose her abdomen. It was embarrassing enough to have these men stare at her, but it was worse to reveal her body bare. "I'm not wearing underwear," she tried to explain as she resisted the doctor's tugging.

The doctor was losing patience. As he felt himself losing control, he also felt humiliated in front of his students. As the patient began to cry, he really lost control and slapped her. "Who the hell do you think is going to look at you, you ugly duckling?" Shoving the gown aside, he bared her legs, pelvis, and abdomen. She pulled it over her face. She gave up. She cried uncontrollably.

"In order to find the organ causing the pain in the

abdomen," he began somewhat shakily and loud enough to drown her sobs, "you should be familiar with the areas of the abdomen and associated organs." Touching the girl's bare skin and drawing imaginary intersecting lines, he proudly shared his expertise, "There are nine such divisions. From the top down in the middle they are: epigastric, umbilical, and hypogastric. On each side, again from top down you find hypochondriac, lumbar and iliac." He continued expounding on the diseases associated with each area.

All I could hear was the this sick young girl's sobs. I could not concentrate on the lecture. Instead of hearing Dr. Zeshtgoo, in my mind I could hear Dr. Meer, a venerable experienced professor of surgery, who constantly counseled his students about the proper way of addressing and examining a patient. "Never," he emphasized, "never disturb the patient. Make sure you never hurt anyone. Your professional demeanor must evince the highest level of integrity and dignity. Should you ever doubt how to handle your patient, put yourself in his position and see what you would want your doctor to do for you." Dr. Meer would never behave as Dr. Zeshtgoo just did. Even I could have told Dr. Zeshtgoo that it would have been so simple to cover the girl's legs and pelvis and still be able to point out pertinent areas of the abdomen.

The lesson that I did learn that day was to NEVER be like Dr. Zeshtgoo .

When Aesop (Loghman) was asked from whom he had learned dignity, he answered, "From the undignified."

57

Dr. Eqbal

As a group of medical students was leaving a medical ward of Pahlavi Hospital, they all seemed to be talking at once, asking Dr. Azizi, their professor of internal medicine, questions about the patient they had just seen with Parkinson's disease. The professor was just as pleased as the students were excited--he with their enthusiasm and they for his knowledge. He felt that their success was his.

Out of nowhere appeared Dr. Eqbal, totally disregarding the discussion in progress and completely ignoring the students. He motioned Dr. Azizi to leave the group. Reluctantly Azizi did so--out of sheer politeness to his colleague, even though he had no inkling of the reason for such a rude interruption. Eqbal spoke in French, assuming that only Azizi will understand what he had to say, which obviously was not to be heard by the students.

The students continued to discuss the patient among themselves until they heard a few French words that they too could understand: "You are wasting your time with these stupid medical students. It won't get you anywhere."

"Where did Dr. Eqbal want to go?" wondered one of the young men.

All of them noticed how he sneered, obviously most dissatisfied with whatever he was doing. He certainly couldn't object to being chairman of the Department of Infectious Disease. That was very prestigious in the world of academia.

Another time he had simultaneously enjoyed the position of Minister of Health. In this position he became a personal friend of the royal family's. Because of his good looks, his underlings even rumored that he had enjoyed a romantic relationship with Princess Ashraf, the Shah's divorced sister. For such political prowess that he thrived on, he would do anything.

Dr. Eqbal was so preoccupied with his political

aspirations, he never had time to fulfill his responsibilities at the medical school. When the fourth year medical students spent 10 weeks rotation concentrating on infectious diseases, the department supposedly chaired by Dr. Eqbal, they rarely ever even caught a glimpse of him. Because of the political power he wielded he could not be replaced at the University. He had become so influential with the royal family that none of the university administrators would dare mention a replacement for him. As the years went by, he cared less and less about medicine and more and more about politics.

By 1957 I worked as a pathology resident in New York City. That January I received an invitation from the Iranian Consulate inviting all Iranians in New York to greet Dr. Eqbal at a tea. "The Embassy of Iran" it read in embossed letters, "requests your presence at a tea in honor of Dr. Manoochehr Eqbal at the Iranian Consulate, Rockefeller Center, 4:00 p.m. Wednesday, January 16, 1957." It was probably that the Shah was going to appoint him to the post of Prime Minister and wanted him to have some public exposure. Having heard rumors that this man was about to be appointed Prime Minister of Iran, I surmised his affair was to influence the citizens by wining and dining them.

Since socializing with fellow Iranians would be a pleasant change of pace, I accepted the invitation. That afternoon I found myself among 100 Iranians. Dr. Eqbal stood by the entrance, ready to welcome his guests. I stepped forward and introduced myself, "Dr. Payan."

He half way bowed, warmly shook my hand, and smiled most charmingly, "How do you do, Dr. Payan. I'm delighted that you could come. It's a real pleasure to meet you."

I too smiled, but not as effusively as he. In my mind's eye I was reviewing the scene of 1946 when he advised Dr. Azizi not to waste time talking to "stupid medical students." I wondered if he had taken me for someone else. I was sure he had absolutely no idea who I was and certainly had no recollection of even seeing me 11 years ago.

Three months later Dr. Eqbal did become the Prime Minister of Iran. He enjoyed the distinction of being the first physician to enjoy this prestigious post. In his acceptance speech to Parliament he declared himself as his "Master's Voice," referring to the Shah as his "Master."

For the rest of his life his obeisance to the Shah which kept him in powerful political positions was remarkable.

As opposition to the Shah increased, however, so did hatred for Eqbal. A few years before the Revolution of 1979 he died.

When Khomeini assumed power, his followers wanted to exhume Eqbal's body and burn it as a public manifestation of their scorn for the Pahlavi Dynasty.

58
Schizophrenia

Medical schools always include a one-semester course in psychology and psychiatry. In addition to theories, explanations in textbooks, as a medical student enrolled in these classes, among other things, I was exposed to the world of reality by spending four hours a week at the State Hospital.

As a matter of routine, Dr. Rezai--a professor of psychiatry, as well as medical director of the hospital--would first greet the class of approximately sixty students and then interview four of the patients for about fifteen minutes each. During the next hour he would explain the art of conferring with patients tactfully, N E V E R getting anyone excited or angry.

Students were rarely allowed to go beyond the closed doors of the "closed wards," where the acutely disturbed patients were treated. Patients assigned to the medical students were in the so-called "open ward," therefore supposedly not dangerous. Nevertheless, every once in a while one would become violent and had to be calmed down. To prevent any unforeseen problem, we were instructed to be with a fellow student whenever we talked to patients. During the last two hours of the day we each teamed up with a partner to walk around the wards or (in pleasant weather) the yard.

The grounds around this hospital were landscaped with many varieties of trees, shrubs, and flowers. Such natural surroundings were very conducive to inner peace and tranquility. Interviews became more productive when doctor and patient could relax side by side, sitting comfortably on lawn furniture or simply leaning against one of the huge trees, rather than in a crowded ward.

One warm sunny day I accompanied a classmate as he talked to a patient in his 50's.

"When I was young, like you," the patient said in a

very loud voice, "I too attended medical school. In Paris," Still louder he added, "While I was taking the fourth-year exams, I fainted. When I woke up, I found myself in a hospital, dehydrated and exhausted. Afterwards I was plagued with auditory hallucinations and eventually diagnosed as schizophrenic. That ended my dreams of a medical career. Instead of a doctor, I became a patient in this state hospital.

"It's really not bad," he mused. "I have food, books to read, a comfortable clean bed. When you don't expect very much, life isn't disappointing."

How profound, I thought. When the patient noticed that my friend was holding a book in French about infectious diseases, he asked to look at it.

"Of course," he obliged and handed him the book.

After flipping through a few pages, the patient began reading loud enough for people all around to hear about pneumonia--in excellent French. The word *penicillin* stopped the flow of French, as he looked up at us to ask whether or not this was some kind of new drug.

I confirmed his assumption and mentioned how effective it was in treating pneumonia and other infectious diseases. I couldn't help wonder how such a logical and intelligent person could be committed to an institution.

My friend must have felt the same. With absolutely no connection with anything else we discussed, he blurted, "What do you think life is all about?".

The patient's face changed. His eyebrows arched. His eyes looked beyond everything in view. Slowly, very slowly, he opened wide his grey hospital robe, exposing his genitals in full view. "This is life. THIS is what life is all about." His face was flushed.

I think our faces were also flushed--in embarrassment. My friend and I did not know where to look.

Luckily, the patient closed his coat. For a few moments he said nothing. He just looked at us. Again we did not know where to look.

Almost in a whisper, almost accusing, he reasoned, "You guys get up early in the morning, rush to school, study very hard, work like hell." He paused. "For what," he asked rhetorically. "So you can call yourself a doctor. Be a successful man. Find a good looking woman, get married, and have children. Then you expect your children to grow up and do the same thing. Only by this time, you are old and you will die. That's what life is all about."

At that point I had no doubts why this man was among the mentally disturbed. Even as an inexperienced student, I could tell that he was crazy! His behavior doomed him to the state hospital for the rest of his life--no doubt about that.

Many times later my friend and I referred to this incident in the garden and even laughed about it.

Fifty years later I still remember the complete scenario, as though it were a movie. I may have forgotten some of the visual details, but I will always remember the patient's commentary on life. In fact, as the days go by, he makes more and more sense. In Biology: The World of Life Dr. Robert Wallace writes:

> Evolution at its basic level is a means whereby certain kinds of genes are perpetuated. . . . Individuals are simply temporary caretakers of their genes. . . . Variability of offspring is one way an individual might be able to leave its genes in a changing world. . . . An organism is simply a vehicle that genes use in order to reproduce themselves. Of course, we would prefer to feel that our lives have a bit more meaning than that, that we are more than carrying cases for our gonads. . . . We are simply our genes' way of making more genes. Therefore, we primp, work, save, worship, rationalize, love, lust, avoid, hate, defend, retreat, and sunbathe. We have a variety of explanations for all the things we do. But perhaps what we are really doing is behaving in such a way that our genes end up in the next generation.

Obviously, Nature has spent billions of years

processing the evolution of the available genetic material in man and animals. The precious genetic material must be protected and transferred from one generation to the next. Every person is a mere carrier of this precious material. The brain is given to each to survive the hostile environment. Sex is one's reward for transferring the precious material. When people grow old and become incapable of reproduction, they are all condemned to death by nature.

The schizophrenic patient seems just as astute as the sceintist philosopher. The difference between them is the medium of expression.

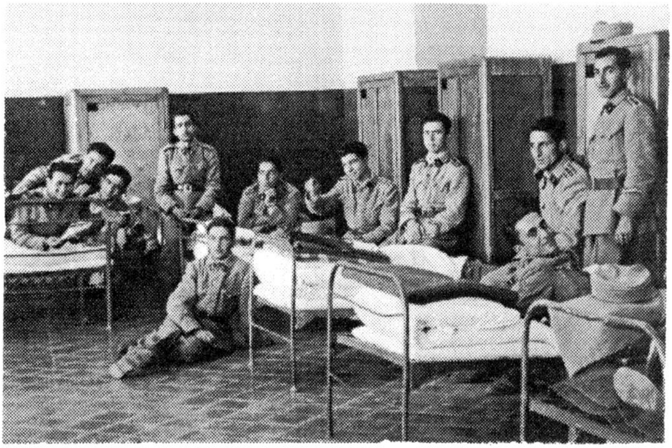

59
Buzzing

On a sweltering summer day a *bazary*, a successful businessman who owned a shop in the bazaar, went to the office of Dr. Jamsheed Aalam, professor of otorhinolaryngology, complaining of buzzing and movement in his right ear. It was even more annoying every time he had to interrupt his routine work every few minutes to poke his finger in the external ear canal, hoping to eliminate the aggravation. While he was settling down to sit in front of the doctor, he simultaneously flashed a wad of bills and said, "Doctor, I'll give you anything you want--50 tumans, 100 tumans, whatever. Just get this damn noisy thing out of my ear. It is driving me crazy."

The doctor looked at the man, then glanced at the ear, paused for a moment, and responded, "Fine, 50 tumans is enough. Just turn your head and let me look."

Dr. Aalam positioned the *bazary*'s head to let the spot light shine in the ear, adjusted his medical frontal mirror, and searched for the trouble. What did he see but a housefly lodged against the tympanic membrane, the eardrum. Within a second with the help of thin forceps the doctor removed it.

The *bazary* was elated, definitely relieved. After the doctor dropped a fly in a small jar, he presented it to the man and asked for fifty tumans.

"What 50 tumans?" he exclaimed. "You didn't even do anything! You hardly spent a second pulling that thing out of my ear. What kind of fees are you charging poor sick people? Here, on the basis of your time, I'm being most generous by giving you this." With that outburst he threw five tumans on the table.

"Fine," the doctor calmly responded, "but before you leave, let me take one last look into that poor ear to make sure that nothing is left behind."

As the patient glowered but sat down quietly again,

within another second the doctor transferred the fly from the jar back into the man's ear. "You can keep your five tumans . . . your fly too. Goodbye. "

Once again the fly buzzed in the *bazary*'s ear. Once again he screamed into the doctor's ear. "Get it out! Please! I'll give you anything you want."

"Fifty tumans . . . before I do anything."

"OK," he grumbled, thumbing his wad of bills and handing the money to the doctor.

Once again the doctor positioned him in the examining chair, adjusted the frontal mirror and with a twist of the long forceps removed the fly.

60

Prime Minister Razmara

While the number of students at the University of Tehran Medical School almost doubled, the number of university hospital beds did not. Under such circumstances it became more and more difficult for the future doctors to acquire clinical experience as there simply were not enough patients. Consequently, in early 1950 the medical students went on strike to have all the public hospitals in Tehran placed under the jurisdiction of the medical school. Dr. Saleh, the dean, was sympathetic to their cause.

For two weeks the students refused to attend classes. Such a public demonstration became negative publicity for the government.

General Razmara, a friend of Dr. Saleh's, was also sympathetic, but for personal reasons. The general felt that he could be influential in bringing about such a change, when (and if) he became Prime Minister. Razmara advised Saleh to encourage the strike until such an appointment was made public. At that time, as the prime minister, he could appoint Saleh to "Minister of Health," and in that position Saleh would have the power to unite all the public and university hospitals and satisfy the needs of the students.

While the students were deprived of their scheduled instruction, Saleh and Razmara were scheming to advance their political ambition.

General Razmara possessed an uncanny talent to achieve personal goals. It was this very strength that weakened his adversaries. While Mussadiq, a member of Parliament, strived to nationalize the oil industry and keep it out of foreign control, the British were confident that this no-nonsense general would sanction their efforts--for political support. The clergy disapproved of Razmara because he flaunted pro-West attitudes that inculcated change. Many Iranians feared that Razmara's self-assurance foreshadowed dictatorship. The Shah was afraid of him because he was extremely intelligent, experienced, self-confident and politically ambitious.

To avoid international confrontation which could lead to national criticism the Shah did appoint General Razmara Prime Minister, whom the British favored. As Prime Minister, Razmara kept his promise and did appoint Saleh as Minister of Health. That very day when Saleh promised unification of the two hospital systems, the strike ended.

Since Razmara spoke French, English, and Russian fluently, he cultivated friendships with foreign ambassadors and politicians. He supposedly received financial gifts from Anglo-Iranian Oil Company.

Such camaraderie with foreigners instigated hostility with nationalist members of Parliament. As he stepped to the podium in the Assembly Hall one day, the Majles greeted him with jeers: " dictator, British-man, traitor." He never had the opportunity to address the group.

One day he was urged to attend the funeral of a prominent clergyman. As he mingled among the large crowd, he was felled by an assassin's bullet.

In an instant the suspected murderer was arrested and taken to jail.

Two weeks later, during a session of Parliament, Ayatollah Kashani, the speaker of the House, hailed the gunman as the Savior of the Country and persuaded the group to grant him a pardon.

61

Surgery in the Mosque

By the dictates of Moslem religion it was customary for patients who died in the hospital after sundown to be transferred from their hospital room to a kind of mosque in the hospital basement. Only during the day were relatives notified to arrange for funeral and burial. Under normal circumstances anyone who died at home after sundown would be taken to the mosque where he would remain till burial the first thing the next day. Since this room in the basement of the hospital served as a holding area just as a neighborhood mosque does during the night, everyone referred to this cold basement room as the "hospital mosque."

In the wee hours of the morning when it was deathly quiet, Javid slipped in and out of this hospital mosque.

One morning a daughter came to claim the body of her mother. When a nurse took her to the basement, the daughter wanted to take one last look at her mother's body. They were both quite surprised to see blood stains on the hospital gown. As they checked further, they discovered a sutured surgical incision on the gall bladder area. Since the mother was hospitalized for pneumonia, there was no reason for abdominal surgery.

The daughter immediately went to the office of Dr. Farzad, Chief of Internal Medicine, and demanded an explanation. The Chief had no idea what they were talking about. This was the first that he had heard of any such incident. For his own satisfaction, if for no other reason, he promised to investigate.

For a few days he questioned the nurses, orderlies, and maintenance people. After a few days as the news spread, a night time orderly mentioned seeing a medical student coming out of the morgue around 6:00 a.m. Now the Chief questioned every medical student.

When it was Javid's turn, he nervously sat down at the edge of the chair facing Dr. Farzad.

The older doctor looked him in the eye and asked, "What were you doing in the mosque early in the morning?"

"Oh, nothing special, Sir. I just like to practice different surgical procedures on corpses. I am getting better and better at appendectomies and cholecystectomies. I learn best by doing, rather than by observing."

"What is the matter with you? Don't you know that tampering with bodies is illegal? Don't you know that you need permission from the relatives to do anything to a corpse? Even religion prohibits the touching of a corpse. What did you do anyway?"

"I only did a cholecystectomy on her."

"And you think this kind of practice is going to make you a surgeon? Where are your brains?"

The next day a padlock was placed on the door of the hospital mosque.

62
Inspection

In 1950 representatives of the American Medical Association visited medical schools around the world for accreditation. Seven physicians, all professors, representing various specialties, came to Iran. Several Iranian physicians understood English on various levels of comprehension, but the most fluent were Dr. Ameli (a British trained neurosurgeon) and Dr. Saleh (an American trained obstetrician-gynecologist). Those who could not communicate verbally had no trouble demonstrating their medical skills.

Dr. Smith, the American neurologist who headed the group, was surprised at the ability of Iranian physicians to make accurate diagnoses strictly on the basis of clinical examinations and limited radiologic and laboratory tests.

One day, as Dr. Ameli and Dr. Smith examined a young man with severe backache that radiated down both legs, their provisional diagnosis was slipped disk. The patient manifested a slightly elevated temperature, normal blood count, and normal appearance of the lumbar spine on X-ray. The history of the patient disclosed a questionable chronic gastric peptic ulcer and abdominal pain associated with eating. Dr. Ameli observed, "I am fairly sure this is a herniated disk. The mild fever and the abdominal pain in the back, however, make me wonder."

The next morning the surgical team was prepared for a diskectomy, the removal of the disk. The patient was already under anesthesia when Dr. Ameli decided to examine him one more time before making any incision. With a large needle and syringe the doctor drew 50cc of pus from the lower back. He then injected penicillin into the area and ordered antibiotics for the next few days. "This is obviously an abscess, the origin of which is not clear at this time," Dr. Ameli pointed out to his observers. Dr. Smith and everyone else were impressed with the strategy. Subsequent examination of the patient revealed a perforated posterior wall gastric ulcer with retroperitoneal extension.

Another day, while Dr. Smith, Dr. Ameli, and a group of students were making rounds in the neurology department, everyone was startled when a young male patient fell to the floor and began convulsing. Dr. Ameli removed the young man's shoe and sock, pulled a pin from the lapel of his white coat, and scratched the sole of the bare foot on the side. (When a person in good health feels a scratch on the sole of his foot, his toes curl under involuntarily, exhibiting the normal plantar-flexion of the toes. A person suffering from certain types of neurogenic disorders would react just the opposite. His toes would flex upward. Such a reflex is called "Babinksi sign.")

"The Babinski is negative. This man's problem is not physical. He's suffering from hysteria," announced Dr. Ameli. He then slapped the patient on the face and shouted, "Get up, you fool."

Immediately the patient stopped convulsing and opened his eyes. He rolled on his side, got on his knees, and stood up. The attending nurse was then directed to escort the patient to the psychiatric ward.

Once again Dr. Smith was very impressed with the way Dr. Ameli arrived at the diagnosis. The other AMA visitors were equally impressed with the superior clinical judgment in determining diagnoses. After a week they left.

About a year later it was announced that the only medical schools approved outside the United States and Canada were those in England. The University of Tehran School of Medicine was found lacking in basic sciences, radiology and laboratory facilities. What was surprising was that medical schools of Switzerland, France and Germany were also found unacceptable. Those familiar with medical schools in Europe were surprised.

About 10 years later the AMA developed an examination commonly called ECFMG (Educational Council for Foreign Medical Graduates). It subjected all foreign medical school graduates to two days of testing to ascertain their proficiency in all disciplines of medicine, as well as communication skills in English.

63
Persepolis

Ancient history came alive when my friend Ahmad and I visited the ruins of ancient Persia in southern Iran. It was a trip into the past, an era about twenty-five hundred years ago. .

In the fifth grade, youngsters learned about Cyrus the Great. In 559 B.C. he began his reign as an obscure Persian who within 30 years changed his status from the king of a tribe to the leader of the world's first empire, which stretched from India to the Mediterranean Sea. Now that we were university students, we wanted to see with our very own eyes where some of this took place.

The only significant remains of the capital *Pasargadae* (Persian camp) is the tomb of Cyrus. The unadorned structure made of white limestone consists of a rectangular room about three stories tall at the top of six steps. Scattered in the sand around this neglected tomb, perfectly carved round and square blocks of limestone about the size of a bushel basket convinced us that at one time another building, most likely a temple, had surrounded this tomb.

Unfortunately, Cyrus left very few documents about himself. Greeks, Babylonians, Egyptians, and Israelites, however, have praised him profusely in their writings. Of the 23 times that Cyrus is mentioned in the Old Testament, the emphasis is on the rebuilding of a temple in Jerusalem.

More than anything else, Cyrus seems to have been admired for his respect for others--be they individuals or nations--in regard to religion, custom, or culture. In all his actions Cyrus never mistreated anyone, not even the people he defeated. He freed the Israelites from Babylonia after they had been held captive for more than thirty years. Before sending all 40,000 of them back to Israel, he gave them all the gold and silver that had been looted from their Jerusalem temple. Cyrus may have been influenced by the teachings of Zoroaster, especially in regard to freedom of choice.

Another great king who was the subject of many historical accounts was Darius who ruled the Persian Empire from 520 B.C. to 486 B.C. He exemplified tolerance just as Cyrus did. His fame, however, rests on his management skills. He organized all the diverse people under his rule into 23 provinces called "satrapies." To each province he assigned a *satrap* (governor) along with a general to command the army in that particular satrapy. To prevent any abuse of power by any royal representatives, he had a controller-general visit each province periodically. Since Darius was in command of all the provinces, each of which had its own ruler (king), he is often called "Shahanshah," King of Kings.

Such power fostered an interest in luxury and grandeur. For himself he built a new capital called Parsa. While Iranians call it Takht-e-Jamsheed, the Greeks named it Persepolis, a name still known around the world.

The overview of the magnificent ruins is a royal complex sitting atop a 33-acre terrace formed of natural rocks. A few columns 65 feet tall still stand, slender and intricately decorated to show symbols of the nations of the time. The predominant decoration at the heads of the columns was double headed animals--like lions, eagles, or bulls. Each of these sculptures on top of the columns stood eight feet wide and five feet tall. Seventy-two of these columns supported the roof of the audience hall called "Apadana." One would enter this hall from either of its two sides by a double reversing staircase. To enable the horses to carry dignitaries to the entrance into the Apadana each of the 111 steps was wide enough and deep enough with a four-inch riser to facilitate their climb. These stone steps are still supported by a nine-foot wall carved with life-sized reliefs of soldiers, animals, and gift bearing visitors.

It took Darius, his son Xerxes and his grandson Artexerxes more than 60 years to complete the construction of this limestone citadel.

In the last year of Darius's reign Persians lost the battle of Marathon in Greece. At the same time a major revolt erupted in Egypt, one of the satrapies. At age 64

Darius died in 486 B.C.

Not far from Persepolis his tomb (carved 75 feet high and 60 feet wide) still stands in a cliff. Stone carvings surround the only door which leads into the interior of this sepulcher. The facade of the tomb is cross shaped. The center horizontal aspect of the cross features a palace. The upper arm of the cross shows Darius on a platform facing a Zoroastrian fire altar. People representing each of the 23 satrapies support this platform. Above the king is a winged, crowned figure, believed to be Ahura-Mazda, the Zoroastrian god.

The demise of Darius began the demise of the empire. In 330 B.C. Alexander conquered Iran. In a drunken frenzy he looted, burned and destroyed Persepolis, the remnants of which have lasted more than twenty-three hundred years.

As the tour of ancient Persepolis came to an end, Ahmad and I began to realize that the truly great geniuses in these ancient times were the architects and artisans who turned the dreams of the kings into functioning reality. There seems to be no record to immortalize these people.

Ahmad and I also wondered what--if anything--Iranians learned from this historical period. Till this day we discuss the steady stream of foreign intervention in Iran and the dictatorship of kings and religious leaders. The obvious answer is "Nothing."

64

Father of Freedom

One of the most revered men in recent Iranian history is Dr. Muhammad Musaddiq. He will always be remembered as extremely patriotic, honest, incorruptible, and anti-foreign--especially in regard to the British. His name will go down in history for preserving Iranian interests, for sanctioning nationalization of oil, and for strongly advocating democracy.

His son was also respected. Dr. Musaddiq, Jr. served the world of medicine as a professor of obstetrics-gynecology. He performed his work meticulously and treated everyone with sincere respect. His prime purpose in life seemed to be to make people feel good, physically and psychologically.

One day, however, he was late for work, definitely unlike him. In the middle of an intersection his Ford stalled when he stopped for a traffic light. Since the car refused to budge, he had to call the nearest service station. Within the hour a wrecker came and towed the car.

By the time the mechanic adjusted the carburetor, he was three hours late for surgery and ready for someone to take care of him. When it was time to pay, he filled out the form with his name, the model of the car, and other formalities of identification.

The man behind the counter happened to be the owner. When he noticed Dr. Musaddiq's name, his eyes opened as he asked, "Really? Are you the famous Dr. Musaddiq?"

"Oh, no. The famous one's my father."

The mechanic tore up his bill and said, "I cannot charge you. Your father is the father of freedom in this country. I will not take your money."

Dr. Musaddiq insisted, but the man refused.

They shook hands and he walked to his car.

65

Sarcasm

My mother's brother Jafar was old enough to be my father, but tactless as a young wolf. When I was accepted into Medical School, all the relatives and friends congratulated me. Only Jafar had nothing pleasant to say.

"I hear you are going to medical school," he almost growled.

"Yes, I am."

"You should buy a large piece of land, you know."

Wondering what he had in mind, I questioned naively, "A piece of land? For what?"

"For all the people you are going to kill. You are going to need a private cemetery for the patients that you will not be able to cure."

Being young and sensitive, I was upset. Considering the source, however, I tried to ignore him.

Six years later one early morning at the beginning of my last year of medical school, Jafar came to the hospital to see me. I was surprised.

"I had to come to see you," he announced.

"What can I do for you?" I really wondered.

"I have had this sore on my penis for some time now, like over a week. It refuses to go away. I probably got it from using public bathrooms. Can you look at it, please?"

"Yes, of course."

I took him to the clinic. After examining him, I said, "This is syphilis. To be absolutely sure, you should have a Wasserman test, a blood test that determines the presence or absence of the problem."

He hesitated about such a procedure because he feared his name would be recorded and then associated with promiscuity. His wife and grown children would be more upset than he, especially if they ever discovered that he had visited a brothel several weeks ago when he was out drinking with his friends. After I suggested that he go to a private laboratory and use a false name, he felt more receptive to my ideas.

A week later he returned to show me that the test result was positive. Once a week for the following eight weeks I treated him with neo-salvarsan. During this time he admitted that he cheated on his wife and often slept with prostitutes.

Even though prostitution is indeed the oldest profession and exists around the world, it is still illegal in many countries, especially where the government is strongly influenced by religion. If prostitution were legalized, the ladies of the night would have to meet standards of personal health and hygiene before they could be licensed. Such laws would control the rampant spread of sexually transmitted diseases.

After Jafar's last injection I explained the dangers of the situation to him. He did seem grateful for my concern. As he got up to leave the office, he asked, "How much do I owe you for your services?"

I looked at him, smiled, and hesitated for a moment. "You owe me all the money I need to buy that parcel of land large enough for a cemetery."

"Oh," he mumbled, turning around to leave. He was surprised that I remembered his sarcasm from six years ago.

66
Loan

With the approach of spring, all Iranians turn their thoughts to No-Ruz, Persian New Year. A few of the medical school students who worked in the same hospital decided to celebrate the holiday together as this was their last year as students. After graduation they would scatter to all corners of the earth.

At an elegant restaurant nearby they enjoyed a cucumber/yogurt salad, barbecued *kofteh*, *khoresh ghorme-sabzi*, mountains of rice, sparkling wine from Shiraz, and an unbelievable assortment of fresh fruit for dessert. It cost about five tumans apiece.

After the meal I pulled out my calendar/notebook, between the pages of which I carried my money--as most Iranians did. As wallets were not commonly used, such a pocket calendar served a double purpose. When Javid, one of my classmates, spied 30 tumans tucked between April and May, he stared and asked soulfully, "Would you pay for me? I don't have money this evening. I will pay you later."

"O.K.," I said and gave him a bill. "You owe me five."

Several times a week I saw him in the hospital, as well as at the university, but he never mentioned the money he owed me and I felt uncomfortable broaching the subject.

Several months later we accidentally met in the office of the Chief Secretary of the school, finalizing graduation requirements. As we each had to pay five tumans for the stamp that would validate our diploma, he pulled out a 20-tuman bill. Unfortunately, the secretary did not have the right change. Instead of giving him 15 back, the man gave him only 10. Noticing the 10-tuman bill in my hand, he suggested that I give Javid five after I get change. "Right now he can pay for yours."

Javid's jaw dropped in silent protest.

I smiled. "O.K.," I said, took my receipt, and

walked out.

He was right behind me, hounding me for his five tumans.

"Get some change and give me the money. Now."

"I don't owe you anything. You owed me five tumans from the restaurant. I paid for your dinner. You do remember, don't you?"

"Ya, but that was long time ago. How come you still remember that? Today I need money."

"Who doesn't?"

He kept harassing me to change the 10-tuman bill and give him five. He said the same thing over and over again so many times, I was ready to puke--right on him.

As we were leaving the building, I unfolded the 10-tuman bill and asked the janitor who was standing in the hall if he had two fives.

He did. I carefully put one between January and February and slowly ripped the other up, piece by piece. Just as I was about to drop this confetti into the garbage can, I decided not to. Instead, I gave the pieces to the janitor.

Javid growled, "You . . . are . . . stupid. You could have kept half and given me the rest. That way you would still have some of my money."

"Your money?" I screamed. Exasperated, I turned away and went off in the opposite direction.

In spite of the pieces, the janitor thanked me as I walked away.

67
Young Physician

Early 1952 as one of the doctors in the Iranian Air Force, I was in charge of the infirmary at the Academy. Young and athletic, the cadets, as well as the soldiers stationed at the base, were seldom ill. The older men who may have needed medical attention would not consult me because I was young. Since they were earning a comfortable salary, they consulted more experienced physicians elsewhere.

Most military physicians worked at their government jobs between 7:00 a.m. and 2:00 p.m. and in their private offices after that. I decided that I should have an office too. Since I was totally unknown and very young, I wanted my office to be in a poor section of the city of Tehran. As a twenty-six-year-old idealist, I was convinced that I could care for the destitute, bring them back to robust health, and prove instrumental in helping them to be self-sufficient.

The only office I could afford was on the second floor of a dilapidated building at the end of Jaleh Avenue, near Doolab. The landing at the head of the stairs served as my waiting room. For this and the room I paid 30 tumans a month for rent and an additional 10 tumans for cleaning services. Utilities were extra. The only time I saw the owner was at the end of the month when he came for the rent--in cash.

The first time I went to my office it was exciting to see a 3' x 2' sign advertising my availability:

دکتر هوشنگ مفخم پایان

٨-٤ بعدازظهر

Dr. Hushang Mofakham Payan
Office hours . . . 4:00 - 8:00 p.m.

For weeks I was the only one to be in that office during those hours. Instead of hearing "Good afternoon, Doctor" from patients in pain, I kept hearing "*Khiar doolab, do-ta be sannar* (Cucumbers from Doolab, two for penny)" from vendors outside.

As I sat behind the small desk near the landing, I spent most of my time reading. Since I was hoping for the opportunity to go to the United States for postgraduate studies, I whiled away the time by concentrating on medical books in English to become more at ease with English terminology. I lamented the fact that I could afford neither nurse nor secretary, but I obviously had no need for either. To make sure that no one had difficulty finding me, I left the door open with me at my desk in plain sight. I did have electricity, but no phone. When I got stiff from sitting at my desk, I got up, walked around the empty office, and sat in one of the two chairs on the other side of the room--one for the patient and one for a possible companion.

It was at the end of the third week that one unkempt man with a stubby beard walked in. He was so weak, he could hardly whisper. He was so thin, he seemed prematurely old.

"Hello."

"Hello, please come in. Have a seat."

The man looked at me and reluctantly sat down, using the desk for support.

As I picked up my notebook to write his name and history, he said, "I am sorry, Doctor. I am really not sick. I just need a little money. I have terrible cramps and stomach ache."

"When did you eat last?" I asked, laying aside my pen and papers.

"Three days ago."

I put my hand in my pocket and pulled out two tumans, "This is all I have. I will share it with you--half and half."

I handed him a tuman, which was good enough for a couple of good meals. He took the money and said, "Thank you, young man. God bless you." Then he walked down those creaky steps that the landlord promised to fix and never did.

This scenario repeated itself several times throughout the summer. It was not always the same man, but different people--all suffering from postwar economic depression. There were many truly hungry people, people who could not get anything to eat for 24 hours or longer.

On another occasion, an hour after my arrival at the office, a man about my age walked in. His rolled-up sleeves, collarless shirt, and baggy wrinkled slacks told me that he was an unskilled blue-collar worker.

"Are you the doctor?" he asked.

"Yes, I am."

"My grandfather is sick. The house is only a five-minute walk from here. Can you come to look at him?"

This I did not expect. Since it was very warm, I did not have a tie or jacket. In the office I wore my white coat, but I did not want to walk out into the street dressed that way. Nevertheless, after I took off my white coat, picked up my bag with sphygmomanometer and stethoscope, I followed him.

As we walked together, I asked him, "How old is your grandfather?"

"Nobody knows for sure, but he seems to be about 90."

"How long has he been ill?"

"On and off a long time."

"Can you tell me approximately how long?"

"Oh, yes, probably a year--maybe even longer. One doctor told him long time ago that he has kidney disease and not much can be done about it."

"Is he on medication?"

"No. He can't even swallow anything but liquids. He's asleep most of the time."

"Did you ever think of taking him to a hospital?"

"No, the family wants him to die at home. They are afraid someone in the hospital will cut him up after he is dead."

"You mean an autopsy?" I asked.

"Something like that," he said, most likely not knowing what an autopsy meant.

By the time we entered the old house, I already knew what the diagnosis was. Kidney failure and chronic uremia.

Following the grandson, I walked into a large room covered with a wall-to-wall rug and about twenty-five men of all ages sitting around. They were all unkempt, sad, solemn, and quiet. I remember Dr. Adl, one of my medical school professors, who repeatedly said, "When you are examining a patient, tell everyone to get out of the room, except for the person who takes care of the patient." Nevertheless, I did not say anything. I simply let these people watch me. Dressed in his underwear and covered by a thin sheet, the emaciated man lay on a mattress in the middle of the room. His breathing was shallow; his blood pressure, elevated; pulse rate, normal; heart sounds, weak with extra beats.

I told the grandson, "Your grandfather has uremia and chronic kidney failure, which may take his life any time soon."

"When?"

"That, I do not know. He may actually get a little better, only to get worse again. If you would like to take him to the hospital, I will write a note for you. You can take him to a government hospital. It is all free. He could rest more comfortably. Nothing more can be done for him."

"No," he immediately responded. "We want him to die at home." After a pause, he scratched his chin and asked, "Would you sign his death certificate?"

"Now?" I gasped.

"Yes, now."

"No. I cannot do that. He is still alive. When he is dead, come and get me. Then I will sign the certificate for you."

He pulled a soiled piece of paper from his pocket, unfolded it carefully, showed it to me and explained, "Three days ago Dr. Sardar signed this, but left the line for the date blank."

In disbelief I read the death certificate twice. Sure enough, it was signed by Dr. Sardar, whose office happened to be closer to town than mine. He was 10 years my senior. I did not know him personally, but I did see him on occasion.

"This is illegal," I sighed. "I couldn't sign it in the first place. Besides, you already have it signed."

As I gathered my stethoscope and blood pressure

monitoring equipment and turned around to leave, the grandson came after me, shoving five tumans into my hand.

"I really did not do anything. You do not owe me anything. When your grandfather is dead, call me. I will sign the death certificate. Then you can pay me." I returned the money.

I was not called back, because the family already had the certificate signed.

When I accidentally bumped into the grandson a few days later, I naturally inquired about his grandfather. Three days after my visit, the old man had died.

Another day a young crying mother came to the office with her baby. "The baby, my baby," she sobbed, "is dead. She won't wake up. My little Zeeba is dead."

Gently I lifted the baby from the woman's arms and placed her on the examining table. The baby then stretched a little and "christened" my new table that cost me two weeks' salary. She was sound asleep. Her respiration was shallow in blissful dreamland, her cheeks were rosy, and her pulse and heart were normal.

"Don't worry, ma'am," I turned toward the mother. "Your daughter is not dead. She's sleeping soundly and will wake up in perfect condition. Everything is all right."

The young woman stared at me almost menacingly, almost accusing me that I certainly did not know what I was talking about. "I could easily wake her up for feeding, but today she refused to wake up."

I wrapped the baby in her swaddling clothes, gave her back to the mother, and said, "Now hold Zeeba near your breast. She will start suckling, even though she's asleep."

The mother pushed her blouse around to place the baby near her bosom. Zeeba could hardly wait. The mother cried with joy. She could hardly wait to pay me for the miracle I performed. After they had left, I noticed a tuman on my desk.

Another afternoon a more excited young man ran into my office, screaming, "Doctor, Doctor, there's a boy bleeding to death in the street. Come, please come."

Immediately I ran after him. A boy, no more than seven or eight years old, was sitting near a pile of broken glass. Apparently his mother sent him to the store for a bottle of vinegar. On his way home, he tripped, fell, and dropped the bottle which broke and cut his hand. The wound was about half an inch on the palm of his hand, adjacent to his little finger. But there was a pumper, a small artery, which had also been cut and needed to be tied. Out in this street (neither in my office for that matter) I had no facilities to do such a procedure. The best I could do was press on the pumper with my clean handkerchief. "Get the boy's parents," I ordered.

Meanwhile, a crowd of all ages gathered around us. The boy kept crying, not only because he was frightened at the sight of so much blood and so many people, but because his hand ached. More than anything else, he was afraid that his father would scold him for dropping the vinegar.

Within minutes both parents were at the boy's side, assuring him that they did not care about the vinegar. I showed the father how to apply pressure on the pumper and told him to rush the boy to the Emergency Room at Seena Hospital. The only way to get there was to walk about twenty minutes to the bus stop and then ride #22 for about a half hour. In that poor section of town, there was no horse-and-buggy service.

As my business acumen was sparse and as I spent more and more of my military salary to support my medical office along with the poor and hungry, I wondered what kind of business being a doctor really was. At the end of the summer I had no other choice but to close the office.

68
Mussadiq

Since I was on call on July 22, 1952, I stayed at the Air Force Hospital in Dowshan Tappeh until 6:00 p.m., later than usual. At this hour military trucks that normally provided transportation to town had stopped running. Neither were buses available, because the drivers had gone on strike. I had no other choice but to walk.

Many other people also declared a strike to make clear their displeasure about the way Muhammad Riza Shah had treated Prime Minister Muhammad Mussadiq. In 1951 Mussadiq had nationalized AIOC, the Anglo-Iranian Oil Company. Since a control of the oil was really control of the country, Winston Churchill in retaliation aligned England with the so-called "seven sisters," the seven western oil companies, to boycott Iranian oil and bankrupt the government of Iran. The British government also imposed a trade embargo on Iran for the sole purpose of subjecting Iran to Western Imperialistic designs. When the United States offered to mediate, Secretary of State Dean Acheson discovered that the British wanted to "rule or ruin" Iran.

Such political maneuvers caused tremendous financial difficulties for Iran. Disregarding these problems, the young inexperienced pro-British Shah kept pressuring Prime Minister Mussadiq for more money for the army--not to protect the country, but to protect himself against his enemies among his own countrymen. On the basis of the way that his father operated, the Shah believed that the armed forces were at his disposal to do as he wished. On the basis of the democratic constitution the Prime Minister should command the Army. The government could not meet the demands of the payroll of an ever-increasing military personnel and still handle other financial responsibilities. Neither could the private citizens meet their financial obligations.

To ease the country's budget problem Mussadiq

wanted to check the expenses of the army. When the Shah refused to relinquish such control, Mussadiq resigned. Mussadiq's resignation triggered a series of strikes, demonstrations and riots. Such chaos continued for a week until the intensity of protest unnerved the Shah, who recalled Mussadiq.

That evening when I had no choice but to walk about three miles, my walk home became more wearisome than expected. At Parliament Square a large noisy crowd of at least two thousand people stood listening to a man talking over a loudspeaker about the weakening of democracy and freedom. "Uncertainty and indecisiveness characterizes every move made by the Shah. If the Shah does not reinstate Mussadiq, Iran will lose the only democratic government we ever had."

In response people cheered, straining their voices and pumping their clenched fists at the sky, "Down with the Shah. Down with the Army. Long live Mussadiq."

One man screamed "Either Death or Mussadiq."

Directly across the Square there seemed to be a showdown with police and army units patrolling with tanks and armored cars. In the distance flames punctuated the trees, as though a car had been on fire. Branches of trees were separated by brandishing bayonets and police night sticks. Casualties were mounting right in front of my eyes. People were fighting each other, not even caring which side each represented. Some young people seemed to revel in the electricity of the excitement, while they didn't even know why the crowd gathered.

While I had no choice but to pass this angry mob, I stayed away as far as possible. On such a day my military uniform definitely was a liability. None of these rioters would calm down for even a second to verify that I was a doctor, not a soldier. Instantly I would be considered pro-Shah, consequently a target.

It was at this time that a cousin of mine with her twin 2-year-old daughters was trying to circle Parliament Square to avoid any confrontation. Without exchanging more than a nod and a whispered "hello" when we met, she picked up one of the girls and I, the other. We looked at each other, knowing the possibility of danger, hoping that the people who have gone wild will spare us along with the children. The farther we went, the faster we walked.

Together we disappeared into the calm of the residential area.

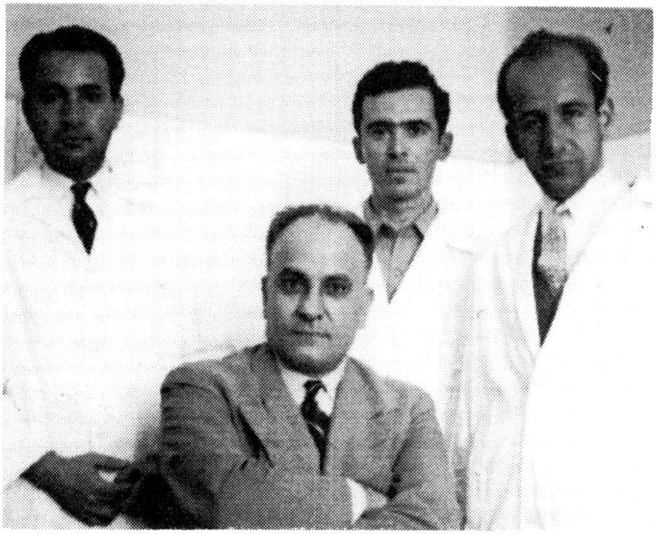

69

Student Pilot

At 5:00 a.m. when the world was still asleep, on the darkest day of December, the alarm clock jangled next to my head. I did not feel like getting out of my warm bed. No one else in our house was awake.

Mechanically I washed, shaved, dressed, and left the house.

It was so cold, I pulled up the scratchy collar of my heavy olive drab military overcoat and pulled down my cap tightly to my ears. I hurried down Sed Hashem Alley making sure that my polished shoes would not be scarred by the bumpy stones in the pavement. The street lights, few and far between, did not help me see where I was stepping.

At Shahabad Avenue I turned left toward Parliament Square, where the military truck driver would pick up passengers for Doeshantappeh, the base of the Iranian Air Force under the command of the Army. Soon I jumped onto the tailgate, slid toward the back of the truck, and quickly found a space on a wooden bench next to others as we lurched along.

Even the most rickety of busses would be more comfortable than these wooden benches. Because of the war, Tehran had lost all its busses to the allied armies. By 1952 replacements gradually came back.

While the busiest routes in the city had limited public transportation, nothing ran to the base where I was stationed. Even though I was a physician and an officer in the Army, I did not have a car. On my salary of $90.00 a month, I could not afford one.

By 7:00 a.m. I was expected at the infirmary to care for young students at the Air Force Academy, the training center for pilots. At 25 years of age, just out of medical school, I had dreams of miraculously curing the severely ill--not boys with headaches, toothaches, sniffles, stomach aches, scratched fingers or sore toes. In reality, these students objected to the confinement of the base. While I went home every afternoon, they stayed on base round the clock for six days out of seven. My primary responsibility was to recognize the malingerers. This was hardly my idea of practicing medicine.

One early morning as I buttoned my coat in preparation of another day of pretended maladies, I glanced out of the window and watched student pilots go through aerial acrobatic routines. A young man in the air was flying solo, apparently practicing different maneuvers. Freydoon was the trainee second in line on the ground, ready to repeat the configurations. Eager to go, he excitedly revved up the engine of his single propeller plane, something left over from World War II. To him the minutes seemed like hours. Finally, Student #1 landed smoothly and taxied onto the runway--to the cheers, applause and smiles of his friends waiting their turn.

Freydoon took off as excited as could be. The plane soared into the air smooth as silk and circled according to the prescribed maneuvers. Since the student pilots were not permitted any higher than 5,000 feet, they were easily observed. In a classroom adjacent to the control tower of the base the students listened to the conversation between the student pilot in the plane and the instructor in this tower. Upside-down he went, into another detail of the prescribed procedures. Those watching couldn't wait to experience the same ecstasy.

"Hey," screamed one of the waiting students. "He fell out of the plane!"

Freydoon spiraled like a javelin. Then his parachute opened and drifted toward the ground.

"Get the ambulance," commanded the instructor.

Instantly four others went off to the site of the crashed plane, now in flames. Two fire trucks jerked their way onto the field.

In a few minutes a phone call to the infirmary alerted everyone to be prepared to treat any emergency. With two benches along the sides, this ambulance was like the truck I rode in--only this vehicle had a couple of cots in the middle. The least bump across the field intensified the pain of the injured pilot. Within minutes the ambulance reached the infirmary.

With utmost care the attendants removed his heavy boots and flying gear and gently lifted him to the examination table. In spite of the pain in the young man's left ankle, there was no evidence of fracture or dislocation. Movements were not impaired, there was no change in any sensation, and there was no swelling in any part of the foot. He had a sprained ankle. Miraculously nothing else was wrong with him.

The instructor surmised that the young man failed to buckle himself properly.

No matter what the reason, I ordered an X-ray to make sure there were no bone injuries. Before the patient was transported to the hospital, this ankle had to be temporarily immobilized with a thin wooden splint and elastic bandages. A pair of crutches helped him hobble out of the infirmary.

Only now did Commander Rokny appear on the scene, ranting and raving, "Where is that miserable kid?"

"He's ..." I interrupted.

"Take that damn kid to jail . . . now. He destroyed one of the few practice planes I have on this base. How the hell am I going to replace that expensive plane?"

Freydoon did not go to jail. After a short stay in the hospital he resumed his duties, but had all privileges revoked for a month.

70

Scholarship in Texas

The gyrations of the small planes never ceased to amaze me. That morning my observing came to an abrupt ending when the phone rang.

It was General Neeknafs, the Commander of the Air Force Medical Corps, reprimanding me for failing to have my papers in order. "Don't you realize that you are supposed to travel to the United States within a few days?" Gruffness seems to be the outstanding qualification of a general.

As long as an ambulance was going to the hospital where the general had his office, I too became a passenger along with the patient.

With the general's abruptness ringing in my ears, I took the steps into the hospital two at a time. He wasted no time reminding me that I had taken the English language examination three months earlier and had been assigned to go to the United States for a four-month military medical course. He apparently had a telephone call from headquarters informing him that if I did not show up by noon, the military police would come to get me.

"General, as I told you before, I certainly want to go to the United States, but not for four months. I want to go for four years in order to qualify for a specialty board," I answered.

"As a lieutenant in the Air Force you are in no position to make such a request. You are here to follow orders. Right now your orders are to go to the main office of the Army Medical Corps and get your papers. Ask for Colonel Shams." With that he turned around, away from me.

"Yes, General," I replied, not sure that he even heard me. More quietly, I added, "If I am forced to go to the United States like this, I will not come back."

This he did hear. "Don't talk like that, young man.

You can get arrested. Go. The ambulance is waiting to take you to town." He looked me in the eyes without saying a word. Then he shook my hand firmly and said, "Good luck."

Once again I jumped into the ambulance. The closer we got to town, the better the roads became--black topped, smooth, and relatively free of holes. Since busses were rare and private cars were virtually nonexistent, traffic was no problem.

At this office Colonel Shams gave me a few papers to sign and copies of them to deliver to Army Headquarters.

Thirty minutes later I had another interview with another officer, Col. Khaki, who gave me more papers to sign.

After a half-hour walk to the police headquarters I had my picture taken and received my passport. The one good thing the Army did for me was having all this red tape unraveled. Under ordinary circumstances it would take at least six months to get a passport alone--after months of paper work requesting such a document.

I became a little excited as I now headed for the American Consulate at the end of Roosevelt Boulevard, a street renamed during Roosevelt's war time visit to Tehran. Since it was somewhat out of town close to the Amjadieh Athletic Stadium, it was already 1:00 p.m. by the time I approached a receptionist.

I was immediately escorted into the office of a well dressed, gray haired lady sitting behind a huge desk flanked by the American flag and a portrait of President Truman. I started to introduce myself, but the lady had already been informed about my coming. As she attached the visa to my passport, she informed me that it was good for six months but could be extended if necessary. Once a passport is extended, any immigration office in the US would approve an extension of the visa. Passports had to be valid for six months beyond the expiration date of the visa.

"Compared with other officers going to the United States, you have a good command of the English language, " she complimented me.

I thanked her and wondered how bad the others must be.

"From now on," she emphatically informed me, "you are under the command of the United States Army. Your orders along with everything else you need to reach Texas are here in this envelope. It is important that you carefully read each detail. If you have any questions, do not hesitate to ask the people who will meet you first in New York and later in Texas. Tonight at 6:00 p.m. in the officers' club you and a few others who are going with you will receive further instructions. On Saturday at 4:00 p.m. your flight on Scandinavian Airlines will depart from Mehrabad Airport. Try to have a good time."

I picked up my package of documents and my passport with the treasured visa, thanked the lady, and left.

71

Gone with the Wind

I still had a 45-minute walk to get home for a delayed lunch and a much needed rest.

That evening I was so excited while trying to stay calm, I was at the officers's club way ahead of time to meet the one other physician and six other officers going to various parts of the United States for various kinds of training. Captain Maafi, about four years my senior, was the one assigned to take the course with me in Texas. Taller than I, he was quite handsome, especially in his uniform.

In a lecture room we gathered to hear Gen. Hedayat tell us about our responsibilities in the United States. "Behave as ambassadors of Iran." One detail that stayed in my mind was his remark that Americans are all very honest people who could be trusted anywhere. "In New York you can give your money to anyone for safe keeping and get it all back whenever you wish." Since we were trained to have implicit faith in our superiors, I did not question what he had said, but certainly wondered about it.

Dr. Maafi and I left the officers' club together. He mentioned that his English was very poor, since his second language was French. Just as I did, on base he worked as a general practitioner. Since he was married but divorced, the stay in the United States would be no inconvenience.

As we walked along Lalehzar Avenue we decided to meet the following night to see the new American movie "Gone With the Wind." Maybe we could also learn some English that way.

The next morning I appreciated having the day off, because I had to gather all my military uniforms and civilian clothes for winter and summer, since it was cold in Tehran, but warm in Texas.

I also had to think about packing a heavy gypsum (chalky material) mannequin. My older brother Mohsen had worn a cast since the age of three to support his deformed back, the result of a broken spine after falling from a height of many steps. My mother wanted me to have made for him a lightweight plastic cast which had become recently available only in the United States. As though there wasn't enough to do that day, Mohsen and I had to find the right hospital which had the right technician who would make the proper form.

First the cast was molded to his body. After it dried, it was cut off and then reattached and filled with the same heavy gypsum. We now had a mannequin of his upper body. Then we needed a special suitcase to transport it. This only added weight to the mannequin. I hoped that it would weigh less as it dried thoroughly.

By the time I met Dr. Maafi at the theater, I was ready to sit down anywhere. Almost all the movies that were shown in Iran were American with Persian subtitles. We were both impressed with this beautiful story, even though it was so long.

That night I dreamed that I was in the United States, where everyone was as handsome as Clark Gable and as gorgeous as Vivian Leigh. I will never forget the sentence, "Frankly, my dear, I don't give a damn." In perfect English, I repeated it over and over again.

I woke up greeting my sister with "Frankly, my dear, I don't give a damn." She looked at me quizzically, wondering about my sanity. Everyone helped me pack my clothes. Even though my passport specified "four months," everyone sensed that it could be longer. I packed everything. The entire family was ambivalent about my departure--happy for me to have such a unique opportunity, sad to see me leave, perhaps forever. This was my first trip out of the country.

Just before we left for the airport, my mother held the Koran, the Holy Book, high above my head, then had me walk back and forth under it three times. This ritual would keep me safe and bring me back home safely. My religious beliefs were nonexistent; obedience to my parents was minimal. At this point I followed my mother's dictates out of love for her and proceeded to the airport.

In 1952 the Mehrabad airport was quite small, nevertheless adequate for the half million people which it served. SAS, KLM, and Air France each scheduled one daily round-trip flight between Iran and Europe. There was no Iranian airline at the time. The largest planes of any airline, probably a DC6 or 7, had four engines and four propellers with a seating capacity of no more than one hundred passengers.

Passport control presented no problem. When I had to show how much money I was taking out of the country, I handled fifty dollars in United States currency.

"You can take $75.00," the official assured me.

"This is all I have. Give me another $25 and I'll take it."

He glowered and mumbled, "You have to be young to have the guts to get up and go to America with only $50.00."

My immediate concern was to check my luggage and board that SAS plane.

So many of my relatives came to the airport to bid me farewell, they overloaded two large taxis. One by one they all said bon voyage with a peck of a kiss on each cheek. My father was the last in line.

He and I seldom spoke to each other. I honestly did not like my father. His harsh personality and strict behavior toward his family kept him aloof. But this is the way at the time the man of the house in Iran was expected to be, always without emotion. Nevertheless, I went through the motions of hugging him, but kept my body half turned toward the plane on the runway.

By the time my plane took off around 4:00 p.m., it was dusk. I did glance out the window for one last look at my family, but saw only silhouettes of their bodies against the mountainous background. I sighed silently as I controlled the lump in my throat.

72
Stockholm

Hardly a few hours away from home, the eight of us were getting more and more excited about seeing Damascus, our first stop. After at least 1,000 miles the plane did land in this city, but only the departing passengers were allowed off. After another 750 miles, the plane stopped again-- this time in Athens, again just for a short time, again for departing passengers only.

When we landed in Rome, however, everyone was permitted to deplane. Everybody was happy to walk around the terminal, if for no other reason but to stretch his legs. This airport was much larger than the one in Tehran. It was also much livelier with gift shops, souvenir stands, restaurants, newsstands, and check-in counters meeting every imaginable need of the travelers. My companions were so excited with the excitement in this place, they began buying gifts. They probably had more money and less luggage than I. I spent five cents on a cup of good hot coffee--with a lot of warm milk, just as I like it. For the very first time in our lives, we all tasted pasta. Thanks to Lt. Meghdadi, one of the officers traveling with us, we had no trouble communicating, because he spoke Italian, rather fluently. Soon it was time to reboard the plane.

Since we were heading west most of the flight, we gained time. While our watches showed 5:00 a.m., it was only midnight in Stockholm. Our airline fare included two nights at a hotel in Stockholm and all the meals before we boarded another plane to New York City.

With only one day to visit Stockholm, we awoke early and had an adequate continental breakfast. When we walked out of the lobby, it looked as though everyone who worked in town neatly parked his bike in front of the hotel--not even locked or tied to anything. Bicycles zigzagged in and out of traffic. Taxis seemed relatively few; private cars, fewer yet. For about five cents one could go anywhere by bus or trolley. We decided to walk, at least for a little while. I had never seen so much snow in my entire life. It covered every inch of everything in sight.

Since Lt. Meghdadi spoke German (in addition to Italian and Farci), as many of the Swedish did, he became our leader. Together we visited museums, stopped in a few shops, and stared in wonder at things, people and places so different from those in Iran.

At the entrance of the Royal Palace stood two young handsome guards--without guns. Children laughed and played on the steps of the palace. For twenty-five cents we toured every room in the building except the private apartment of the royal family. We were told that we may even see the king, for he often rides his bicycle around town and mingles with the people. (What a surprise for an Iranian, whose royal properties were guarded by soldiers with guns, guns ready to be fired for the least trespass--willful or accidental. In contrast, the Shah of Iran was chauffeured in bullet-proof cars and was surrounded by body guards.)

By evening we must have felt homesick. In spite of an extensive menu in the dining room, we chose fruit for dessert and tea for our beverage--typically Iranian. Meghdadi overheard the conversation of the four other people--the only other diners in the entire restaurant. Having understood their Swedish, he advised us to eat slowly because they commented on our eating habits and concluded that we must have been starved.

During the entire meal Razavi turned in every direction, looking around for women whom he expected to swoon over him. He was very proud of his captain's military uniform. It made him handsome, he believed, in spite of his very ordinary looks.

After dinner he was determined to have a massage--by a good-looking masseuse. He was so eager, he left our group before the rest of us had finished our meal.

The next morning Razavi walked as though he had been hit by a truck. He could hardly walk. The good-looking masseuse he dreamed of turned out to be an Amazon of a woman who massaged his muscles as though she were kneading bread dough.

At 6:00 a.m. we left Stockholm for New York with stops in London, Reykjavik, St. Johns, and Boston.

73

Angel of Freedom

"We are about to land in New York," announced the stewardess over a loud speaker. Her pronunciation was much different from my teacher's. She must have been a foreigner. At 5:00 p.m. the sun had already set and the city lights sparkled for miles and miles beneath us. I had never seen so many lights in any one place. For that matter, I had never seen such an expanse of lights and buildings. And the buildings! I almost feared that they would touch our plane. The center of the world must have surely moved from western Europe to America. The capital of the world definitely was not Paris, London, or Berlin anymore. It was New York City!

I strained my eyes and neck, hoping to see that famous statue on a little island, "Angel of Freedom" as the Iranians called it. To anyone living under oppressive dictatorial governments this was a symbol of opportunity. Tiny as it seemed beneath our plane, my hope for freedom loomed large. The excitement increased as I pointed it out to Maafi sitting next to me. Within a few minutes our plane touched ground.

Going through customs, I held up the line with my mannequin. I had to open this huge suitcase.

"What's that?" asked the officer.

"A mannequin," I answered.

"What," wondered the officer, squinting his eyes.

"A mannequin, " I repeated. Then sensing that he did understand my English, but not the contents of my luggage, I proudly and confidently began to tell the story about my brother.

Before I hardly got started, he waved me on, "Go ahead." When I hesitated because he really didn't hear the entire explanation, he almost yelled, "GO! Go, man, go!!!"

La Guardia bustled with activity that filled the air with all kinds of strange sounds of people speaking many strange languages. The usual busyness was compounded by something Americans kept referring to as "the Christmas rush." The quick pace was infectious. In every direction there were people, not just one or two, but thick knots of people. Unbelievable! In comparison, Rome and Stockholm seemed like sleepy villages.

If the terminal offered so much to do and see, I wondered what could possibly happen in the city. My traveling companions couldn't wait to see this place. First we roamed the airport in search of the recommended USO, where we were welcomed to the country and served coffee and donuts. A lady wearing a tag, which identified her as "Sally Jones, volunteer," informed us that military cars will meet us in about 45 minutes to chauffeur us to a base in Brooklyn. In less than an hour a tall young blond welcomed us to New York. His uniform was so perfectly creased, it looked like cardboard. After so many days traveling, my clothes looked as though I had slept in them all my life.

After winding our way through throngs of people along many hallways, we finally reached the parking lot where two military cars were waiting for us. We almost hated to move along as we found the shops in this airport quite interesting. Liquor was available as easily as flowers. We could have bought everything from toys that hopped around the floor to at least 100 different kinds of knives which seemed to come as a set that every household in the world desperately needed to survive.

Along the way we did stop to go to the bathroom. I had problems flushing the toilet. Nothing looked familiar; everything was different from that of Europe and the Middle East. Aware of my dilemma, a young man neatly dressed in a crisp uniform of blue slacks, blue jacket, white shirt, white gloves and blue tie came to my rescue and flushed the tank. Obviously, he had the job of flushing toilets. I watched carefully. I didn't want to hold up our group another time. I had to remember to look for a little shiny lever on the side of the water tank. There was no knob in the middle of the tank cover or no chain to pull from a box up high.

As I left the men's room, one worker who watched the young man help me commented, "What a lousy job! What work for a bunch of lousy foreigners!"

I knew they were talking about me, a foreigner. It didn't exactly sound complimentary, but I didn't understand "lousy." Even Meghdadi, whose English was superior to mine, did not know this word.

Outside the terminal I welcomed the fresh air, even though it was brisk--colder than Rome, warmer than Stockholm--it was clear and cold, the same as Tehran. Within minutes we were careening along the highways of New York, weaving in and out of hectic traffic that defied description. The heavy traffic of private cars was mind boggling. I had never seen such large cars before, except in a military parade when the Shah rode by in his Rolls Royce. Here in New York, not only was there such a variety of vehicles, there was a variety of license plates. How could one country have so many different kinds of identifications? The pleasant young driver explained how each state of the United States has its own design.

Since he was so knowledgeable, I asked him, "What does lousy mean?"

After a pause, he turned sideways to stare at me, "Where did you hear that?"

"I heard it in the men's room."

His light laughter encouraged me to relate the experience in the men's room. It took so much effort to say all this in English, I was actually tired.

"Don't worry about it," he advised. "You'll hear more things like that in New York, even though 30% of the people here are foreigners themselves. Do you know what a louse is?"

"Of course, I do. I'm a doctor. I know how parasites thrive on other forms of life. But this man said 'lousy.' The word had a z sound."

"True," he nodded his head. "That's *English* fer ya. No rules."

After winding our way through extremely busy highways for less than an hour we reached a military base in Brooklyn around 7:00 p.m..

74
Brooklyn

At the base the eight Iranian officers were led into a spacious room, where two ladies welcomed us. They gave each of us our orders and train tickets to our individual destinations.

Maafi and I were assigned to Fort Sam Houston, which is in San Antonio, not Houston, as we firmly believed. Our first class tickets specified a room with a private bath on this "Pullman." These reservations between New York and St. Louis were confirmed. As soon as we reached Missouri, we were to have the Station Master confirm our space to Texas.

The receptionist in Brooklyn urged us to contact anyone that we possibly knew in the New York area to make sure that we were able to enjoy the city as much as possible over the weekend. She even offered to help us locate the people and call them for us.

I happened to have a cousin who worked for United Nations. I even had his phone number--written right there in a little pocket calendar. When I pulled it out of my jacket pocket, the lady noticed that that's also where I kept all my money--the $45.00 that I had left from the original $50.00.

She stared at my calendar, then at me. "Keep that in your wallet."

"Wallet?" Now it was my turn to stare.

"Yes, your wallet. You know, where the rest of your money is."

"This is it," I fanned it out in front of her. "This is where I carry my money."

Hardly anyone in Iran owned a wallet. That may make a good souvenir.

In the process of this confusion I managed to point out the phone number of my cousin Satrap.

This woman suddenly took all my money. I was horrified. "Sir," she scolded, "I don't know how things are in your country, but in this country you make sure that you keep your money hidden in your pocket with your hand on it. If you don't, you may lose it. You may even get killed for it. Be very careful. Don't let anyone know how much money you even have!" Immediately I recalled the comment of Gen. Hedayat, who told us that in New York one could trust anyone else with his money.

She returned my $45.00 and called my cousin. Fortunately, he had the following day off and agreed to pick me up. Maafi had a friend in New York who offered to show him around town.

We were then driven into the business section of Brooklyn. For two nights and one day our entire group enjoyed meals and rooms in a fancy hotel.

Even though Maafi and I were tired, we decided to walk a bit before retiring for the day. In the lobby quite a number of well-dressed elderly women chattered away. As I think about them now, they were probably some senior citizen group touring the Christmas festivities in New York.

We also noticed Razavi roaming around the lobby in his military uniform, preening himself as he noticed his reflection in the mirrored pillars. These ladies must have included him in their conversation, for many of them turned to stare at him. Razavi was delighted. Maafi predicted that Razavi was going to get into trouble being so eager to pick up a woman. Maafi and I walked away. Later we heard that Razavi was not successful. In fact, he wasted $2.00 getting his trousers quick-pressed in preparation for a conquest.

Maafi and I took a walk in the fresh air. It was so cold, we soon felt like having some hot coffee and a bite to eat. We noticed how well lit the streets were and how lit-up the movie theater was. When we neared a coffee shop, we went in and sat down.

"What's gonna be?" asked a waiter.

For the first time in my life I had to order and I had absolutely no idea what to say. I knew no words for food of any kind. The man interpreted our hesitation as indecision, so he put a menu in front of each of us. "Menu," I tried to sound out. "What's this?" I whispered to Maafi. In all the English books I had read--like Silas Marner, or David Copperfield--I never saw "m-e-n-u." I did remember the word "weaver," but that didn't appear anywhere among these pages now in front of me. I did recognize d-o-g. Did Americans really eat dogs? I also recognized f-r-e-n-c-h. Could this be an international restaurant? In desperation we each huffed as we looked around the room.

The waiter came to our table again. "What'll it be?"

I had no idea what he was saying, and I didn't dare ask what a "what'll" is. I simply pointed to a picture of a sandwich with some meat, cheese, lettuce and tomato. Next to it on the picture were some orange strings and a glass of coke. "That," I ordered for 89 cents.

"Ham and cheese sandwich," said the waiter.

Maafi looked up from the menu and said, "Same thing."

When we returned to our hotel rooms we had no trouble falling asleep immediately.

75
Manhattan

At 8:00 a.m. Sunday my cousin Satrap met me in the lobby. Our Middle Eastern greeting of cheek-to-cheek touching on both sides had a few people stare at us.

Crossing the Brooklyn Bridge on our way to Manhattan, I was amazed at the height of the buildings against the horizon. Having lived here for six years, Satrap was able to tell me about everything in front of us. He explained how these tall buildings were appropriately called skyscrapers because they really are so tall that they do scrape the sky. By the time we reached Times Square, so many people were crossing all of the streets that meet here that we had to inch our way through the crowds. At every traffic light in this area the numerous lanes of traffic screeched to a stop, then squealed to a start. About 10 blocks south it was especially exciting to see the Empire State Building, because I had seen it in a King Kong movie.

Around noon we turned toward the United Nations complex where Satrap worked. He treated me to a brief tour of the assembly halls and a quick lunch in the cafeteria. The outbreak of World War I led President Woodrow Wilson to strongly support The League of Nations. Originally located in Geneva, Switzerland, it later moved to New York City and flourished as the United Nations. More political and less legalistic, the organization now relies on diplomacy, rather than judicial procedures, to prevent wars and promote higher standards of living throughout the world.

That afternoon we continued to Rockefeller Center, where the enormous tree decorated for Christmas, the gilded statue of Prometheus, and the ice skaters in the rink provided more attractions that I had never even imagined. Satrap mentioned that one day a year a street in this Center is closed to assure the Rockefeller family that their private ownership continues.

Late afternoon we stood in line nearby to buy tickets

for the show in Radio City Music Hall. Never before did I stand in a single file in such an orderly fashion. This line stretched around the corner as far as the next corner of the block.

Once inside I was again surprised. With a seating capacity of 6,000, Radio City Music Hall is the largest indoor theater in the world. Even the rug was carefully planned in rectangles with designs of musical instruments. Should one part show wear, it can be easily replaced simply by removing just one piece, not the entire rug that covered acres of floors. Between features of Moulin Rouge the famous Rockettes held me spellbound with their dancing. Even the Iranian Army did not have such military precision and discipline.

As we left the theater and walked up Fifth Avenue, we had to dodge a man who appeared to be drunk. He kept yelling, "We need a soldier in the White House, not a piano player." I knew that Eisenhower was president-elect, but I wondered who the piano player could be. My cousin explained that Harry Truman, the outgoing president, was quite an accomplished musician. The man kept yelling the same thing as he staggered from one side of the sidewalk to the other. To my surprise, a policeman who went by said absolutely nothing to him. In Iran the drunk would be picked up and put in jail instantly. In a government of mullahs, the man would be whipped in the public square.

Satrap was nonchalant about the incident. He's seen many such people. Never do the police bother them unless they seem to intend harm--which is rare.

Back at the hotel Satrap and I shook hands and went our separate ways.

As I waited for the elevator, Maafi came along. We both had such an exciting day, we were both talking at the same time. When we reached our floor, we must have said "Good Night" at least 10 times as we kept telling each other about the exciting details of our day.

76
Train Ride

We may have left the hotel half asleep, but the crowds at Penn Central Station quickly jolted us to attention. Eventually we found our rooms in the Pullman car. We had never seen such comfort so compact. In the dining car we were relieved to see that our meals were limited to either #1 or #2. We didn't even have to know the words. Every meal on our way to St. Louis was a surprise. We had no trouble eating while we enjoyed the scenery that blurred by on this speeding train.

As we sped along to the rhythm of the click clack of the train, Maafi and I sat together either in his room or mine and soon got to know each other better. We swapped memories of medical school, life in Tehran, and crazy childhood experiences. He was quite apprehensive about his limited English and repeatedly coaxed me to help him with our class work. I promised.

A newspaper seemed like an excellent beginning textbook. So we went to the porter and bought the Sunday New York Times. For all I knew, sections of it could have been Chinese. Maafi understood less. We had trouble not only in understanding the gist of many articles, but even in holding that Sunday's edition. Iran newspapers were about four pages long. This one was several inches thick! Forget about counting the pages. Maafi's English didn't go that high. The number of ads surprised us even more.

Twenty-four hours and a good night's sleep later we detrained in St. Louis and hurried to the ticket office for confirmation of our sleeping space on the next leg of our journey. No sleepers were available till five days later.

Five days! We had to report to Brooke Army Medical Center and start classes in four. Besides, we had no money to cover the cost of hotels and meals that long. The only alternative was to accept 2nd class and hope to find a seat. The cavernous waiting room that echoed every announcement from the loud speaker was jammed with travelers. As soon as the doors opened to the platforms, the people swooshed through like a flood through a broken dam.

By the time Maafi and I reached a coach, there was no place available, not even standing room. How could we stand all the way to San Antonio! We never even climbed the steps of that coach.

We were literally pushed back into the waiting room, my luggage turning into lead with every step I tumbled. This time we parked ourselves immediately in front of the doors, ready to catapult onto the train that was scheduled to arrive in two hours.

During this time we took turns guarding our possessions and leaving our post to go to the bathroom, get something to eat, or just walk around. Fortunately, my English was good enough to have people behind a food counter understand "ham and cheese sandwich and coke."

At the sound of the train we sprinted, not an easy feat with suitcases and my brother's mannequin. By the time we sat down next to each other, the coach was jammed. Some passengers even appropriated the toilet seats, while others stretched out in the aisles.

It didn't take long for us to realize that we were on a local train, one that made stops at every station, one that took 48--not 24--hours to reach San Antonio. Since this train ran for the convenience of local passengers, there were no facilities for handling food. When the train stopped, anyone who was hungry would jump off the train, rush to a counter in the station, and order from the take-out menu. Since the bathrooms on the trains were used as space for the passengers, it was quite a challenge during these short stops to go to the bathroom, as well as get our meals.

For 48 hours Maafi and I indulged in ham and cheese sandwiches for breakfast, lunch, dinner, and even bedtime snacks. Since we were young, like most of the others on this train, we were able to sleep in these seats--which would hardly merit the Good Housekeeping seal of approval for neatness by the time we reached our destination. Almost all the passengers were men, all on their way to Fort Sam Houston. By the end of the second day people used the aisles for dressing rooms as they changed into uniforms.

Obviously, Maafi and I looked like foreigners "just off the boat."

The only thing we realized was that it was a relief to leave that train.

77
Texas

The warm Texas air was most welcome. No need for winter clothes of any kind. People walked around in sweaters or just short sleeves. Maafi and I, dignified officers that we were, still wore our double-breasted suits, white shirts and ties--not exactly neat and crisp at this time. The creases in our slacks were horizontal. Since our hands were already overburdened with our luggage, we had no choice but to wear our overcoats--in spite of the record breaking heat wave of 80° that day.

To avoid the crowd, Maafi and I skirted to a side door. Out of nowhere a policeman appeared, "Who are you? Where are you going?"

"Fort Sam Houston," I mumbled.

Apparently he was accustomed to foreigners. He directed us to another door that we should have used and called the base for us. The kind officer pointed out a sign showing us that we had used an area specified "For Negroes." We did not understand the reason for such preferential treatment for "Negroes." Why would anybody have a special entrance? Nevertheless, we followed the officer's instructions and used another door.

Within minutes we were greeted by a driver who chauffeured us to Fort Sam Houston, which was about 25 minutes away. By this time it was around 4:00 p.m.. At the main office of the Medical Field Service School at Brooke Army Medical Center we presented our papers and received instructions in regard to housing, meals, classes, bus schedules, maps, and identification. On the base we were expected to wear our Iranian uniforms, but outside the compound, civilian clothes.

In the United States not only my routine, but my name, was changed. In Iran where double surnames were customary, I was Hushang Mofakham Payan. Now I became H. M. Payan. I really had no choice. Furthermore, I had to listen carefully to respond to my name pronounced phonetically: pay-anne.

Once again we were chauffeured--this time to the junior officers' quarters, housing for men only. These two-story wooden buildings had 10 rooms on each side of each floor. Each room was minimally furnished with a bed, chair, table, and clothes closet. The middle of each floor had a large bathroom with multiple stalls with adequate bathing facilities. (Men often walked to or from the bathroom naked or with minimal cover.) For all this plus maid service we paid $10.00 per month.

Every day we relied on excellent scheduled bus service to take us between the officers' quarters, the classrooms and the hospital. Since the cafeteria served dinner between 5:00 and 6:00 p.m., our driver was so considerate, he would wait for us while we quickly changed into our uniforms, required during meal times, and then take us back to the Officers' Mess Hall. Until this experience I had never heard the word "mess."

Our military uniform was not much different from the Americans'. The Garrison hat which the US servicemen wore was soft and able to be folded flat like an envelope, whereas ours was more like a cap with a visor. Soon we were able to identify other foreigners, including a few Iranians.

78

Brooke Army Medical Center

Bright and early on January 2, it was off to breakfast and my first class at Brooke Army Medical Center. At 8:00 a.m. promptly, gathered 27 physicians--mostly young, mostly lieutenants and captains. From Iran came Maafi, Doneshvar, and I; from Canada, Lt. McAuley. The rest were Americans, including one Negro.

When roll call was taken, I was almost marked absent. What a way to begin! But my ears snapped to attention, the second time the syllables of my name boomed through the still air.

"Pay-anne," called the instructor.

In the split second when my peripheral vision gave no signs of anyone answering, I raised my hand and responded, "Here."

After roll call, someone yelled, "Attention!"

Instantly, everyone in the class stood up. I soon learned to follow the crowd, do what everyone else was doing--even if I did not understand what was going on.

A tall elderly gentleman with perfect posture and a full head of white hair entered the room, walked up to the podium and quietly said, "Please sit down." We were being welcomed by Gen. Martin, Commandant of the Base.

"I wish to welcome all of you to the course. I assure you, it will be very informative. I particularly welcome the foreign officers. I am sure your American classmates know how to make you feel at home." I listened very attentively to this humble, down-to-earth general and was amazed to have understood most of what he had to say.

Next, Col. Glass, director of the postgraduate courses, welcomed us and introduced other personnel of the program--lecturers, office staff, and coordinators of various services and facilities.

He advised us not to walk around certain sections of town, especially late at night, especially alone. Like any big cities, San Antonio had its percentage of people who defy the law just for thrills and even go so far as committing murder. The advice took me by surprise, since I never heard of such a problem in Tehran. Perhaps such problems never made the news.

Courses that challenged my academic prowess included clinical psychology, psychiatry, and neurology. Reading textbooks consumed much of my time, as I had to refer to the dictionary often. Furthermore, the seriousness of some of the lecturers in neurology almost intimidated me. It was a spark of "comic relief" when the lecturer of psychiatry added a bit of humor to his explanations. I was beginning to wonder about myself when one of the experienced psychiatrists imparted the amazing fact that 90% of the people of the world are psychologically disturbed enough to need professional attention. Was I becoming a statistic?

One professor of psychiatry talked nonstop the entire period. The words sounded familiar, yet I could not focus on their meaning. As a conclusion he wrote the topic on the blackboard: "Senile Psychosis," not exactly pronounced as I had learned the term with a French pronunciation: *psychose sénile.* I was fluent enough while reading English, but my listening skills were quite deficient. While the objective was to learn military psychiatry, I was definitely improving my English.

As the courses continued, I managed to get copies of the lectures which were available in the office a day ahead of time. This way I could read them at my own pace and then be able to understand the lesson and follow the lecture more easily. That strategy not only helped me understand the classes, but improved my conversational English as well.

In addition to classroom discussions, we learned from hands-on experience. Making rounds with a neurologist at Brooke Army Medical Center, I examined a 45-year-old white male born in Panama and having served in North Africa. He had a peculiar skin lesion on his left leg, on the antero-lateral aspect midway between the knee and ankle. The patient mentioned that he had a history of "bad blood." That disease never surfaced in my medical textbooks.

When I asked the neurologist about it, he explained that it was "positive serology for syphilis." In addition to the ulcer, the patient had an area that had no sensation. In the differential diagnosis list syphilis appeared first.

I commented that in Iran I had seen a similar case and that turned out be leprosy. I was surprised that the experienced physician was really interested in what I had to say.

A few days later after the results of all the tests were determined, this case likewise was diagnosed as leprosy. Never having seen anything like it before, the neurologist thanked me for helping. That incident was among the proudest moments of my life in Texas.

In the psychiatric open ward, patients had all kinds of anxiety, mostly the result of the war, with various degrees of severity. Some constantly had to be encouraged to relax, during the interview, as well as the examination. One asked me whether I was a Republican or a Democrat. I was quite proud of myself when he understood what I said when I answered, "Neither. I'm a visitor to the United States."

Maafi wasn't the least bit disturbed when he wasn't understood. In fact, he told me, "I'm glad these people are crazy. When they don't understand my English, they think it's their fault."

One of the requirements of the course was a term paper. The topics were of our own choosing. I concentrated on alcoholism, because it was a problem in the United States, but not in Iran. Since Col. Brown was also interested in addiction, he not only offered to help me, but volunteered his secretary to type the report.

Preparing these papers was another lesson in American culture. The use of libraries was a necessity. In comparison with the medical school library in Tehran this library on base had more professionals to help students handle more books on more topics. It also had one librarian who kept eying Maafi.

Maafi could not resist her charm. About once a week he would disappear and go out with her, never telling anyone where. She was not only attractive and single, but intelligent and efficient. Maafi produced an excellent paper--thanks to her.

Thanks to Maafi's poor English and Doneshvar's seniority, I was pushed to read my paper first. Those two wanted to see how things would work out. My three-page report held the interest of everyone in class, even Col. Glass and Gen. Martin, who sat in the back of the room. I maintained that most Iranians did not suffer alcoholism because they could not afford liquor and because they adhered to the restrictions of their Moslem religion. I was very flattered when a few of the students talked to me about my paper. They obviously understood my English!

I was fast becoming an avid student of American language and culture. Some of the people amazed me, like the gray-haired ambidextrous professor of neurology who used both hands simultaneously as he diagramed on the board the two sides of the brain.

While this man was an expert at saving time and motion, the rest of the Americans seemed programed to waste. During the breaks I was introduced to disposable paper cups, a nonexistent product in Iran. Almost everyone smoked at least one cigarette per break and almost everyone used the machine which dispensed coke in those paper cups. After drinking the coke (sometimes not even finishing it), people dropped the cup into a trash can. After only a puff or two on the cigarette, they would toss that out too.

We attended class between 8:00 and noon in the morning and between 2:00 and 5:00 in the afternoon. Class lasted fifty minutes and had 10-minute breaks between them. On occasion guest lecturers added a change of scenery.

Near the end of the course, we had a group picture taken with Gen. Martin. As guests, the Iranians sat in the front row with the celebrities, while the others stood behind them. The arrangement showed complete disregard for rank--lieutenants sat, captains stood. After the photography session, Gen. Martin approached the Iranians, shook hands, and once again asked if everything was O.K. As usual Doneshvar spoke for us, thanking him profusely.

79
American Ways

The Officers' Mess Hall yielded an endless source of surprises. The very first time that Maafi and I approached the building, he worried that our unfamiliarity with American table etiquette would create a negative impression. Nevertheless, we walked in. We couldn't exactly skip our meals because customs were foreign to us.

"What the hell are we going to do?" worried Maafi. "We don't know the names of any foods and really don't know what to do. You go first." He pushed me ahead of him in line.

I told him that we would simply follow an American and do exactly what he does. Luckily, this was a cafeteria. We were able to see every item and then point.

As the weeks went by, I apparently often pointed at items that made strange combinations, so strange that the man behind the display of food often asked whether or not I really wanted what I had chosen, like a hot dog on top of a hamburger in the same sandwich. My stomach had adventures with brussel sprouts, broccoli, sweet potatoes, grits, mayonnaise, catsup. *Cat soup?* "Cat soup" over everything! I really had my doubts about this "catsup." Why was food for cats among food for people? Completely missing from this vast array of food, however, was exactly what appeared in abundance in Iran: fruit, rice, and yogurt.

Col. Doneshvar, one of the Iranian physicians already at the base, considered American coffee absolutely delectable, not so much for the coffee, but for the cream. Such delightfully rich cream, along with many other dairy products, was rare in Iran. Every time he ordered coffee, he would fill his cup half with coffee and half with this rich cream. Before even reaching his place to sit down, he would sip it and savor every drop that trickled down his throat. "Full of vitamins, " he observed. "Good for you."

Nevertheless, we ate. We were satisfied. We

enjoyed. We were glad to have something different from ham and cheese, which I never ate again in my entire life.

Eventually Maafi discovered that all the sandwiches we ate on the train included ham. "We had sinned," he mournfully whispered to me, almost chanting. Ham was pork, a forbidden item according to Moslem law. "Were you aware of all that pork we had eaten?" This he said almost yelling, definitely accusing.

"Of course," I answered. "I also know that if we hadn't eaten those sandwiches, we would have starved." I assured him that American ham was different. In a country like this, with all the money and latest facilities, it is O.K. to eat ham because the government inspects every aspect of the food industry to make sure nothing is tainted. There is no danger of trichinosis.

"But what about God?" he worried.

"Don't worry," I tried to ease his fears. "God is understanding and forgiving."

Every time we sat down to eat, no matter where, we got our silverware all mixed up. While everyone else used a fork for a particular item, especially vegetables, Iranians used a spoon. While everyone else used one utensil at a time, placing another on the plate before picking up the next, foreigners usually held the knife in the right hand and the fork in the left simultaneously. To signal the end of a meal, Americans placed the used utensils at an angle across the farther edge of their plate. Foreigners, on the other hand, placed these utensils in the form of an inverted V in the center of the plate.

At the cash register we could hardly believe that a whole tray of food cost slightly more than 50 cents. Undoubtedly the cafeteria was subsidized by the government.

The greatest surprise, however, involved a man dressed in a white jacket and a chef's hat at the beverage station. One day he looked at me longer than most people did. In Farsi with a Ghazvini accent, he asked, "Would you like *kick a kola*?" Ghazvin, a city not far from Tehran, had its own undeniable accent, a combination of Persian and Turkish.

I was so startled to hear it, I asked in English, "I beg your pardon?"

Again he repeated in his Ghazvini accent, "Would you like some *kick a kola*?"

He was definitely a fellow countryman, but he was in the service of the US Army. I was a physician, an officer. What should I say to this underling? "Yes, please," I answered politely in Farsi. Maafi and I were most surprised to see this Iranian in Texas--at this base yet.

As the days went by, we learned that this Iranian with the Ghazvini accent was Mahmood, Americanized to Mammy. In the kitchen in Amir-Abad, an American military post outside Tehran, he was employed as a cook. After the war an American officer who was impressed with his honesty and efficiency invited him to go to the United States with the Army. Wearing an army uniform, he didn't even need a passport or visa.

Mahmood eagerly accepted the offer of his American superior and in the process became an American soldier and citizen. Not before long he married the sister of an American soldier with whom he worked in the kitchen. His wife was a seamstress.

Many foreign officers from different countries with different uniforms and insignias were easily noticeable. The Iranian uniform was similar to that of the American, but stars on the shoulder of an American uniform indicated the rank of general, whereas in the Iranian army, stars identified lieutenants.

One day an American major, a physician who looked older than I, was ahead of me in line for the Mess Hall. The appearance of his brand new uniform made me believe that this was his first day in the Army. After fidgeting a few moments, he turned around and saluted me. I then introduced myself as Lieutenant Payan, shook hands with him, and informed him that I was only a lowly lieutenant from Iran, not a general.

Another time we came across two Iranian colonels who said hello to us. What a surprise to chit chat about the weather and the Texas scenery! In Iran senior officers were expected to keep their distance from the junior officers. These two had been in the United States for around six months. Maafi and I decided that they had become Americanized.

It was surprising to experience the levity with which the American military personnel treated each other when not on duty. One day during a break Gen. Martin came into the hall from one of the offices. Immediately I snapped to attention and saluted him. He smiled and returned the salute. A few steps farther down the hall a soldier rested on the steps and smoked a cigarette. As Gen. Martin went down the steps, he touched the soldier on his shoulder, greeting him, "Good morning, Son."

"Good morning, Sir," answered the soldier, not even bothering to get up or give up his cigarette.

Early in the course I approached Col. Brown to discuss my brother Mohsen's illness and his need for a brace. He gave me a letter of introduction and sent me to a place in the hospital where artificial limbs were made. The people were so accommodating, they made two corsets--one from plastic and one from aluminum, never charging me anything for the materials, their work or their time. I shipped both of them to Iran. Such generosity was most welcome, as I had hardly any money left from my monthly stipend of $150.00. (Mohsen was very pleased with his braces, which he used for many years.)

Another building for socializing and dining was the Officers' Club. Besides a bar, this club was equipped with a pool, tennis table, and other facilities for enjoyment. Everything but the food and drinks was free. It seemed that Americans usually drank beer and sometimes even hard liquor. Since the Moslem religion forbids the use of liquor, Maafi and I usually enjoyed coke, something else that was not available in Iran. As Maafi and I were on our way there one evening, we realized that Americans rarely walk. They ride their cars or take buses. We also noticed that almost all of them smoked heavily, no matter where they were. A pack of cigarettes tucked into a breast pocket almost seemed like part of the uniform. We thoroughly enjoyed socializing with officers from all over the world.

Among the Iranians we met was a corporal about 20 years old, whose uncle--a colonel in Iran--had enough influence to arrange this young man's studies at the base in Texas. Besides his military courses he learned about life in the United States.

This young man was housed in a barrack that accommodated about 25 soldiers. He found it most shocking to learn that most of them supposedly slept naked. To protect their bed sheets which were changed once a week, a tray of condoms sat near the front of the room to be worn by everyone to prevent ejaculations from soiling the linens. In Iran such openness about bodily functions would have created quite a scandal.

Another oddity was the number of women in uniform. In Iran women in the army served only as nurses in the hospitals. In our class, however, there were no female physicians.

I noticed many other differences between Americans and Iranians. More and more I learned to appreciate people on the basis of personality, rather than on social status or professional accomplishment. By the time I left Brooke Army Medical Center, I was also enjoying hot dogs, hamburgers, and apple pie.

80
Entertainment

Captain Brown, one of our classmates from New York City, had a way of putting us foreigners at ease. One day after a rather difficult lecture in psychiatry, he wondered how much we understood.

Maafi smiled and said, “About half.”

“You must be good!” exclaimed Brown. “I understood less than that, and I didn’t have to struggle with a foreign language.”

One weekend, when Brown was in the PX with his wife and children, we had a pleasant visit in this small store, open only to military personnel. Mrs. Brown took one long look at Maafi and said, “What a handsome man!” Maafi got all red in the face. Brown minimized Maafi’s embarrassment by finding some reason to leave quickly.

In Iran, no respectable woman would ever compliment a man about his appearance.

Outside the classroom and away from the hospital we discovered a different world. Late in January Maafi and I were introduced to the concept of a stag party and learned the meaning of BYOB. At that time restaurants in Texas did not serve liquor. That evening only officers in uniform were admitted to a private clubroom. We spent four hours exposed to drinking, dirty jokes, and a burlesque show.

For the first time in my life I saw a stripper. The highlight of the performance was a voluptuous brunette wiggling and twirling gracefully in time with the music, gradually removing her bits of clothing one by one. Without a stitch on, she then left the stage to continue dancing around the tables. Wherever she moved, the spotlight followed. Near our table she smiled at Maafi and sat on his lap, still wiggling and twirling in time with the music. Now Maafi too was in the spotlight. The crowd of about 350 male officers went wild. “Kiss her,” they chanted. “Grab her,”

Maafi wiggled too, but not exactly with the music.

Beet red in embarrassment, he was sweating bullets. He couldn't even look at her. He didn't know where to look. The party-goers kept whistling and cheering. After what seemed like an eternity to Maafi, she stood up, still wiggling, coaxing Maafi to return to the stage with her. Maafi refused. The crowd went wilder.

When the lights dimmed away from our table, Maafi and I slipped away from this crowd for a breath of fresh air.

Most of the time our social life was extremely different. A volunteer group, mostly elderly women, arranged parties and provided hospitality of all kinds to international visitors. Similar to present-day Councils for International Visitors throughout the United States, this group depended on a network who invited people to their homes for dinner, provided scholarships, conducted local tours, and tried to see that visitors had some personal attention during their stay. (Since my stay in Texas this group has evolved into the San Antonio Council for International Visitors.)

Even though the director appeared to be about 70 years old, she was always impeccably dressed in extremely good taste and never had any difficulty making everyone feel welcome. She was such an amiable hostess to people from all over the world, she was given the title "Mother of Texas." She was so down-to-earth, many people called her "Mamie." This gracious hostess was obviously quite influential. Her guest list often included judges, generals, politicians and businessmen. On one occasion we even became "honorary citizens of Texas." We were given a certificate signed by the Bexar County judge, Charles Anderson, and made official with a gold seal.

It was customary for the guests to stand up, introduce themselves, and share an observation or two. Most foreigners usually commented on the beauty of the United States, particularly Texas, and the amazing warmth of the Americans, particularly Texans. More interesting than the comments were the accents, many of which made what was being said completely unintelligible.

At one of these get-togethers when one woman and I found ourselves forced to find a common topic for small talk, she asked whether or not I was a Bahai. When I replied, "No, I am not," she was so surprised her big brown eyes became even bigger.

Her reference to this relatively new religion had me equally surprised. Even in Iran, where it had its inception about 150 years ago, it had a very small following. She believed that all educated Iranians were automatically Bahais. Apparently quite a number of Americans profess this faith. After she confided that she subscribed to this religion, she further surprised me with her knowledge about its history and about Iran. At this time hardly anyone in the United States even knew where Iran was.

Another weekend Maafi and I accepted an invitation to lunch at the home of an Iranian American lady who had lived in the United States a long time selling Persian rugs. After visiting this family several times, we got to know her husband, son, daughter-in-law and grandchildren. There was no doubt about the head of that family. The lady bossed everyone in a most powerful tone of voice and with gestures that rippled every inch of her chubby body. When the five-year-old grandson tried to pick up a piece of food that had fallen to the floor, she reprimanded, "No, dear. Don't eat that. That's for Negroes." In spite of her origins in Iran, she had no hesitation discriminating. Could this be a part of being Americanized?

As part of our program it was arranged that Maafi and I spend a weekend with a typical American family. After a few-hours' train ride to Houston, we were greeted by our hostess, Mrs. Craig, the wife of an ophthalmologist. Later we met their delightful family. The wife seemed about 45 years old; one daughter, about 10; and another, about 18. Their Black maid served the meals. They were all very curious about Iran--where it was, what the people were like.

Dr. Maafi, who spoke French well, exchanged a few sentences with the older daughter who was studying French. The father interjected that people in the US don't pursue foreign languages because they don't need them. "This is a very vast country and we have everything we need right here."

As we discussed languages, I told them how the Iranians hated the British and those who studied English maintained that they spoke "American," not "English." Dr. Craig became curious about British and Russian involvement in Iran. I commented that the British used a small percentage of the enormous sums of money they made from Anglo-Iranian Oil Company to bribe the government and religious leaders. The corrupt pro-British leaders in turn promoted ignorance. Oppression and religious fanaticism, causing division among the people, then helped the British to rule indirectly. Dr. Mussadegh was still struggling to deter the British influence by nationalizing the Iranian oil.

Dr. Craig sympathetically equated such problems with those that instigated the American Revolution.

On Saturday morning when Dr. Craig was leaving to make rounds in the hospital, he invited us to join him. First we stopped at a recently built private hospital, where everyone was White--patients, as well as staff. Next we visited a city hospital, where one section admitted White patients, while another, Black. Here large rooms accommodating about 25 patients comprised an old-fashioned ward. Nurses were White, but nurses' aides were Black.

Staying with the Craigs two nights and one whole day, Maafi and I noticed that the family had two big new cars including the Cadillac that the doctor drove. Their Black maid had her own car.

Neither Maafi nor I ever owned a car even though we were both of middle class in Iran. We didn't' even know how to drive. Obviously, the United States was a very rich nation.

Racial discrimination that we noticed in the hospital was not unusual in Texas. When Maafi and I took the bus from the base to downtown San Antonio, above the driver there was always the sign: "Front seats for White patrons."

Discrimination in Texas was not limited to race. It included negative attitudes toward strangers and foreigners, especially Mexicans. While Maafi and I were browsing in a jewelry store one day, the owner overheard us discussing a gold bracelet that Maafi found interesting for his sister.

"Are you Mexicans?" the man asked, hearing foreign words.

"No," I answered, "we are from Iran."

"Is that part of Mexico?"

Instead of the "No" that I answered, I felt like asking, "How stupid can you get?" I am sure that he thought we were lying.

To avoid confrontation we left the store without buying anything.

One day during a break, while drinking coke, Capt. Filips from New York City told me and Maafi that "We Americans like foreigners to come to the United States to learn our culture and then go back to their own country. We don't like them to stay in the US." At that moment I could not understand why he even brought up the subject. No one said anything about staying in the US. Stranger yet was the fact, as Brown told us later, that Filips himself was not American-born, that he came to the United States from Eastern Europe as a child with his parents before World War II.

Among our classmates, Dr. Alexander, the only African American, seldom talked to the foreigners, but often argued with the White Americans about discrimination against Blacks on all levels of life everywhere. The Whites maintained that discrimination existed only in the South. Alexander, however, was convinced that the problem existed likewise in the North, perhaps in more subtle forms, perhaps even stronger in certain circumstances.

Discrimination also existed in Iran. It was directed against Sunni Arabs, Bahais and Jews. Since there were no Negroes, there was no discrimination against them.

The longer we stayed in Texas, the easier it was for us to understand what everyone was saying or doing. Most complicated, yet never easily discernable, were the innuendos of American culture. Not only was it frustrating to not understand what others were saying, it was embarrassing to not know what to do. Listening skills certainly required more concentration and effort than filling in the blanks of a textbook exercise with the correct verb forms. I owe some of my success, step by step, to the movies. Anyone stationed at this base was able to enjoy first-run films for only 25 cents. The feature changed every three days.

I would sit through three showings of the same film.

Matching the activities on the screen with the stars' perfect articulation taught me more than textbooks. Movies also showed me the unwritten laws about life in the United States--culture. Fortunately, I was not only eager to learn, I was at an age when accepting change and adapting to it were relatively easy.

Learning was a continuous process, encompassing far more than medicine. Most interesting, indeed, was American culture.

The Medical Field Service School

United States Army

This is to certify that

FIRST LIEUTENANT HUSHANG M. PAYAN, MC
IMPERIAL IRANIAN ARMY

has satisfactorily completed the

MILITARY NEUROPSYCHIATRY COURSE

GIVEN AT BROOKE ARMY MEDICAL CENTER, FORT SAM HOUSTON, TEXAS THIS 24 DAY OF May 19 53

Lieutenant Colonel, MSC
Secretary

Major General, Medical Corps
Commandant

TO CONSERVE FIGHTING STRENGTH

81
Back to New York

On May 2, 1953, Graduation Day, I tightly held my diploma with the impressive gold seal (about two and a half inches in diameter), proving that I had successfully completed the course in neuro-psychiatry at Brooke Army Medical Center. Suddenly I recalled Dr. Shaafi in Iran boasting that he was a recipient of a gold medal from the United States government. Even his prescription pad listed this unique accomplishment. Somehow, I always questioned his delusions of grandeur. Being trained to respect one's elders, I never even dreamed of prodding him about this dubious honor. The split second that I saw my own gold "medal," I realized that neither mine nor his had any true value. They were just pieces of decoration, paper at that.

Along with my fellow Iranian physicians, I was given instructions, train tickets to New York City with a stop in Washington, DC, and vouchers for accommodations for those four days. At the end of this short vacation, unfortunately, I had to leave the United States and return to Tehran.

Between San Antonio and Washington Maafi and I luxuriated in first-class accommodations on the train. In the dining car we now knew that a hot dog was not the animal served hot, a hamburger contained no ham, and french fries were not imported. We were amazed how much our English had improved in those few short months. My thoughts jumped back and forth from the numerous pleasures we experienced in Texas to the many wonders I could experience if I stayed longer.

As early as a year before I left Tehran I kept in contact with an agency and a hospital in the United States, hoping to pursue internship and residency in this country. Accepting the offer to study at Fort Sam Houston facilitated my departure from Iran, but complicated my involvement in a program at Jewish Memorial Hospital that also began in

January, the very same time that I started in Texas. The administrator at the hospital in Manhattan understood my obligation to remain at Fort Sam Houston and had no objection to my delaying the beginning of the post graduate studies till May. All I had to do now was find a way to stay in the United States legally to complete my surgical residency.

I was still an officer in the Iranian Army. Without its official permission to postpone my return I would be considered AWOL--worse yet, a deserter. Taking such a tremendous chance to stay in the United States could have disastrous consequences. What or how, I didn't exactly know; yet I was sure that they would be major.

While such thoughts raced through my mind, I kept thinking about a friend of mine, an Iranian military physician who defied orders by pursuing his own interests in the United States. Instead of attending a two-month military medical training session at Walter Reed Hospital, he reported for an ENT (ear-nose-throat) residency at another hospital in Washington.

Naturally, administrators at Walter Reed wondered what had happened to him. Was he ill? Did he die? Was he lost? Rather than solve the mystery, they relegated the problem to the Immigration Office.

When he was found after a month or so, he was notified that his visa had expired. This time his orders stipulated that he was to return to his native country within a month. Should he refuse to do so, he would be deported. Deportation incurs the denial of any request to return at any time.

When I reached Washington, I could hardly concentrate on sight seeing. I was preoccupied with my possibilities of staying in the United States and my friend's confusion doing so. No way did I want trouble. I found my way to the Iranian Embassy and convinced the military attache, a colonel, to grant me an extension of two more weeks.

In order to be independent of both armies, I definitely needed professional help. I needed a lawyer, one well versed in immigration law. A lawyer in Texas had assured me that the American government, unlike the

Iranian government, did not operate as one gigantic singular entity. Every segment of the government in the United States had its own department with its own unique concerns. The Immigration office had absolutely nothing to do with the Army.

In Iran, if the Army went looking for me, I would be hunted down by the entire government. In Iran, any suspect was immediately guilty. There was no such law that a person is innocent until *proven* guilty beyond a shadow of a doubt. An accused person in Iran spent his time in jail until a friend or relative of his was able to bribe or influence an official for his release.

Since such "officials" in Iran considered themselves above the law and twisted any law to their personal advantage, the written law was ignored. What ruled was personal power. Such absolute power is always absolutely corrupt. In the United States it is the law, not a person, that prevails. I desperately needed a lawyer.

Two days of touring DC only added more mixed-up, ambivalent thoughts. Now that I legally had two more weeks in the U. S., I felt somewhat relieved. Having that extension tucked between the pages of my passport, I had peace of mind. On the train to New York City I was able to relax.

While at Grand Central Station I bade Maafi and Doneshvar goodbye. They were on their way back to Iran, while I headed toward Upper Manhattan. Maafi was kind enough to carry my military clothes and a few small gifts back to Tehran. My mother would be happy to see the hand tooled leather bag. I bought everybody everything imaginable in tooled leather: purses, belts, wallets, and coin purses--treasures never seen in Iran.

When Doneshvar spied a $20.00 bill sticking out of my calendar in my pocket, he asked to borrow it. "You don't need it," he rationalized. "You're going to the hospital. I want to buy more gifts to take to Iran for my wife and children. I promise to return the money to your brother." Since my brother Mohsen had a photo shop on Shah-Abad Street in Tehran, he was not difficult to find.

(A while later after I had written to Mohsen about the $20.00, I heard that Doneshvar never even mentioned my money. What really disgusted me was that Doneshvar took about $30.00 worth of pictures and prints from my brother's shop without ever paying. This was the typical behavior of an Iranian who had power, but I never expected a friend, especially one of mine, to take advantage of another.)

By mid-afternoon I found my way to Jewish Memorial, a 250-bed hospital on Broadway and 192nd Street. As I entered the building, lugging my suitcase, there was no doubt about my being a foreigner. I was wearing an out-of-fashion, unpressed, double breasted suit.

The telephone operator/receptionist directed me to the office of Mr. Miller, the administrator.

At the sight of me, before even saying "hello," Mr. Miller asked, "Do you speak English?"

"No," I responded--boldly.

Mr. Miller turned red, jumped out of his seat, bracing himself with his two hands firmly on his desk, and yelled, "What do you mean? What do you speak?"

"American," I responded--meekly this time, utterly amazed at his behavior.

He soon calmed down, only to look at me sideways and ask, "What's this supposed to be? A joke?"

Only then did he smile, shake hands, and invite me to sit down. When he sat down, his 5'2" frame almost disappeared behind his huge desk. Across from him I admired his extremely well tailored suit. The dark blue wool was punctuated with a red carnation in the lapel of the jacket. As he picked up the phone to call the chief resident, he used his fingers to comb the few hairs on the top of his head.

While waiting for this doctor to show me around, Mr. Miller told me about Isik, a young doctor from Turkey who indicated on his application that he spoke English well. When it came time to communicate, all he could say was "yes" and "no."

When Dr. Elahi joined us, I was quite surprised to see an Iranian. This relatively short and prematurely bald man was an internist working on his medical license, as well as a permanent visa.

Instantly we accepted each other. When he heard about my visa problems, he referred me to Mr. Avocat, a lawyer who could possibly help me.

At this hospital eight of the twelve intern positions were filled, and I would be #9. Because of the Korean War there was such a shortage of young physicians, half of the interns were foreign graduates, none of whom had a license. There were three residents: an American in Medicine, another American in Obstetrics-gynecology, and a Filipino in surgery. Of the two chief-residents, one was Dr. Elahi and the other an Eastern European surgeon. Since both were trying to get their license, they became close friends, even working similar schedules: 24 hours in Emergency and 24 hours off. At night the interns were expected to help them.

In that capacity I as an intern earned $30.00 a month with room, board, and uniforms as fringe benefits. I never gave lawyer fees a thought.

82

First Day of Internship

Exactly as I had placed my wake-up call, the telephone jangled at 6:00 a.m. By this time, thanks to my military training, I had the self-discipline of a robot. Within fifteen minutes I was shaved, showered, dressed in my whites, and on my way to the basement cafeteria for breakfast.

The chubby 70-year-old elevator operator greeted me, "Good morning! *Mange, mange*?"

"Good morning," I responded. "Yes, the basement, please."

In the doctors' dining room I joined Dr. Kaplan, a surgical intern from Argentina. I could not help staring at the dark lenses of his glasses.

Before I even had a chance to place my order, Christine, the 50-year-old overweight lady in charge of this part of the dining room, brought me orange juice, two eggs, bacon, toast, butter, jam, a glass of milk, and coffee. As though she were my mother, she reprimanded, "Eat everything on your plate. You work hard. You need energy." Gently she placed all this in front of me and adjusted my silverware and napkin, then asked if I wanted anything else.

"Anything else!" I wondered. In Iran breakfast consisted of a piece of bread, some cheese, and a cup of tea. "No, thank you," I said.

Over coffee and rolls Kaplan and I exchanged tidbits of our lives. He had already done a few years of general surgery. When I told him that I had just finished medical school two years ago, he called me a "spring chicken." Having never heard the expression before, I had no idea whether that was an insult or a compliment. I bristled over his self-imposed superiority. After all, I was a doctor and should be treated seriously.

No sooner had I buttered my toast, I was being paged, "Dr. Payan . . . 739. Dr. Payan . . . 739."

"Oh, oh," said Dr. Kaplan. "That's the OR. They're looking for you."

I jumped up to use the phone nearby and dialed 730. "Hello, this is Dr. Payan. Are you looking for me?"

"Yes, Dr. Payan. This is Gloria in OR. Miss Cook would like you to come right away."

"OK." I hung up, returned to the table, picked up a piece of toast to eat as I left, and took the elevator to the seventh floor.

Before I even got through the swinging doors of the OR, a middle-aged nurse greeted me, "Are you Dr. Payan?" She almost seemed to be scolding me, her words as crisp as her white nurses' uniform.

"Yes, I am," I answered meekly.

"I'm Miss Cook. Come with me, please."

She led me to the doctors' lounge, pointed to the locker where I should hang my uniform, and showed me where to find scrub suits, booties, hat, and mask. "Get dressed quickly, please. They need you in Room 2."

After doing what I was told, she accompanied me to Room 2 and introduced me to the anesthesiologist and two nurses. "This is Dr. Payan, our new intern. He will help you get the patient onto the operating table." She added this sternly, as though she were giving me orders.

"This isn't my job," I mused. In Iran orderlies did such work. Didn't she realize that I am a doctor? She introduced me as one.

It took four people to transfer a 65-year-old overweight female onto the operating table. As she was secured to the table, I was ordered once again, "Go and scrub."

Luckily, Dr. Kerzner appeared.

"You must be Dr. Payan," he said. "Hi, I'm Kerzner."

"Good morning. Yes, I am Dr. Payan." It was about time someone treated me with respect due a real doctor.

Dr. Kerzner, a native New Yorker, was in his last year of obstetric-gynecology residency.

"What's your first name?" he asked.

"Hushang."

Almost freezing in position with one hand holding a brush and his blue eyes staring at me, he asked in disbelief, "What?"

"Hushang," I repeated.

"Hmm. That won't do." Rinsing the suds off his hairy arms, he decided, "We'll call you 'Payan'."

He never even asked me where I was from or how I felt. He just gave me orders to follow him and go through the routine of scrubbing as he was showing me. This was not much different from that in Iran. The emphasis here focused on cleanliness and sterility. No one was permitted to take one step into the operating room, wearing street clothes.

Instead of chit chat, Dr. Kerzner rattled on about the patient--a private patient of Dr. Olds's who was scheduled for a hysterectomy because of bleeding.

"Have you ever helped in surgery?" asked Dr. Kerzner.

"Not in the United States, but I did in Iran."

"Well, just do as you are told by the surgeon. You'll be just as good as anyone else."

He abruptly turned around and entered the operating room. I followed him. The circulating nurse helped us with the sterile gowns and gloves.

Dr. Olds walked in and cooed "Good morning" to the patient and assured her that everything will be all right. He ignored me completely. As he went to scrub, the anesthesiologist worked on the patient.

Kerzner cleaned the lower half of the abdomen first with iodine, then with alcohol. I helped drape the patient. Dr. Olds soon returned. As second assistant I stood to the right of the surgeon who stayed on the right of the patient. Kerzner, as first assistant, stood on the left.

"Has she been bleeding long?" Kerzner asked Olds.

"Oh, about a year. Two curretages showed benign hyperplasia. Hormone therapy was carried out, but did not help."

By 10:00 a.m. the uterus, cervix, ovaries, and tubes had been carefully dissected and removed. Dr. Olds pointed out tumors on the uterus, commenting, "She has fibroids."

Dr. Kerzner noticed that the ovaries were also slightly enlarged and cystic.

"But there is no evidence of malignancy," said Dr. Olds.

For longer than three hours I stood on the same spot--observing, listening, pulling retractors, and getting more and more tired by the minute. I wondered how 75-year-old Dr. Olds managed.

Kerzner asked, "Are you going to remove the appendix?"

"Oh," Olds answered with uncertainty, "I guess we could." After clamping the root of the appendix, he cut it and coated the exposed surface with a drop of iodine. After the root was tied, the clamp was removed.

Just as Dr. Olds was cleaning the area with a piece of gauze, a bleeder appeared near the root of the appendix. Blood was pumping. Three times Dr. Olds tried to clamp the bleeder. Three times he failed. He was getting nervous. Perspiration poured from his forehead. The circulating nurse mopped his brow.

Kerzner was reluctant to interfere, but kept cleaning the tissue.

Finally Dr. Olds asked the head nurse to call one of the general surgeons.

Dr. Vesson came immediately, not even changing from his street clothes. With the help of the nurse he pulled a pair of sterile gloves over his skinny hands. After a masterful stroke, the pumping artery was clamped. Dr. Olds put a tie around it, and Dr. Vesson's clamp was removed.

"Thanks, Bob," Dr. Olds quietly said to Dr. Vesson. After the muscular layer of the wall of the abdomen was closed, Dr. Olds left, leaving the rest of the suturing (as was customary) to Kerzner.

The incident left Kerzner mumbling, "The old man should quit doing surgery."

The thought was soon interrupted when the head nurse announced, "Dr. Walsh's case, tubal pregnancy, is here. You two better not disappear."

One hour later the second case was finished. "Let's go get a bite to eat. We have to start grand rounds at 1:00," reminded Kerzner.

In the elevator smiling George greeted us with "Mange, mange."

Mange, mange we did--quickly. We almost inhaled our orange juice, soup, salad, meal loaf, mixed vegetables, potatoes, milk, coffee, and apple pie.

The grand round took about an hour. About 10 attending physicians between the ages of 30 and 65 participated, discussing OB/Gyn patients in general, but each patient briefly.

After grand rounds Kerzner took me to the fourth floor to show me how to admit patients and how to write up charts. "You are responsible for all new admissions of the day. You must take the history and do physical examination. Write routine orders and have the written reports up to date every day by the end of the day." He smoked constantly, just as everyone else seemed to do. "If you have any questions or problems, call me. I am in the hospital till 10:00 or 11:00 p.m. After that anyone at the switchboard will connect you with me at home. They have my number. For particular orders for private patients, you call the private physicians involved."

That evening I had five patients to be admitted. I kept going back and forth to the nurses' station in search of the dictionary for words I did not understand. Then in order to learn the system of reporting these details I had to look up charts reported by others, like Kerzner.

Even though I hesitated to disturb anyone, I had to phone Dr. Kerzner twice. I had more trouble understanding and expressing myself over the phone than I did person to person. From the minute I stepped off the train in Grand Central Station, everyone seemed in such a hurry to say what was on his mind. Only four days out of Texas and I already missed the Southerners. At least they spoke slowly.

Around 5:30 the head nurse noticed that I was still struggling with the dictionary. She pointed out the time and reminded me that the dining room closes at 6:00.

In the dining room I shared a table with my roommate Dr. Lambert. Originally from Holland he was doing his rotation in medicine. His accent made understanding a bit of a challenge, but at least he spoke slower than most of the others in the hospital.

We were soon joined by Dr. Isik, the new intern from Turkey, whose English was most limited. In spite of his deficiency in English, he and Lambert were able to communicate in French. As best as he could, he told us that he was assigned to the laboratory.

Eventually I finished all my admissions and charts by 10:00 p.m. My bed was never such a welcome sight. I fell asleep before my head touched the pillow.

Around 1:00 a.m. the phone rang.

"Dr. Payan?"

"Yes."

"We have a new admission on the fourth floor."

"O.K. I'll be right up."

Up I went, said hello to the head nurse of the midnight shift, and inquired about the patient.

"Room 423," she pointed and gave me the chart.

"The 30-year-old pregnant patient had a history of two previous normal pregnancies and deliveries. This time everything appeared to be fine too. Her pain was regular and fifteen minutes apart. Her cervix was three fingers dilated.

Over the phone Dr. Diamond advised me to take her to the delivery room. He would be here in about half an hour.

The patient was transferred to the seventh floor. Again I helped the anesthesiologist and the nurse to put the patient on the table. By the time Dr. Diamond arrived, everything was ready.

Dr. Diamond kept calling the patient "Honey." I wondered how closely they were related. Daughter perhaps? Later on I noticed that some obstetricians were in the habit of addressing their patients by similar terms of endearment.

By 3:00 a.m. I was able to go back to my room. I marveled at the efficient system which worked just as well in the middle of the night as it did during the day. In contrast with Iran, here the center of attention appears to be the patient, rather than the hospital officials or the doctors. The goal is for every person involved in every area of the hospital to work as a team for the welfare of the patient.

83
Embryonic Fluid

A few weeks into the internship I became quite comfortable with the duties in OB/Gyn service--in spite of the expectation to be ready for anything any split second.

Around 6:00 p.m., dinner with Dr. Lambert came to a halt when the paging system screamed, "Dr. Payan . . . 418 . . . Dr. Payan . . . 418."

Lambert identified that as fourth floor. "They probably have an admission for you."

Mechanically I picked up the phone and dialed 4-1-8. "This is Dr. Payan. Were you looking for me?"

"Yes, we have an admission for you. No rush."

By this time I was finishing my meal anyway. Dr. Lambert, having the last puff on his cigarette, commented, "A woman delivering a baby isn't really sick. She's going through a physiologic process."

"I was born at home, " I told him, "with the help of a midwife. There was no doctor involved."

"Me too, and I didn't cost my parents as much as babies cost today--like $250.00 to the obstetrician and another $250.00 for the week's stay in the hospital."

We both walked toward the elevators--Lambert heading to the Doctors' Recreation Room on the seventh floor to watch the news; I, to the obstetrical floor to meet another challenge of my training.

At the nurses' station I received the chart, "Mrs. B. Schroeder. Room 408. Bed 2."

Since English words always led me to the dictionary, I now owned my own which fit into my back pants pocket. The dollar that I spent on it was the best investment of my entire life.

"Good evening, Mrs. Shroeder."

"Hello, Doctor," quietly answered this 35-year-old pregnant woman about to give birth to her fourth child.

Since her previous deliveries had no complications and her physicals were normal, I assured her that everything will be ok. As her pain became regular about every fifteen minutes, gradually intensifying and occurring more often, she didn't exactly agree with my predictions.

As I examined her, everything was normal. Her legs were slightly swollen, but in this circumstance, that was within acceptable range. Soon her pains jolted her about six minutes apart and her cervix was three fingers dilated.

I talked to Dr. Kerzner, who suggested that the patient be taken to the delivery room.

"Is anyone else in the delivery room?" he asked.

"No," I said.

"Who's her doctor?"

"Dr. Gershman is the private physician, but he's on vacation. Dr. Silverberg is covering for him."

"OK. Send her upstairs and call Silverberg."

As I sprinted up the stairs to the Delivery Suite, I marveled at the fact that I did not have to resort to my dictionary that evening. I had to listen carefully, but I managed to understand. I wrote down the results of my conversation with the patient just as we spoke--even though she had a slight accent. I was elated.

In the delivery room I phoned Dr. Silverberg to keep him abreast of the progress of his patient. He expected to join me in about an hour, when the patient would definitely be ready.

Just as expected, Dr. Silverberg was arriving on time. So was Mrs. Schroeder's baby. As the mother was being transferred to the table, Dr. Silverberg and I scrubbed and got ready.

Going under anesthesia, the patient started yelling, "*Akh kamaram! Akh kamaram*!"

Dr. Kirsh, the old anesthesiologist from Hungary, wondered, "Anyone know what she's saying?" He was concerned about the patient.

"She's complaining about her aching back," I translated.

"You understand that?" He was surprised. "I'm glad that someone here knows what's she's talking about."

Dr. Silverberg was likewise impressed. "How many

babies have you helped deliver?"

"About 50 or 60," I surmised.

"OK. It's about time you deliver one on your own, all by yourself."

"Thank you, Doctor."

"OK. Now get close to the table. The most important thing is that you do not drop the baby. Put your knees close to the table, just in case that happens. This way, the baby would fall on your lap. That's all you need to worry about--catching the baby. The mother will do the rest."

I moved as close as I could get. Just at that moment the embryonic sac broke and water spilled everywhere, splashing right into my face. My mask got soaked. The water even reached my tongue. My taste buds informed that it was salty.

"Shit," I grumbled. I recalled my professor of medicine telling how long ago doctors would taste the urine of a diabetic patient to reach a diagnosis. If it was sweet, the patient definitely had the disorder.

Dr. Silverberg simply smirked. "I told you to bring your knees, not your head, close to the table. Don't worry. That water is sterile. You have now learned another lesson in obstetrics."

Waiting for the mother to push the baby out gave Dr. Silverberg the opportunity to lecture. At the age of 60 he considered himself the Voice of Experience. "You know Haldane?"

"No," I answered.

"He was a naturalist philosopher who believed that life started billions of years ago in the warm salt waters of the ocean. He called it primeval soup. That's how life starts and is sustained in the embryonic sac. When living creatures left the ocean, they took salt water with them. It runs in their veins--electrolytes."

His tale was interrupted when the patient needed an episiotomy, the cutting of some tissue to prevent tearing. She had experienced this procedure during the previous births.

The delivery went well, adding a sister to her daughter and two sons.

The next day when I made rounds, Mrs. Schroeder

and I conversed in Farsi. She told me how she had married an American soldier during World War II in Iran and came to the United States.

"You could have made my history-taking much easier if you had spoken in Farsi," I told her.

She dismissed my comment by reminding me that I had to practice my English.

84
Violence

The visitors' lounge hummed with the television set turned low while relatives of patients, waited for news--good or bad. Some were curled up in comfortable overstuffed chairs, some had their heads bowed in light sleep, some had eyes glued to light reading material in books or magazines. With a slight squeak of the doors Dr. Lee asked quietly, "Mr. Montana?".

"I'm Montana," replied a man almost twice the size of Dr. Lee--certainly twice his weight.

Close to the man's ear Dr. Lee began to almost whisper.

Suddenly the man grabbed Dr. Lee, spun him around, applying a wrestling hold and wound his burly right arm around Dr. Lee's neck, choking him.

Dr. Lee gasped, unable to say anything at all. His eyes turned red; his face, blue. The more he struggled to loosen the man's hold, the tighter the man squeezed.

A woman screamed, "Help! Help!" The ruckus had everyone spilling out of a nearby conference room--interns, as well as their lecturer Dr. Schwartz. Visitors in the waiting room stood around helpless. 50-year-old Dr. Schwartz, a prime example of physical fitness, was the only one big enough to take on the attacker. "Let him go," he repeated in his authoritative voice. "Let him go!" Mr. Montana seemed deaf. The only thing he wanted to do was strangle Dr. Lee.

Dr. Schwartz then raised his knee and kicked the assailant in the crotch. Dr. Lee fell to the floor, huddled on the rug, gasping for air. After the young intern gained his composure, two doctors nearest him each grabbed his elbows and lifted him to a chair.

Now it was Mr. Montana's turn to choke and gasp for air, all curled up in the corner of the room. Beating his fists against the wall, he sobbed violently, "They killed her, they killed her. Dear God, why did they have to kill her?" His anger turned to grief, his grief to total weakness.

In the conference room adjacent to the visitors' lounge the interns were having their weekly meeting with Dr. Schwartz. These pathology lectures usually focused on recent or current unusual hospital cases. The subject of that day's lecture was drug sensitivity and anaphylactic shock. It was about Mrs. Montana.

At the age of 38 Mrs. Montana already had five children. Her many episodes of bleeding indicated the need for hysterectomy the previous Monday morning. Everything with surgery and postoperative care went well. Tuesday, however, her temperature jumped to 99°. Dr. Solaric, her private physician, ordered aspirin.

Forty-eight hours later her temperature went higher--to 100°. When Dr. Solaric made rounds at 7:00 a.m., he ordered 200,000 units of penicillin to be injected intramuscularly. This dosage was to be repeated the next two mornings.

Within an hour a nurse administered the penicillin and left Mrs. Montana resting.

No sooner had the nurse gone down the halls about three rooms, she heard a scream from Mrs. Montana's room. The other patient in this semi-private room, also recovering from a hysterectomy, pleaded for help. Something was wrong with Mrs. Montana.

The efforts of Dr. Kerzner and other physicians to resuscitate Mrs. Montana failed. The patient was pronounced dead. Her husband was contacted at work and told to come to the hospital as soon as possible. Early that afternoon he arrived. In the lobby he was asked to wait for the doctor. Dr. Lee, the doctor, had the task of telling him the bad news and asking him to sign the autopsy consent required in such cases of unexpected death.

Death in the hospital is not unusual, but this particular death was.

85

Disappearing Pleasure

As I was finishing the report on Mrs. Bertucci, a 38-year-old lady expecting her fifth child in a normal delivery, the paging system screamed, "Dr. Payan . . . 105. Dr. Payan . . . 105."

At the nurses' station I picked up the phone and dialed 1-0-5. "This is Dr. Payan."

"Dr. Payan, there is a Mr. Bertucci in the visitor's lounge on the first floor. He would like to talk with you--when you get a chance."

"OK, I'll be there in a few minutes." My answer was mechanical.

Within minutes I reached the visitors' lounge. A man about 50 years old, rose slightly from his chair, anxious to meet the doctor he called for.

"Mr. Bertucci?" I surmised.

"Yes, Doc." He stretched his arm from the sleeve of his well-made striped suit as we shook hands. "Let's get away from all these people," he suggested nervously. "What I have to say is a little personal."

"OK," I agreed and we moved toward the hall.

He almost whispered, "Doc, can you sew it a little tighter?"

The blank expression of my face told him that I had no idea what he was talking about.

"You know what I mean, don't' you?"

"No," I dragged out my answer.

"Well, don't you have to cut the vagina to let the baby come out?"

"Oh, yes, that is episiotomy, an incision of the perineum and introitus of the vagina. We do that almost routinely. That is to prevent laceration."

"OK. Whatever it is that you cut, sew it a little tighter. That's all I'm asking."

For a split second I had to decode what he was

saying. Then I smiled and said, "OK. I'll talk to the resident about it."

"Thanks, Doc," he sighed in relief. "Don't tell my wife I said that."

"Of course not. Don't worry."

We shook hands and left in opposite directions.

Back in the maternity ward I discussed the matter with Dr. Kerzner, the obstetric gynecology resident. Chuckling, he remarked that we could not do anything like that in association with the childbirth. Such a procedure may create scarring and pain later on. If she has prolapse, plastic surgery could be done at another time.

"But she has no evidence of prolapse," I reminded him.

"What he is probably missing, " observed Kerzner, "is her youth."

"Maybe his own too," I added.

86

Americanisms

The little English dictionary soon became a permanent fixture in my back pants pocket. I seemed to have used it at least once every hour. Unfortunately half the time the words I looked up made no sense in the context of what was said. Other times I could not even find them. When it came to Epsom salts, Witch Hazel, grubby, yep, or other grunts that defy spelling, I was still at a loss.

Early one morning a man about fifty years old was brought by ambulance to the emergency room. The policeman who accompanied him told the nurse that someone must have tried to kill the man, who was now lying limp on a stretcher, in a state of shock. His arms and legs extended in odd positions, suggesting multiple fractures.

Immediately he was treated with adequate fluid and blood. X-ray examinations revealed seventeen fractures which were taken care of in the operating room. Eight hours later he emerged in a body cast extending to his arms and legs. One arm and one leg were in traction.

When his general condition improved and he was settled in his room, it became my task to take his history. With so much of his body in casts, physical examination was almost impossible. I asked him, "How did this happen?"

"I got into a fight."

"With whom?" I asked, imagining some kind of monster seeking revenge.

"A friend of mine," he answered nonchalantly.

To myself I said, "Some friend!" and wondered if the word *friend* was another of those American expressions that have different connotations.

* * * * *

That afternoon a female patient needed my attention. While examining her in preparation for admission, I kept telling her "sit down." All she did was twist her body and look at me strangely from the corner of her eye. "Sit down, please," I repeated.

Her response was the same. She twisted her body and looked at me strangely from the corner of her eye. She looked so confused. I finally held her gently by the shoulders and helped her to sit up.

"That's 'Sit up'," she grumbled. "Where the hell did you learn English?"

I bristled. In Iran patients did not use that tone of voice while talking to a doctor. I quickly realized that I was no longer in Iran and I used the wrong expression.

* * * * *

At the nurses' station while I was recording the history and physical of another patient, Dr. Thompson, chief of obstetrics/gynecology, walked in. As a fledgling physician I certainly respected my superiors. At the sight of him I instinctively stood up and offered him my seat at the desk. He simply remained standing. After a second of dead silence he shook hands with me and said, "Son, no one in this world is important enough for you to interrupt whatever you are doing--not even the president of the United States. Sit down and get on with your work."

* * * * *

Early one evening in the ER I admitted a man about 50 years old. This one had a sprained ankle, the result of trauma. He told me how he accidentally banged his ankle against a step at his house. "Now it hurts like hell every time I step on it."

"When did this happen?" I asked.

"About three days ago."

"Did you see your physician?"

"Sure. That same evening. The damn pain was killing me."

"What did he recommend?"

"Soaking it in hot water and taking a couple of aspirins."

"Did they help?"

"Yeah. It feels like a million bucks when my foot's in hot water."

"Like what?"

"A million bucks, Doc. Really. A million bucks."

Since he had no relief in spite of the rest and

medication, he was admitted to the hospital for X-ray and further treatment.

The opposite of "like hell" was "like a million bucks." Having a million dollars just had to be close to being in heaven. He may have learned how to care for his pain, but I learned a new American expression.

* * * * *

Around 10:00 one evening I was called to help in the ER. A man in his early 30's came in with a two-inch laceration above his left elbow.

"How did this happen?" I asked routinely.

"My wife did it."

"Your wife?"

"Yes, my wife. I work afternoon shift from 3:00 to 11:00. Today I was able to leave early. When I got home, I found my wife in bed with another man. I got mad. Then she got mad. She blamed me for ruining her evening. So I hit her. Then she hit me. While we chased around the apartment she picked up a knife in the kitchen and threw it at me."

The laceration was superficial. Without a word but plenty of questions in my mind I sutured the opening and sent him on his way. I wondered whether or not he went back home.

* * * * *

Shortly after midnight my sleep was interrupted before it hardly began. A man about 35 years old staggered up to the reception desk in the Emergency Room, complaining of abdominal pain and headache. He insisted on being admitted to the hospital. He was neither nauseated nor feverish. Every time the nurse tried to explain that he had no reason to be admitted, he let go a steady stream of loud cursing and bad breath from liquor. Drunkenness was not a medical problem that warranted admission. Drunkards simply created problems by disturbing other patients, requesting sleeping pills, and disrupting any routine in progress.

This man presented a real dilemma. It was impossible to satisfy him, as well as hospital regulations. Fortunately the 50-year-old nurse was experienced enough to be in control. She called the police station, requesting Sgt. Strong.

control. She called the police station, requesting Sgt. Strong.

Within 10 minutes the officer walked in and ordered everybody but the drunken man out. "Everyone out," he shouted. O-U-T." From inside that room came a few mysterious thumps. Within a few more minutes Sgt. Strong came out of the room and suggested that we call the patient's wife and send him home.

I was amazed at the success of Sgt. Strong's treatment. Like a miracle, the patient became very subdued and most cooperative.

* * * * *

An hour later I was again back in the ER. This time several people were brought in after a car accident. The police officer indicated that there were nine people--all men, all drunk, all from the Bowery. Apparently they stole a car, took it for a joy ride, and rammed into a telephone pole in Upper Manhattan.

While the nurses were preparing examining rooms for them, the policeman went around asking each one, "Who was driving?"

Every single one of them answered the same thing, "I don't know. I was in the back seat."

One of these men decided that sprawling on the floor and leaning against the wall were better than sitting on any of the chairs. I leaned over him to see what the injury was. What I felt was a fracture of this man's tibia.

"You have a broken bone," I told him.

"Is that right?" he smiled at me in a stupor.

During the examination the nurse noticed how I took extra effort not to add to his pain. She leaned over and whispered, "Don't worry, Doctor. He's feeling no pain."

"But he must," I thought. "Is she using another expression that does not mean what it says?" Apparently "Feeling" and "no" and "pain" taken separately meant something altogether different from "Feeling no pain" connected.

This patient was admitted, while the rest of his friends were released and taken to jail "to sleep it off."

How does one sleep "it off"? "Off what?" I wondered before I finally went to sleep myself.

87
Christmiss Cards

Since the majority of Iranians are Moslems, only a few of my childhood friends were Armenian Christians. I noticed that they celebrated a holiday called Christmas, during which they became very subdued. While they participated in some ritual in their church, they all dressed in their latest fineries in colors as subdued as their mood--either gray or brown. On such an occasion an entire family would spend the day together. The celebration seemed more solemn, than joyful.

The main holiday in Iran had a different mood. It was Now Ruz, the Persian New Year which took place on the first day of spring--March 21 of the Gregorian calendar. It was indeed a time for the greatest celebration of the entire year. People wore their best clothes (often brand new), visited relatives, and feasted on sumptuous gourmet delicacies. Children, not adults, received new silver coins as presents. It was customary to recognize the most important person, which automatically was the eldest relative, by going to that house first. Since most relatives lived near each other, it was easy to walk from one house to the other. To visit the few a little distance from our home we relied on horse and buggy for 20 cents. By the time I was a teenager buses provided public transportation. To those who were out of town, people would write letters wishing them well. Everyone was especially pleasant.

Poverty, perhaps, limited the gift giving. Most families were headed by a hard working father who had to support several children and a harder working mother who devoted every second of her life to her family. Furthermore, without the benefit of mass media, the world of business had little control over people's lives. People bought what they needed, not what was suggested by persuasive advertising. For that matter, radio and newspapers, under the scrutiny of the government, broadcast mostly news, music and educational programs. Newspaper advertising was minimal.

In the United States, however, Christmas was quite different from Christmas in Iran. Instead of the somber tone of the Armenians, the Americans permeated everything in sight with happiness to the extreme.

During that first Christmas that I experienced in the United States I was working in Jewish Memorial Hospital. To be unaware of this holiday in December, one would have to be comatose. Decorations, advertisements and activity bustled everywhere among all people--Christian or not. Stores, houses, even the hospitals were decorated with bright green, fluorescent red, shimmering silver, and sparkling gold. People exchanged gifts wrapped in the same colors. And these were not limited to children. As December dwindled, the excitement heightened. The frenzy was infectious.

"What's this all about?" I asked a senior resident who had already been here a few years. Even though he was a Moslem from Iran, he seemed well acquainted with the customs of this noisy holiday. "Am I supposed to do something?"

"Not really," he answered. "You can send a few cards if you wish . . . to people you respect or are grateful to."

"All right," I mused. "I can easily come up with a few like that."

As part of my education, he added, "In this country everybody sends cards to everybody else for every occasion imaginable: Easter, April Fool's Day, Mother's Day, the Fourth of July, Halloween, Thanksgiving, birthdays, anniversaries, when a person is born, when a person dies. This is the only country in the world where a Moslem like me would send a Christmas card to a Jewish guy like the hospital administrator. Last year the office staff made a Santa Claus out of the assistant administrator, who is Jewish, to visit the pediatric ward and deliver presents to the children."

He laughed and went on his way down the hall.

As I walked out of the hospital, I was reminded of the courtesy of the hospital administrator, the professors of surgery and medicine, the senior physicians, and the head nurses in the various departments. I was now driven by social pressure. I was immediately on my way to get some cards.

I went to a J.C. Penny store near the hospital. Right at the entrance was a huge table with cards--all kinds of cards in all sizes, shapes, designs, and colors. Those nearest the entrance were quite colorful, almost gaudy. They seemed like jokes most likely for children or maybe girlfriends. I ignored these as I had my scientific minded superiors on my mind. I couldn't discern any order to the display of cards. There seemed to be no purpose behind the stacking of these thousands and thousands of cards, except for selling them. Perhaps it was a special sale inspired by the holiday. Nevertheless, I had very important, serious people in mind, so I was drawn to those cards in more subtle shades, those that looked a little more dignified.

After I paid for my selections, I went back to my room. To make sure that this obligation was done and out of the way, I immediately signed them, addressed the envelopes, attached the stamps, and dropped them in the mailbox on the corner.

A week went by. No one acknowledged my efforts.

Another week went by. Still, no one commented on my thoughtfulness.

A few days later the chairman of the department of surgery put his hand on my shoulder and most sincerely thanked me for the card I had sent. He went on to say how important it was to have people show friendship, especially during traumatic times. It just happened that his mother had been killed in a car accident.

A few days after that a young surgeon about to be married greeted me with the biggest smile I ever noticed on his face. "That was some joke! I never thought you had it in you! That card you sent was something else. Everybody's still laughing about it."

"Oh?" I shyly commented, wondering what in the world he was talking about.

The next day I literally bumped into Dr. Veston, one of the senior surgeons, who greeted me enthusiastically. "How did you know that my cousin died?"

For a split second I too wondered how I knew that his cousin died. Did I? Really? I answered--and lied, "One of the nurses told me."

Suddenly I became suspicious of myself. What kind of cards did I send? I really did not read the message on any of them. They were all the same. Just then I remembered that Dr. Elahi mentioned that Americans send cards for every occasion, including "when a person dies." I had mailed sympathy cards to everyone.

88

Desirable Curves

With an interest in architecture, Kavoos and Daryush came to New York City in the 50's to pursue professional courses at Columbia. For these two young men the buildings in Manhattan were so spectacular, they were constantly in awe no matter where they walked. They had never seen anything as tall as the 102 floors of the Empire State Building. They marveled at the triangular windows set in arches on top of the Chrysler Building. They were repeatedly inspired when they experienced the openness of Frank Lloyd Wright's Guggenheim Museum. During the course of all their meanderings they often commented on the fact that curves were usually more aesthetically pleasing than sharp angles.

At times the people of New York aroused more curiosity than their buildings. No matter where they went, everyone had to rush. Men and women alike, young or old, always created a blur of bright colors, never the slow stream of conservative grays, blacks, and browns that dotted the landscape in Iran. The difference was so remarkable, they found themselves honing their powers of observation and voicing their reactions. Since very few Iranians were among the crowds in the United States at this time, these two young men felt that it was safe to exchange such ideas in public because they did so in Farsi. Certainly, no one else would understand them.

One Saturday, Kavoos and Daryush were invited to dinner to the house of an Iranian family on East 95th Street. That same afternoon they decided to buy a gift for their hosts. Like typical visitors they leisurely made their way to the department store, marveling at the enticing displays, the decorative arts, and the inviting entrances of each store. Inside Macy's, while waiting for the saleslady to help them, they couldn't help notice the very attractive blond at the same candy counter.

"Look at those curves," said Daryush in Farsi. "What a behind for an old broad."

"Her ass gets a 10 from me," commented Kavoos.

Slowly this lady turned around, glowering at them. In Farsi she scolded, "You miserable contemptible kids. You come to this country, spend your parents' money to go to school, and all you can do is walk around and talk about women's behinds."

Kavoos and Daryush felt the heat rush to their faces. They didn't know where to look. Without a word they turned around and headed to the opposite side of the counter.

A few hours later each one of them with a gold box of Godiva chocolates in hand began to feel the excitement about meeting other Iranians and spending the time in effortless conversation, as everyone would be speaking Farsi.

Eventually they found 12C, the apartment of Mr. and Mrs. Yazdi. They touched the door bell and heard a few notes of a sprightly melody.

Who should open the door for them but the same elegant blond lady whom they annoyed at the candy counter. "Welcome. I'm Maryam Yazdi. Please come in."

Daryush and Kavoos turned to stone. Once again they felt the heat rush to their faces. Instinctively they turned to escape another embarrassing situation.

Mrs. Yazdi simply smiled and assured them that they were most welcome.

89

Sleepless Nights

As daytime winds down, Mother Nature permeates the night with calm. Against the sky only the stars interrupt the darkness. Day colors fade into shadows. Daytime cacophonies become the secrets of the whispering trees.

Only man, however, dares defile the serenity of Nature, especially when people try to turn night into day.

One late evening a chauffeur-driven Cadillac pulled up at the main entrance of the hospital. The driver hopped out of the car to help a pregnant woman from the back seat. For some reason, the husband never appeared--that night or that week.

In the lobby a nurse was already waiting for Mrs. Enceinte to take her to her private room in Obstetrics. Since her husband was a member of the hospital's board of directors and a multimillionaire businessman, this patient's reputation preceded her.

As soon as she was settled in her room I was called to do the history-physical. Mary Dunn, the afternoon nurse who jokingly referred to herself as MD, mentioned that this lady was a VIP.

"What's so special about her?" I asked.

"She's a triple threat: money, board-member husband, patient of Dr. Shervin."

"Isn't he the gynecologist known to charge the highest fees for his services?"

"Absolutely," she nodded her head.

"Is he really better than any other obstetrician?"

"I doubt it, but he does have this reputation."

I was thankful to be working when an experienced nurse was on the floor. With chart in hand I proceeded to Mrs. Enceinte's room. For a thin 36-year-old, she didn't look like anything special to me. She was, however, most pregnant.

"My three previous babies were delivered by

Caesarian section. Vaginal deliveries are too traumatic for me," she informed me immediately--without even letting me introduce myself.

I recorded as much history as her aloofness allowed. As I was about to examine her, she turned on her side. "No one in this hospital touches me except Dr. Shervin."

"OK," I agreed and left her room. According to protocol, across the sheet where the details of her physical examination were to be noted I wrote, "Patient refused to be examined." I left the chart at the nurses' station and tended to other patients.

It was one of those days, a day that extended long into the night. By 11:00 p.m. I was so exhausted I just plopped across my bed--for a few minutes.

The next morning at 7:00 a.m. Dr. Shervin performed the Caesarian Section on Mrs. Enceinte. He directed the nurse to send the placenta to the lab to be examined by a pathologist, even though it was not customary to do so in the 1950's.

Later that afternoon when I made rounds, I visited Mrs. Enceinte's room. Before I was able to catch sight of her, I was greeted by dozens of floral arrangements. Since she was sleeping, I walked out and returned to the desk.

After another busy day I could not wait to get a good night's rest. My sleep, however, was interrupted. AT 3:00 a.m. the telephone operator told me that I was urgently needed in the Emergency Room.

I was soon speeding along in an ambulance with flashing lights and screeching siren, slaloming around cars and disregarding traffic lights. During this thrill ride I sat between the driver and a nurse. "Where are we going?" I asked the middle-aged.

"To the East Side," she responded, "a poor neighborhood. The police who called will be waiting in front of the building."

"Why couldn't the mother go to the hospital to deliver the baby?" I asked.

"Who knows? Some of these people have so many problems, they don't want any more excitement in their lives. Only when they suddenly have uncontrollable pain do they call the hospital or, if they have no phone, the police.

Anyway, the police called us and here we are."

The three of us jumped out of the ambulance and hurried up to the eighth floor--on foot. There was no elevator in this old apartment building.

A beautiful 36-year-old pregnant woman was curled up on a worn couch in a very small apartment. Her three children (3, 5, and 8 years old) were asleep in one bedroom. The nurse and I helped the mother to the other bedroom. Nothing was very clean, not even the people. Both husband and wife were barefooted--no socks, no shoes. The nurse and I put on our gowns and gloves and prepared the bed with towels and sheets.

With one more loud gasp the mother let everyone know that she was ready to deliver. The cervix was wide open, the water broke, and the baby's head showed. Most emphatically she told me that her other babies presented no problems. "No one cut me up either." Her comments were interrupted by one more sudden gasp. The wrinkled face of the baby appeared. Another little boy became the member of this happy family. Then out came the placenta which I placed in a pan. The husband took it out of the bedroom.

I let the nurse take over in the bedroom, while I filled out the forms in the living room. The family name was "Colon."

"What will the baby's first name be?" I asked.

"You give him a name, Doc," suggested the father.

He caught me off guard. A name? I didn't know what to say.

At that moment the nurse joined me and suggested, "Call him Sigmoid. That way he'll be sigmoid colon."

The nurse and I smiled, looking at the father jokingly for approval. "Is that all right?"

"Oh, sure," he smiled back, "like Sigmoid Freud." We were surprised because while we were joking, he was serious. Sigmoid colon is a part of the large bowel, but Mr. Colon obviously thought Freud's first name was "Sigmoid," rather than "Sigmund."

We didn't pursue the discussion.

Then I turned to the nurse, "What do we do with the placenta in a case like this, a home delivery?"

Before the nurse could tell me about routine

procedures, the father broke in, “I threw it out the window. The dogs will get it, Doc. Don’t worry about a thing.”

Mr. Colon’s reference to the dog made me recall words of wisdom by Confucius. When he was asked what he would like done with his body after his death, he replied, “Don’t deny the birds a meal.”

On the way back to the hospital the sky was turning pink-blue, the street lights were dimming, garbage cans clattered as they were tossed into trucks, and taxi cabs squealed around corners. Manhattan was giving birth to another day.

90

Epsom Salts

Most of the memorable experiences of my clinical years in the hospitals seem to have occurred during the darkest hours of the night. During the day it was routine work that occupied my concerns.

In the middle of one night the phone jangled unmercifully. The operator said, "They need you in the ER. There is a demanding young woman who would like to see a doctor--immediately."

I splashed my face with cold water, hoping that I could at least look awake. I wondered what kind of emergency could erupt at 3:00 a.m.

In the ER sat a 22-year-old woman, chewing gum in rhythm of her swinging right leg crossed at the knee.

When I tried to follow the normal sequence of questioning, she cut me off. She was in a rather foul mood. "Look, Doc, I've had this before. All I need is a little bit of Epsom salts to soak it." As she bent down to show me her swollen red toe, her blond hair fell forward, exposing black roots.

Her discomfort looked like an ingrown toenail, a problem usually the result of improper care of the nail. "You've had this for four days?" I asked, trying to confirm what she had told the nurse.

"Yes," she replied, "I have."

"Why didn't you see your doctor during the day?"

"I was busy. I have to go to work during the day. Since I was passing this hospital on my way home from a date, I figured I'd drop by for a doctor to check my problem. I don't need your barrage of questions. I'm not on trial for anything. All I need is a little bit of Epsom salts."

Never having heard of Epsom salts before, I turned to the nurse and asked, "What are Epsom salts?"

Now the patient jumped up, sore toe or no sore toe. "What? You don't know what Epsom salts are. What kind of doctor are you?"

Before the nurse answered, I continued, "Are there any available or do we have to call the pharmacist to fill a prescription?"

The nurse mentioned that it was a simple over-the-counter remedy for relief of swelling. "I have the key to the pharmacy," she obliged. "I'll get some."

When she brought the package, I recognized Epsom salts as magnesium sulfate (Mg SO_4.7 H_2O). I knew that it is used as a cathartic, as well as a mild anti-inflammatory agent for topical use. "Make a 4% solution," I said. " Forty grams of magnesium sulfate and a liter of warm water."

To the patient I suggested, "See your doctor tomorrow or come to the hospital clinic during the day. You have an ingrown toe nail. The Epsom salts may make you feel better temporarily, but this problem needs attention."

The patient took the powder and went home.

As I walked back to my room I couldn't help wonder why this woman had to wake me up in the middle of the night.

91

Endless Learning

Dr. Maghrur, an internist, was lecturing about liver function tests in patients with jaundice. His presentation was punctuated with technical jargon, like "conjugated and unconjugated bilirubin, alkaline phosphatase, serum glutamic-oxaloacetic transaminase (SGOT) and serum glutamic-pyruvic transaminase (SGPT)." This was like another foreign language. Not only did the new terminology and the equivalent abbreviations strain my brain, the thorough understanding and clinical application compounded my problem of feeling inadequate.

In the United States diagnoses have depended heavily on laboratory tests, while in other parts of the world (definitely in Iran) if they were available the cost made them prohibitive.

Eventually I recognized and learned the proper use of many laboratory tests. Interpreting the results was most crucial in determining the diagnosis and treatment of the patient.

Such dependence on scientific and mechanical procedures minimized the necessity of the physicians to use their own hands, eyes, and ears. Outside the United States much time was spent on such examination. Perhaps American efficiency lessened the chance of human error.

That evening as I was struggling with my biochemistry, trying to understand enzymes and coenzymes, I was called to admit a patient.

On the third floor a seventy-year-old man complained of acute abdominal pain and vomiting. His condition had gradually worsened during the past forty-eight hours. His boardlike abdomen suggested an introabdominal inflammatory process.

As the internist, Dr. Maghrur already saw the patient in his office and made the diagnosis of acute appendicitis. In the hospital the second physician, Dr.

Friedman, an experienced surgeon, likewise noted "acute appendicitis." Dr. Aguiree, a surgical resident, became the third physician to examine the patient and naturally concurred. As the lowest ranking physician, I had the responsibility to see the man in order to fill the history-physical forms. The patient mentioned that he has occasionally felt some pain in the right upper quadrant of the abdomen for the past few years.

I therefore used a bimanual technique that I had learned in medical school from Dr. Adl, my professor of surgery in Tehran. With the right index finger in the rectum and the left hand on the right lower quadrant of the patient's abdomen, I pressed simultaneously with both hands toward the appendix. If the patient has appendicitis, he will experience excruciating pain. This patient did not. I felt positive that each of these three senior physicians made a faulty diagnosis. I was sure that the patient was suffering from acute inflammation of the gall bladder.

I had no choice but to disagree with my superiors. Dr. Aguiree and Dr. Friedman had no comment, but Dr. Maghrur smirked.

As soon as the patient was anesthetized, the abdominal muscles were relaxed and no longer boardlike. Now the gall bladder stood out hard and large. There was absolutely no question about the problem. The surgeons removed the infected gall bladder and stones.

Dr. Maghrur, watching Dr. Friedman, asked, "Are you going to remove the appendix too?"

"No. There's nothing wrong with it. Because of the inflammation in the gall bladder area, I would rather not handle anything else."

Dr. Maghrur was somewhat disturbed to be proven wrong by a young, inexperienced foreign physician who could hardly speak English.

An hour later in the doctors' lounge, where I was changing from scrub suit to my white uniform, Dr. Maghrur tossed a half dollar to me and said, "Here, go get yourself a beer."

I threw the money back at him, "No, thank you. I don't drink beer."

* * * * *

A similar case occurred about a week later. This time the patient with a fever, acute abdominal pain and vomiting was 13 years old. Once again boardlike muscles made proper examination difficult. Once again I did my bimanual maneuver and once again decided against appendicitis.

Every other physician involved was certain that the appendix was the source of the problem. Dr. Richards, who was to perform the operation, asked why I had questioned the diagnosis of appendicitis.

"I really do not believe this is appendicitis, but since I do not have a definite diagnosis, I questioned it."

"Why do you suspect something other than appendicitis?"

I related the previous experience to him and explained the bimanual maneuver. He had never heard of it, but was quite impressed. He was sure that he would follow the procedure in the future.

When he did make the incision over the appendix of this young boy, he found food particles and fluid in the abdomen. "You're right," he said. "This isn't appendicitis. It's a perforated stomach ulcer."

He then closed the first incision. After making another over the stomach, he cleaned the abdominal cavity and sutured the perforation.

"Isn't it unusual for a thirteen-year-old boy to have a stomach ulcer? A perforated one at that?"

"It sure is," he commented, "but even a new born can have one. It's probably due to stress."

Within two weeks the boy recovered and went home.

92

RiskyTreatment

My mother was the only daughter of 12 children. My grandmother was widowed around age 50. Such circumstances naturally brought the two of them together often, usually at our house. For each new baby, many a chore, every holiday, or any crisis . . . Grandma was there.

Jahan, one of my cousins, also visited often to play with me and a few neighborhood children. We weren't old enough to go to school yet. Just a year older than I, he had a penchant for enough trouble for 10 kids. His mind was always spinning--off at a tangent.

One day he decided to make his own dart from a toy windmill that he had broken. At the broken end of the stick he attached a straight pin that could pierce any target. Since I helped him, I was quite proud of "our" accomplishment. Since it was his idea, he naturally insisted on playing with it first. I was only allowed to watch as he started throwing it around, rarely hitting any intended target. Most of the time it would hit the wall, stay put for a second, and then fall down.

As he became more skillful with his throwing, but still not too good at hitting his target, he jumped around a bit, like an acrobat--maybe a real dancer. During one of such gyrations his dart slipped out of his hand and found my three-year-old cousin as the target. Cousin Touran screamed and cried. The pin landed right under her right eye and hung there, defying gravity. Jahan and I both panicked. Touran kept screaming and crying, louder and louder. She refused to allow any of the kids even to come near her, let alone try to remove the dart.

Jahan ran to hide so he would not be blamed for the accident.

I ran inside the house for Grandma. She could fix anything and never get excited. She never yelled either.

Before Touran had a chance to object, Grandma

had my little cousin on her lap, talking to her to distract her and calm her. Just as Touran turned her head to look at Grandma, Grandma gently and deftly removed the pin. She wiped the spot where only one drop of blood appeared, applied a little pressure on it, and kissed it. Within minutes everybody was quiet. As Jahan noticed the confusion subsiding, he appeared. The world which was falling apart a few minutes ago suddenly got together again, thanks to Grandma.

Of course, Grandma confiscated the dart and gave us a lecture about the danger of playing with sharp objects.

I couldn't imagine life without her.

Twenty-two years later I was an intern in a small New York City hospital. One Friday night, around 10:00 p.m., when I was on call, I made my night rounds to make sure that all was well and the patients were resting comfortably. I was making sure that the nurses would have no reason to wake me up in the middle of the night to prescribe a sleeping pill or an aspirin.

In a box-shaped fixture hanging from the ceiling, a paging system contained numbers which would light up according to a particular doctor's code when he was needed. #12 began to flash. That was mine. Immediately I picked up the phone. "This is Dr. Payan. Are you looking for me?"

"Yes, Doctor. There's a young man in the Emergency Room with a knife in his neck. They want you right away."

I ran down three flights of stairs to the Emergency Room. A young policeman approached me and directed me to the examining table where the injured man lay. "The patient is here, Doc."

I stepped into the room, the door closing behind me. Fortunately, one of the most efficient nurses, around 50 years old, was on duty. (On many occasions I followed the suggestions of an experienced nurse. At this stage of my profession, such a person was more knowledgeable and more capable in many instances than I was.)

The patient, around 20 years old, just lay on the table with his eyes fixed on the ceiling, terrified. Completely through his neck from left to right was lodged an eight-inch carver knife. To support the knife and prevent it from moving, the nurse placed balled-up towels on both sides of the man's neck.

The patient allegedly got into a fight with some of his friends after a few rounds of beer.

"Who did this to you?" I asked.

"My friend," he whispered.

I felt the urge to scream, "Friend?" but said nothing.

This young man had no pain, no evidence of significant bleeding. He was pale from fright, but his blood pressure, heart rate, temperature were all ok. He had no trouble breathing or swallowing. Apparently, the knife cut no important structures, just slid between them.

Tugging at it to pull it out, however, could cause real trouble, like major bleeding. It seemed to be a case for an experienced surgeon to be done in the operating room. I had the nurse page the surgeon on call.

We were told that he was in another hospital in the OR, removing someone's bowel because of intestinal obstruction. That meant that he couldn't even come to the phone for the next couple of hours.

I was on my own!

I tried to recall some lesson . . . or some professor's advice . . . or some chapter I had read about such a situation. My mind was blank . . .

until I recalled the dart under Touran's eye. I had flashbacks of Grandma holding this little girl on her lap, distracting her, and gently removing the pin in the opposite direction of the exact path that it had entered.

I proceeded to clean the exposed tip of the knife with plenty of peroxidase and kept talking to the patient, pulling at the knife at the same time--the smallest fraction of an inch at a time. It took forever. I can't even remember what I talked about.

I do remember, however, that the knife slid out. There was no bleeding, no pain, nor any trouble with breathing, swallowing, or talking.

I was the one who suffered some discomfort, sweating bullets even though the room was actually cold. The nurse dabbed my face with a piece of gauze, while I cleaned the wounds on both sides of the young man's neck and sutured them.

In order to have his blood pressure and his breathing monitored every hour and antibiotics administered every six hours, the patient remained in the hospital for 48 hours.

Hardly two steps out of the ER, I was paged again. It was the surgeon on call, returning my telephone call.

He couldn't believe the situation. "How's the patient?" he asked.

"Fine."

"Good job! I'll see you tomorrow. Good-bye."

At the same time, the policeman was leaving with the knife. "Good night."

"I hope so," I mumbled. "What would I ever have done without Grandma?" I thought.

93
Pleasant Surprise

"Mrs. Grossinger, who was just admitted, is now in Room 412," reported Mary, the young nurse. "She's ready for her history and physical."

As an intern rotating through OB/GYN service, I immediately wondered whether or not she was pregnant.

"No, she's not. She's 50 years old. According to her chart she's here for hymenectomy."

I sat at the desk, looking at the chart, trying to read the illegible handwritten note left by Dr. Collins, her private physician. In the background two young nurses were whispering and giggling.

Apparently Mary and Mrs. Grossinger lived in the same apartment building. Furthermore, since the patient was also a hospital employee, both nurses knew her. They also knew the husband, because he was a police officer who often reported to the emergency room with people involved in accidents.

The nurses enjoyed gossiping about the Grossingers. Everyone was interested in this elderly couple because of their recent marriage. Mrs. Grossinger had never been married before and Mr. Grossinger had been married to her sister until the latter's death. Neither had any children.

"A hymenectomy?" mused Margaret, the other nurse. "At her age? I thought this marriage was for companionship."

"Obviously not," Mary giggled. "Otherwise she would not need a hymenectomy."

"I certainly wouldn't wait that long. I made love to my first boyfriend when I was fourteen."

When I went to examine the patient, I met a pleasant lady who looked much younger than her age, in spite of the fact that she was slightly overweight for her 5'2" frame. Healthy red chubby cheeks added to her youthful appearance. Five years post menopausal, she was in good health. Commenting on her siblings, she mentioned that she had a sister who died in a car accident a year earlier.

The following day the hymenectomy was done under general anesthesia. Twenty-four hours later she was discharged.

One early morning about 10 months after the hymenectomy, I again happened to be on duty when Mrs. Grossinger came to the hospital. She complained about excruciating cramps and was perspiring profusely.

"I can't imagine what I ate that could cause such pain," she moaned.

While she was being registered in the ER, her husband had to leave for work. In fact, they arrived in the police car. He asked the nurse in the ER to let him know when his wife will be ready to leave. The nurse was to phone the police station and then he would come to take her home.

"Show me where the pain is," I said.

"Here," she said as she touched her lower abdomen.

"Is it periodic?"

"Yes," she gasped as she felt one of those stabs just as she pointed to it.

"Are the spasms getting more and more frequent?"

"Yeah, absolutely."

"When was your last menstrual period?"

"Six years ago."

Since she was overweight, it was difficult to determine whether or not she was pregnant. After a brief examination, I noticed that her cervix was flattening. Through the stethoscope came faint heart beats, different from the patient's pulse.

"You're having a baby," I told her.

'Oh, God," she gasped. "That's impossible. Not at my age. I haven't menstruated for the past six years!"

"No doubt that's true, but right now you're about to deliver. At times such pregnancies do occur, and this time it's happening to you."

I immediately called Dr. Kerzner, the OB/GYN resident. When he examined Mrs. Grossinger, he confirmed my diagnosis and had her admitted to the maternity floor.

The ER nurse who knew the husband phoned the police station as requested. When he called back to say that he was on his way, she congratulated him. "You're about to be a father!"

Within minutes a police car approached with the lights flashing. To reach the hospital that soon, he must have wormed through Manhattan traffic at 60 miles per hour.

Dr. Kerzner greeted him at the nurses' station on the maternity floor, "You're about to be a father."

"Oh, my God," mumbled Mr. Grossinger, grabbing a chair where he flopped. "Oh, my God," he kept repeating. "I feel dizzy."

One week later 63-year-old Mr. Grossinger and 51-year-old Mrs. Grossinger left the hospital cooing over their brand new baby girl. She's the only one they saw on their way through the swinging doors. The rest of the world was a blur.

94
Love

In Iran boys and girls attended separate elementary and high schools. Only university classrooms were coed. In my medical school class of 160 students only five were girls. In spite of the oddity of female classmates, the boys either respected them from a distance or disregarded them completely. In school, at the approach of a girl, such a tense and unnatural relationship made the boys abruptly end any conversation among themselves. The few girls likewise avoided the boys. These girls stayed together and did everything together as though they were Siamese quintuplets. A few of the boys were bold enough to speak to the girls, but only most formally and probably to discuss something educational.

Most Iranians were brought up to think that any contact with a woman was reserved for personal interests. Therefore any other relationship was awkward, sinful, illegal, immoral and anything else that was wrong. Other than grandmothers, mothers, sisters, aunts, nieces, or girl cousins, there was no socializing between male and female. As I began to mature my mother constantly reminded me that I should look upon girls the way I would like other boys to look upon my sisters. When she caught me eyeing some good looking girl, she would gently swat me on the back of the head and whisper, "Think of her as if she were your sister."

"If all boys looked at girls," I once asked her, "as if they were sisters, would anyone ever get married?"

"You're not ready yet," she reprimanded. "First you have to finish your studies. Later on you can look for a wife."

"When does love enter the picture?"

"Stop dreaming, young man. Love is for poetry, fiction, songs, and movies. In real life there is no love. When you are ready for marriage, you need to find a decent woman with whom you can spend the rest of your life, someone to bear your children and look after them, as well as after you. In the real world there is no place for love." As I thought about her comments, I noticed that no married couples whom I knew ever talked about love or ever publicly showed any expression of endearment.

In my studies of English during the explication of a literary work, the word *love* was literally translated as عشق (eshgh). Later I discovered that the connotation of عشق (eshgh) implies a sublime relationship. Since the word was never used in ordinary conversations, I assumed that such an emotion should never be mentioned frivolously.

In contrast with Iran, in New York I found myself in the middle of everybody loving everything. The head nurse would greet me with a smile and the schedule for the day. Then she would comment how she loved the smell of freshly brewed coffee and sip it in ecstasy. (I wondered how anyone could have a sublime relationship with coffee.) While making rounds, nurses would keep each other up to date on their personal lives with observations like, "Didn't you just love Gone With the Wind?" (I was beginning to suspect that *eshgh* and *love* were not synonymous.) Dr. Walthe loved his new Sports Mercedes. I overheard one of the patients telling his roommate how his grandmother loved The Arthur Godfrey Show. Even when doctors would relax in the lounge and watch TV, someone would react to something clever with "I love it!" not even hinting what "it" was. (Obviously, *love* in the United States meant liking something intensely.)

Besides finding myself in the middle of loves, I found myself in the middle of women everywhere--in the hospital, in the stores, in the offices, in the dining room, in public restaurants, even out on the streets at night. I not only had to get used to working with them, I had to get used to taking orders from them. I kept my distance. Every time I noticed any girl somewhat interesting, I heard my mother's voice, "Are you ready to get married?" I certainly was not. I hardly had any money to rent a room, buy food, and pay the lawyer. Never mind supporting a wife. According to her rationale, though, I was already married--to medicine.

Occasionally the nurses would love to throw a party

in one of their homes and invite whoever worked with them. At the first party I attended I was surrounded by unmarried nurses and interns. As soon as Dr. Lambert and I walked in, we were met by our hostess, a divorced senior nurse about 35 years old. Before we hardly entered the room, my friend and I were offered a drink.

"What is it?" I asked, twirling the cold glass in my hand.

"It's a highball, basically whiskey." answered Dr. Brown. "Drink it. It's good for you."

I gulped it down just to get rid of it. No sooner had I finished my drink, someone took the glass and refilled it. This was a very unusual and exciting night. I soon began to feel relaxed, very American. I even laughed when others did, without knowing why. Then I began to feel dizzy and tired. I was convinced that I was overworked. But that's what happens when one is conscientious.

There were so many people and so few chairs, everyone was walking around eating, drinking, smoking, talking, even dancing--all at the same time.

At 4:00 a.m. I woke up with a pounding headache. I found myself in a strange dark room in the corner of a couch. As my eyes adjusted to the darkness, I noticed others in this room too, but no one else was alone. All the others were entangled couples, twisted like the pretzels that they consumed all night.

The only one on two feet was the hostess. "How do you feel?" she asked.

"I think I'm all right, but I have a terrible headache."

"Come with me to the kitchen. Have some orange juice. You drank too much on an empty stomach."

After I sipped the juice, she asked, "What would you like to do now? Sleep here till morning?"

"No, thank you. I better go back to the hospital. I have to cover the emergency room at 7:00 in the morning."

"OK. Don't take the subway. Take a taxi."

"How much does that cost?"

"About a dollar,"

"Good. That's about all I can afford. Good night."

95

Tough Cookie

In the male medical ward one day I followed Dr. Friedman, a very reserved, no-nonsense, elderly surgeon, as he examined a patient suspected of having intestinal obstruction. If this were the problem, he would detect no "bowel sounds" as he listened to the abdomen with his stethoscope. While he carefully examined this man, tiny explosive sounds interrupted his concentration. He was more disturbed by the fact that he could not determine the source of the little outbursts. Were they inside his patient's abdomen or from some outside source? Repeatedly he jerked his head upright and asked Mrs. Gintho, the nurse, "What was that?"

Before she had time to answer, he asked again, "What was that?"

"It's the patient in the next bed," she answered, adjusting her bra straps that kept slipping down her arm.

"What was that?" he asked, losing his customary dignity and not paying attention to her answer.

Again she told him, "It's the patient in the next bed."

Like a broken record, these two repeated the question and answer until her patience ran out.
She turned to the neighboring bed and with all her might yanked open the curtain around the other bed, took a deep breath, and yelled, "For God's sakes! Can't you stop farting for a minute? Will you let this doctor examine his patient?" She screamed, reaching a higher decibel with each word.

Matching her pitch, the man screamed back, "I can't help it. What goes in has to come out."

Most people objected to Mrs. Gintho's mannerisms, even though they occasionally envied her results. At this point she pronounced her success by pushing her loose strands of gray hair under her cap.

To avoid Mrs. Gintho's uncouth and rude behavior everyone who knew her in this hospital tried to walk in a different direction at her approach. One night it was my luck to have Mrs. Gintho accompany me when I was called to check on an elderly patient with rheumatoid arthritis. Nine p.m. signaled lights out. Individual beds, however, had lights controlled by the patient. To get around the wards and patients' rooms, we used flashlights.

This lady's complaints about her pain had other patients complaining about her complaining. Late evening was time to go to sleep, not to make noise. To mitigate her discomfort the patient asked for a sleeping pill. I approved the request and had Mrs. Gintho give it to her.

As we left the elderly woman somewhat calmed down, Mrs. Gintho said, "You know what the old bitch really needs, Doc?"

I stood still just then, wondering, "Now what?"

"She needs something big and hard--like this," pointing to the flashlight handle in her hand. Did she really mean what I thought she was implying? Was that flashlight another phallic symbol to her? I heard that American women were frank and outspoken and nurses especially were "tough cookies," but I never expected anything this vulgar to come from the mouth of a somewhat educated person. At 11:00 p.m. Mrs. Gintho's shift ended and so did my uneasiness.

96

Love at First Sight

With Mrs. Gintho's voice still ringing in my brain, I continued making my midnight rounds to make sure that every patient was asleep and comfortable. Since I had admitted 68-year-old Mrs. Bexter, a victim of a stroke, I naturally wondered how she was doing, especially since her prognosis offered little hope. Her hypertension of many years caused her brain hemorrhage and coma.

"Hello, Doctor," a statuesque attractive nurse greeted me. "I'm Eleanor, Mrs. Bexter's private nurse."

"Hello. I'm Dr. Payan, an intern," I said, staring at her shiny blond hair and penetrating blue eyes. "How's your patient?" Instead of hearing her answer, I heard my mother's voice, "Are you ready to get married?"

"Disregarding my mother, I enjoyed the few minutes with Eleanor. What a soothing voice, so sincerely concerned with her patient. What a pleasure to see a crisp, clean uniform on such a perfect body. Since this woman was spending her free moments with a book, she obviously had more of a mind than a mouth. "What are you reading?" I asked, anxious to hear her voice more than the answer to my idle question.

"Gone With the Wind."

"Oh, I saw the movie. A beautiful story," I sighed--more over Eleanor than the story.

On my way out, I stopped at the door, took a deep breath, turned around, and asked, "Are you going to be here tomorrow night?" I couldn't believe that I really did ask that.

"Most likely."

"I'll see you then perhaps," I smiled and left.

"Good night," she smiled.

I left walking on air.

The following night I couldn't wait to check on Mrs. Bexter. The patient was worse, but the nurse looked even better.

Eleanor came from a small town in northeastern Pennsylvania. She and her girlfriend decided a big city would be quite an exciting change after graduation from nursing school. To me every word falling from her mouth became exciting, even though my mother's admonishment haunted me.

Reluctantly I left the patient's room, walking out backwards and almost crashing into the door frame. I dared not stay too long for fear of being the subject of hospital gossip. How would Mrs. Gintho react?

A day later Mrs. Bexter died and I lost track of Eleanor. I never even asked for her last name, let alone her phone number. Instinct told me to ask her out on a date, but my mother interfered.

Weeks later while making midnight rounds in pediatrics, I bumped into Eleanor again. This time she was covering for a nurse on vacation. Just as before, her presence alone lit up the patient's room. I was thrilled to see her, but dared not express even a hint of satisfaction. My Middle Eastern background was interfering with my American lifestyle. "Will you have dinner with me Saturday night?" I blurted. Now I felt like a real American--bold and to the point.

"Fine," she hesitated. "There are a couple of problems. First, I have to start work at 11:00 p.m.. I have to come home early to get ready."

"What's the other problem?" I wondered.

"My girlfriend Shu. We sort of go everywhere together. Can you get her a date too? Can we double date?"

"Sure," I agreed, having absolutely no idea what a *double date* was. Could it mean that first I go out with Eleanor then go out with Shu?

Within the next few days one of my friends not only educated me on the fine points of a double date but agreed to go with me. When he offered to use his car, I was doubly happy.

Saturday came much too slowly. Around 6:00 p.m. Fred and I picked up the two girls in GreenwichVillage. Dinner was interesting, more so for the company than for the food. Unfortunately, the time went by too fast. We had to make sure these nurses were at the hospital on time.

A little after 9:00 Eleanor and I were dropped off at her apartment, while Shu and Fred went for a little ride. An elevator took us to the 10th floor, where Eleanor rented a room from an elderly woman and had kitchen privileges.

"Would you like something to drink?" she asked.

"No, thank you."

As she pulled out a cigarette, I helped her light it. As I silently objected to this habit which I found disgusting, I was sure that I would some day change her. I kept wondering what I really wanted from her, why I even asked her to dinner. All along I was aware of my mother's comments on love.

I stared right at her, my very first date, and asked, "Would you marry me?" If she accepted my proposal, we could be engaged for a couple of years, during which time I would have earned a little more money before we were married and she would quit smoking.

With blue eyes larger and bluer than ever, Eleanor looked at me as though I had three heads. "Are you kidding?"

"Of course not."

She smiled. I couldn't tell whether she was smiling because of me or at me. "Heavens, NO! I can't get married yet. I'm only a baby. I have some real living to do first."

I was now rejected and dejected. We shook hands. "Good night," I said politely.

"Good night," she said politely.

Two weeks later on a Saturday afternoon I was called to the phone. The sound of Eleanor's voice excited me down to my toes. From her sister's apartment not too far from the hospital she asked me to visit her while she babysat her niece. "We can listen to music or watch TV while we take care of the little girl."

I accepted the invitation. After dinner I walked along Broadway, loving everything in sight. At a toy store I bought a mechanical toy monkey that walked and jumped.

Fifteen minutes later I greeted Eleanor. "Hello. Since you told me you were a baby, I brought a toy."

She laughed with pleasure and gave the monkey to her niece.

Too soon it was 10:00 p.m. and I had to leave. We shook hands. "Good night," I said politely.

"Good night," she said politely.

A few nights later when we saw each other in the hospital, for lack of something to say I asked, "How's Susie?"

"Susie was unhappy because you did not kiss her goodnight when you left."

I never saw Susie after that, but I did see Eleanor a few more times. Not long after, she mentioned an offer to work in a psychiatric hospital in Connecticut for more money.

By the following Christmas I was totally preoccupied with my surgical residency in Brooklyn. One of the greeting cards I received contained a note--from Eleanor.

By the time I got around to answering her it was way after Christmas. As an apology for my procrastination I sent her a present, a fancy Iranian-made cigarette box, enough cigarettes to fill it, and a book: <u>How to Stop Smoking</u>. Debating about the right thing to say in a note, I simply mentioned how busy I was with surgical residency.

Eleanor did respond to this note--six months later with a phone call. By this time I was doing a pathology residency and she was visiting her sister in New York City. "Can we have lunch together?"

"Of course. I will pick you up around noon."

Early afternoon I had to take her back to her sisters' because she had to leave for Connecticut. In the car we lingered over our goodbyes.

"I wish I could kiss you," she said.

"Here?" I gasped. "In the middle of the street with all these people coming and going in broad daylight?"

Before she could answer, I got out of the car and opened the door on her side. Without further comment, she told me about a Marine lieutenant in Connecticut who wanted to marry her.

"I wish you luck," I smiled and shook her hand. "I will always think of you as my American sister," I added and thought of my mother. "Invite me to the wedding."

She never did send me an invitation--or anything else, for that matter.

97
Typhlitis

Late one evening during my four months of rotation in surgery I was called to the surgical floor to see a 70-year-old man brought in with acute abdominal pain in the right lower quadrant. He complained of vomiting and diarrhea. His temperature was 103°. His abdomen felt like a board with a questionable mass. Dr. Karsh, an experienced surgeon, who had seen the patient in his office, diagnosed the problem as a ruptured appendix with acute focal inflammation and abscess formation.

In Iran such a patient would have to wait until the next day when hospital personnel return to work. Procrastination was the norm. "It can wait till tomorrow. He won't die before morning."

I soon learned that in the United States there is no tomorrow. Everything is "immediately, if not sooner." Here the patient is the star and for his comfort everyone must go to work instantly. Within an hour the operating room was in full swing to care for this elderly man.

I scrubbed with Dr. Karsh, since no surgical resident was available at the time. For me the opportunity to be first assistant was exciting. When the abdomen was opened, a tumor was discovered involving the cecum and part of the ascending colon. Dr. Karsh labeled the problem "cancer."

"The patient has not been prepared for bowel surgery," said Dr. Karsh. "We can't remove the tumor, but we must relieve the obstruction."

"Ileostomy?" I asked.

"Exactly," nodded Dr. Karsh.

After the terminal end of the small bowel was cut, the opening was attached to the skin and the abdomen was closed.

Dr. Karsh recommended that the patient be put on antibiotics with intravenous and liquid diet. "Within a few days we will go back and remove the tumor."

After the surgery we gathered in the doctors' lounge. "You did a good job," he complimented me. He then looked at me and asked, "Have you ever been to the Yankee Stadium?"

"No, I haven't," I answered.

"Are you off this weekend?"

"Yes."

"Good, take these two tickets. There's a great game Sunday. These are good seats, but I can't use them. Take one of your friends and have a good time."

"Thank you . . . very much, Dr. Karsh. I appreciate this."

A week later, early in the morning, Dr. Karsh was operating on Mr. Olds again to remove his tumor. "How did you enjoy that great game?" he asked.

"It was fine," I lied.

"It's a great sport," he commented with enthusiasm. He almost seemed to be ready to swing a bat himself.

But there he was--opening up Mr. Olds's abdomen. For a split second he was motionless. "The tumor disappeared," he gasped. "This was an inflammation. It was a pseudotumor, not a tumor."

"Could it have been 'typhlitis'?" I meekly inquired.

"Why, of course," responded Dr. Karsh. "That's inflammation of the cecum. Very rare. Very rare, usually secondary to appendicitis."

The patient's bowel was reattached, the appendix was removed, and the man was discharged in a few days.

98

Baseball

A few days after Dr. Karsh gave me the tickets, I invited Dr. Ebrahim to go with me to experience this American passion called baseball. That Sunday he and I got all dressed in a suit with white shirt and tie. We felt like ambassadors from the Middle East showing our acceptance of the culture of the West. Together we reached Yankee Stadium, climbed the cement steps and eventually wormed our way to our seats. Not a soul around us was dressed as we were. We removed our jackets and ties and sat on them so nobody could notice. Had this been a night game, our white shirts would have shone like the 1500-watt bulbs that light up the field. Yes, indeed, we were foreigners.

Neither one of us had ever watched a baseball game. Neither one of us ever had any explanation of what goes on during such a game. So, like everyone else in the stadium, we sat and watched. Unlike everyone else we remained sitting, very quietly, while the rest of the crowd jumped out of their seats, yelled and screaming at the umpire, shouting advice sprinkled with obscenities. Perspiration ran all over their bodies while food and drink poured into their mouths.

Beyond the walls of the stadium a huge billboard type of sign pulsated the time and temperature. At 2:00 p.m. it was 95°.

Dr. Ebrahim and I stole glances at each other--as we sat quietly, as reserved physicians should behave. Finally, in a whisper I hinted, “Should we leave?”

“By all means.”

We got up, grabbed our jackets as though they were rags, tripped over at least two dozen knees, stepped on a few toes, and made a few people miss something that was going on on that field. It must have been monumental, because one man seemed to swear at us--more words that I’d have to look up in my dictionary.

It felt good to breathe fresh air, rather than someone

else's body odor.

"What's the score?" asked a man outside the stadium.

"I don't know," I shrugged my shoulders.

"What! What the hell were you doing there?" he screamed in my face.

Dr. Ebrahim and I moved away from him and left quickly. We sprinted toward the subway on our way back to the hospital.

99
Situs Inversus

When I was on call on a weekend, there wasn't much else to do Saturday evening but watch television and wait.

One evening, Dr. Shift, the only other physician in this lounge, tried to catch up on his reading of newspapers while waiting to be called. He commented how nice it was to have the hospital quiet.

Before I finished nodding my head in agreement, the phone rang. Into the phone he answered, "Hello, this is Dr. Shift." To me he turned, "They want you on the surgical floor."

Immediately I left Dr. Shift and hurried to greet the new admission, a twenty-two-year-old man with acute abdominal pain. He was referred to the hospital by his family physician, a general practitioner, Dr. Olden, who reported a diagnosis of diverticulitis. Dr. Karsh, the senior surgeon, and Dr. Aguiree, the surgical resident, each recorded complaints of severe pain of the left lower quadrant of the abdomen and vomiting. The patient also had fever and a high white blood cell count.

When I spoke to the patient, I learned that he had been living with his grandmother since the death of his parents in a car accident when he was about 10 years old. In the 10th grade he dropped out of school because everything seemed too difficult. As an assistant cook in a restaurant he was able to earn some money. His aversion to needles and doctors kept him from ever visiting a clinic or a hospital. When I examined his abdomen, the pain was on the left side. Everything else seemed like appendicitis, but the pain was on the left, not the right. As I listened to his heart, I noticed that his heart was on the right side. "Could this be dextrocardia?" I wondered. "Could his appendix likewise be on the opposite side?" Upon closer examination I felt his liver on the left. It too was on the opposite side, not where it should be. Only in textbooks did I read about rare cases like this. The chance of a physician ever experiencing the phenomenon may occur once in a lifetime. Medical jargon for such complete transposition of the viscera is "situs inversus viscerum."

I finished the examination and walked out of the ward. At the nurses' station I noticed that Dr. Karsh and Dr. Aguiree had ordered antibiotics and liquid diet. By now both physicians were gone. I was faced with the dilemma of their observations versus mine.

Fortunately, Dr. Aguiree left his girlfriend's phone number with the hospital operator. I called him immediately. When I described the results of my examination, he almost doubted my word. "Are you sure?"

"Yes, I am," I stated most emphatically.

"Well, I actually did not listen to his heart, because I didn't have my stethoscope. Dr. Karsh probably didn't either."

To myself I thought, "Excuses, excuses."

He continued, "To be sure that the heart is on the right and the liver on the left, why don't you order a chest X-ray and a flat plate of the abdomen?"

"I already did. The technician is on his way."

"Good," he sighed. "I'll be on my way too. See you soon!"

Within the hour we had X-rays that showed a mirror image of the organs.

Within the same hour both surgeons were back in the operating room. From the left side of the abdomen Dr. Karsh removed the appendix, acutely inflamed.

Before he left the hospital, he approached me, "I should have considered the problem myself. The patient is too young to have diverticulitis. You really deserve a pat on the back for your accurate diagnosis. How would you like a couple of tickets to a football game?"

I hoped he couldn't read my mind as I thought, "Not again!" When he looked at me, I said, "Thank you very much. I appreciate these."

100
Spelling Difficulty

When Dr. Izik, a fledgling physician from Turkey, first came to the United States his English was limited to "yes" and "no." A vocabulary of two words presented quite a challenge for communication with colleagues and/or patients. No way could Izik apply his medical skill exclusively. And no way would he hire an interpreter to accompany him all day long. Until he improved his communication skills, he had to work in the laboratory. At night, however, he attended classes at a nearby high school to study English as a second language. Such an intelligent person became more and more fluent with remarkable speed.

When he finally began his internship in the wards, he was quite pleased with his progress. One morning he tried to express his empathy for Dr. Cohen, who was on call all night delivering three babies in succession. Izik sincerely felt sorry for the obstetrician who looked very disgusted with such a work schedule. Meaning to tell him how *disgusted he looked,* Izik approached him and said soulfully, "You look *disgusting* today."

Dr. Cohen stared at him and said nothing. He became more disgusted than Izik even thought him to be.

Izik, however, kept practicing his English every chance he got. When the interns were moved into a large rented house near the hospital because of the renovation of their usual quarters, the hospital provided two large rooms on the top floor for those on call. Each was furnished with sleeping accommodations.

One morning when I went to one of these rooms to change into my uniform, this note was on one of the beds:

For clining laidi--

Change this shit. I slip here tonight.

Dr. Izik

101

Cigarette Money

According to a recent obituary in the Pittsburgh Post Gazette a 30-year-old physician in his last year of residency, having completed at least fourteen years of training after high school, had become one more victim of cancer of the lower esophagus.

People who knew him praised him for his athletic, as well as intellectual, prowess. To relieve tension--more likely to obey peer pressure--he developed the habit of chewing tobacco.

For the past 30 to 40 years medical studies have confirmed the correlation between tobacco (smoking or chewing) and cancer.

When I interned at a hospital in Upper Manhattan in the early 1950's, I was given room and board plus $30.00 a month for "cigarette money." Having lived in the United States for only four months, this was the first time I heard the expression "cigarette money." In the world of my youth, such small sums of money were called "pocket money" or "allowance." It seems that American tobacco companies coined the expression to encourage young people to smoke and feed their addiction at an early age. Many people tell about their experiments with tobacco even before their teens. One of my colleagues boasted that he had smoked since the age of 9.

No matter where I went, everyone smoked. The habit defied professions, age, gender, or ethnic persuasions. Many of the physicians from whom I was supposed to learn were chain smokers. I soon felt that I too must jump on the bandwagon and . . . smoke.

In those days a pack of cigarettes cost 20 cents. Quite often pretty girls would stand outside public buildings or on busy corners and distribute samples of four or six cigarettes in a small box. Representatives of the tobacco companies would even come to the hospital with free packs for the doctors and nurses, who gladly accepted them. With my allowance I could budget my dollar a day for five packs of cigarettes.

Apparently, smoking was an American thing to do. In my determination to assimilate I took up smoking. Within a week I also started coughing. Within two weeks I started hacking. When I lamented my miseries, I was encouraged to try a pipe. This called for milder and more aromatic tobacco. I was further encouraged when I overheard one of the good-looking nurses tell another with a sigh, "I just love the smell of that pipe tobacco. I could follow a pipe-smoking man for miles and miles and miles."

At that point I was ready to walk for miles and miles and miles just to get a pipe and the most aromatic tobacco on the market--no matter what the cost. I splurged several days' allowance, puffed constantly, and kept looking backward, waiting for those girls to follow me--preferably the good-looking ones. I soon learned, as President Clinton did, that it isn't necessary to inhale. At least I tried not to do so. Somehow occasionally I did. Inhale or not, I kept coughing. This certainly would not have pretty young nurses follow me. If anything, they turned away, especially when I coughed so much so hard that I resorted to cough syrup. At this point, my throat hurt. Most of the time it was on fire.

That did it! To hell with Americanization! I am what I am. And that is not a smoker.

By this time smoking was among my chief curiosities. The incidence of cancer of the lungs in the United States was higher than that in Iran. I mentioned my observations to several fellow physicians, but had no statistics to prove my point. Perhaps fewer people in Iran smoked. Those who did indulge may have smoked fewer cigarettes. Each of my parents smoked two a day, one after lunch and another after dinner. The high cost of cigarettes and the low income of the people could account for the difference in the habit.

And "habit" it is. When I asked people, especially chain smokers, if they enjoyed smoking while I almost coughed myself inside out, they usually replied, "No, it's just a habit."

In Iran a respectable woman would never be seen

smoking in public. This was considered a bad habit. For men, however, this was considered "cool" as they would dangle a cigarette from the corner of their mouth imitating Clark Gable or Humphrey Bogart. (Most movies shown in Iran were produced in the United States.)

In the early '50's respectable young American women in the United States likewise did not smoke in public. That gradually changed as gorgeous movie stars like Grace Kelly were shown with cigarettes. The logical (maybe) assumption is that anyone who smokes would be just as attractive as this movie star. Later I learned that she was one who definitely did not smoke.

Besides noticing people smoking, I noticed more and more articles in medical journals about the disastrous effects of smoking. Cancer of the lung became a popular research topic. In spite of this scientific approach, many doctors continued to smoke. In 1958 the AMA Journal printed studies by Drs. Hammond and Horn indicating a higher death rate as a result of lung cancer among smokers. Nevertheless, it took another 15 years to convince the government officials and the general public to stop smoking. By now even the surgeon general seemed convinced.

On the other hand, the tobacco companies were devastated. They tried to deny the medical findings. During an interview on television when one official of a major tobacco company was asked about his smoking habits, caught off guard, he replied, "I don't use the garbage. I only sell it." The purpose of any business is to sell, regardless of the consequences for the buyer.

The habit is so addictive that many medical people still smoke. In one conference room it must have been extremely irritating. Scrawled across a blackboard was "Please do not smoke. We would like to breathe." Under that comment appeared another: "Please do not breathe. We would like to smoke."

Forty years later most of these highly educated doctors seem to accept the fact that smoking is deleterious to one's health. It leads to various forms of cancer, hypertension, cardio-vascular diseases, premature births, and other problems. While the habit of smoking in the United States has weakened--thanks to the concerted effort of public health agencies, government, and the media--reports indicate that 30% of Americans still smoke, with more teenagers than ever falling into the habit. Nevertheless, this habit seems to have run rampant in other parts of the world. When my wife and I visit other countries, we see this ourselves.

Tobacco is an American institution. It's been an American crop for over 2,000 years. Christopher Columbus learned all about it from the Indians and took the plant, as well as the habit, to Europe, where tobacco was first enjoyed in pipes. Jean Nicot, a European botanist at the time, classified the plant, named it Nicotiana, and coined the word nicotine. Around 1850 cigarette making machines were invented in the United States. Just as the production increased, so did the habit. Today, the United States Department of Agriculture still subsidizes tobacco growers with tax payers' money in a price support system because of economic consequences, thus proving the saying "Money talks." In this case, however, it even rules, since money is the basis of the subsidy laws.

Tobacco leaves are said to have 6,800 different types of chemicals, many of which are carcinogens, i.e., cancer causing. The most psychoactive of these is nicotine. Large doses for a nonsmoker may cause confusion, tremor, dizziness, cramps, vomiting, or diarrhea. A psychiatrist friend of mine believes that many people, especially the young, are so unhappy with the mind that Mother Nature has given them that they try hard to alter it with cigarettes, alcohol, or illegal drugs. They think in terms of immediate consequences, not the long term.

My daughter was no different. One day as a teenager she flatly told me that she wanted to look chic. She was going to smoke.

"OK with me," I told her. "I'll help you do it properly." I sat with her and helped her light up and inhale two packs of cigarettes within two hours. First she felt dizzy and then giggled over the sensation. Then she felt so sick, she spent the next few hours bent over the toilet bowl, vomiting. It took her 24 hours to recover, a whole week to speak to me, and many years to thank me.

102
Lawyer

Now that my life as an intern quieted down into a routine, I began to untangle my difficulties with the immigration bureau. To be on time for my appointment with Mr. Avocat, the lawyer, I had to leave the hospital an hour early. I made sure to have change including the dime I needed for the subway from Upper Manhattan to Times Square.

The office was located on the 17th floor of the largest building I had ever entered. Four secretaries took care of the paper work for him and his two associates, all of whom seemed extremely occupied with their work. Mr. Avocat seemed about 50 years old, very self-confidant behind his mountains of papers on his desk.

After the customary introductions, I blurted, "I am in the Iranian Army, but do not want to return right now. I would like to stay in the United States at least till I finish my post graduate studies required for the specialty board."

He listened, then examined my passport and visa, both of which were about to expire within the next few months. "Your case is somewhat difficult," he commented slowly, "but it can be managed. I can get you a permanent visa. Of course, it will take time. My fee would be $500.00."

I was speechless. "As an intern I get only $30.00 a month. I have no other income."

"But you are a doctor and you eventually are going to make enough money. You can pay me $15.00 a month. As your salary increases, you can increase your payments."

"OK," I agreed and paid my first $15.00. In Iran no lawyer would be so trusting. He would never take a case without absolute assurance of being paid up front.

My payment led me to a secretary who helped me fill out immigration forms.

When the lawyer instructed me to have my passport extended at the Iranian Consulate, I worried about the possibility that they would refuse to do so. Mr. Avocat wasn't worried at all. "Get a letter from them stating that they refuse to extend your passport. That would be good enough."

The following Thursday I again left the hospital an hour early, headed for the Iranian Consulate in the Empire State Building. Just as I had expected, after searching through a file, a gentleman told me that my passport cannot be extended. "We have a list of about twenty people whose passports cannot be extended. Your name is among them. By order of the Iranian government your request is denied."

"May I have this refusal in writing, please?" I asked.

"If you request this extension in writing, I will respond the same way. Right now, however, I suggest that you return to Iran since you no longer have the permission of the Iranian Government to be in the United States. The longer you stay here, the more problems you will meet upon your return."

As soon as I returned to the hospital, I wrote the letter and within the next few weeks my answer came.

Immediately I took it to the lawyer. "On this basis," he announced, "I have to declare you 'stateless' and work on getting you a 'green card,' a permanent visa."

"Will the permanent visa allow me to return to Iran after my post graduate studies?"

"Of course, it will. You don't have to worry about the American government. It's the Iranian government that should concern you."

"Oh, yes," I responded, "but in Iran anything can be settled with a bribe--or influence."

"That works here too, maybe not as commonly as in other countries, but as the expression goes, 'Money talks.' Get a letter from the hospital administration indicating the need for you to continue working here because of the shortage of young physicians."

Mr. Miller, the hospital administrator, saw that I had such a letter immediately. Within the week I delivered that and another $15.00 to the lawyer.

I now walked around "stateless." I had no passport of any kind. I had no visa to be in this country. With my Iranian mentality, I had a morbid fear of policemen. I had visions of being questioned and arrested by any one of them, even the school crossing guards. At the sight of one, even a half block away, I would hide in the doorway of some building or deliberately cross the street and continue down another. I even memorized a response should a policeman stop me and start questioning me as was the custom in Iran. "I am a stateless political refugee. My lawyer is Mr. Avocat." To prevent such a possibility I stayed in the hospital as much as possible. I never even told any of my friends that I was "stateless." In Iran the expression was a curse meaning fatherless-motherless, tantamount to useless.

Mr. Avocat, on the other hand, had no doubts that I would eventually get my visa. "Eventually" was the key word because the quota for Iranian immigrants was limited to a hundred per year and there were probably thousands waiting to come to the United States. Somehow I began to feel more at ease, realizing that waiting in the United States was better than waiting in Iran.

103
The Shah

By 1953 Iran had been suffering British exploitation for 200 years.

When Muhammad Mussaddiq became the prime minister of Iran in 1951, at the age of 70, he was recognized as a democratic, nationalistic statesman who disapproved of British policies that interfered with internal affairs in Iran. He was incorruptible. By nationalizing the Iranian oil industry, he terminated the operation of the Anglo-Iranian Oil Company. Within a year political relations between Iran and England were terminated, the British Embassy was closed, and all British subjects were advised to leave.

Nevertheless, clandestine British operation flourished. Iranians and those holding dual citizenship continued to serve England. The British contemplated military action, but the American government strongly objected. The Military Intelligence of Great Britain devised a scheme to topple Mussadiq. Winston Churchill, however, realized that his government without the help of the United States could not succeed. As an incentive to the United States, England agreed to share the profits realized from Iranian oil with the American oil companies. Meanwhile Prime Minister Churchill convinced President Eisenhower that Mussadiq was a Communist and should be replaced. British Military Intelligence plans were released to Kermit Roosevelt, a member of the Central Intelligence Agency, who became the director of the operation.

By transferring the plan to the CIA, Mr. Churchill burdened the CIA budget with the heavy cost of the operation and made it seem like a project of the United States. Such strategy transferred Iranian hatred of Great Britain to hatred of the United States.

According to the British plan, the Shah issued a royal decree dismissing Mussadiq and appointing General Zahedi as the new prime minister. To prevent an uprising that would jeopardize their plans, the Shah attempted to arrest Mussadiq and his cabinet members. Since many members of the armed forces supported Mussadiq, this attempt failed. The news of such illegal action brought tens of thousands of Mussadiq's supporters into the streets.

On August 15, 1953, the Shah, fearing for his life, fled the country in his private plane.

One day later American Ambassador Loy Henderson, talking to Mussadiq, complained about disorder in the streets and threatened to move all Americans out of Iran.

Dr. Mussadiq ordered the security forces to restore order in the streets.

The day after that, a well-orchestrated coup d'état under the direction of Kermit Roosevelt brought paid mobs from southern Tehran with army units including tanks under the apparent command of General Zahedi. Tehran radio was occupied and controlled by military forces. Dr. Mussadiq's house was looted and damaged heavily. Mussadiq was taken away by supporters for his own safety. Nevertheless, two days later, he surrendered to the new government.

A week after he fled, the Shah returned to Iran, hailed as the ruler of the country. He was welcomed by military government and Ambassador Loy Henderson. In the meantime a new tyrannical dictatorship had begun. Anyone suspected of pro-democratic sentiment definitely met punishment. Five thousand people, including the foreign minister of Mussadiq's regime, were killed. Five times as many were imprisoned or exiled. Mussadiq was condemned to jail for three years. After that he remained under house arrest until he died.

Iran's short period of democracy came to an end.

104
Insurance

I usually kept my money in the inside pocket of my jacket which hung in the closet in my room while I wore my hospital uniform. One late afternoon as I hurried to change into street clothes, I noticed that my lone twenty-dollar bill was missing. Now I had to call the lawyer's office to postpone the appointment.

I dared not tell anyone about my missing money for fear of getting the police involved. The last thing I needed was a policeman asking me a series of questions, which would eventually lead to my passport, visa, and all kinds of other details about being a foreigner, a displaced stateless one at that.

The following day, though, I did mention it to Dr. Elahi.

"Never leave cash or booze in your room," he reprimanded. "They will surely disappear. Those are two things you keep out of sight of the cleaning people or any others who have access to your room." After a minute, he suggested, "You could file a report with the administration. The insurance company will probably reimburse you."

"I certainly would not do that," I answered. "It may involve the police."

Elahi, however, did not heed my advice. He went ahead and reported the incident to the administration, who in turn reported it to the insurance company. Several days later I was most surprised to receive a check for twenty dollars. This would have never happened in Iran. The incident was one more lesson in American culture.

In Iran the insurance industry was in its infancy. The only kind of insurance that I knew of whose premiums only a few wealthy people could afford was life insurance.

Later the assistant administrator explained that the hospital pays for liability insurance for the medical staff as well.

"What does such a premium cost for a person like

me?" I asked.

"About $10.00 a year for the house staff, but about $35 for a practicing physician. Some surgeons probably pay up to $100.00 a year."

Health insurance was new, even in the United States. Underwriters advertised while the government encouraged it.

During the summer I met Mr. Smarthe, who firmly believed in this new health plan. Each week he brought one of his four children for a tonsillectomy. After they recovered, he brought them back again, one at a time, for appendectomy. Classified as "preventive measures," the surgery assured a person of never having problems with those organs. The practice was quite common.

Mr. Smarthe expounded on the benefits of such a procedure. Not only were the children protected from further discomfort, he collected more money than the health care cost, because he submitted claims to five different insurance companies. It seemed like a money-making scheme.

I was surprised that a father would use his own children to make money. "Did you have your own tonsils and appendix removed?" I asked.

Smiling, he answered, "Not yet, but I'm thinking about it."

Such abuse of health insurance became so prevalent that it soon became illegal to register a claim with more than one company at the same time for the same procedure.

Whatever the rules were, I was happy with the system. I was thrilled to have my $20.00 back. Now I was able to keep my appointment with Mr. Avocat and pay him another $15.00.

105
Surgical Residency

In June 1954, one year after my initial application for a permanent visa, my legal status in the United States remained vague. I had no visa, no passport, no legal document to identify myself. "Don't worry," the lawyer advised me, encouraging me to continue my education.

At this point the four-year surgical residency seemed imperative, not only as an opportunity to learn, but also as a necessity to stay in New York City, close to the lawyer. The subway stations located near the hospital made it convenient for me to meet with him in Manhattan. Luckily, Wyckoff Heights Hospital in Brooklyn needed a second surgical resident for the first year to complete their quota of eight, two of whom completed the program every year. Half of the residents were foreign graduates and half, American.

I was interviewed and accepted by Dr. Zoller, chief of surgery. After speaking with this elderly gentleman I was placed under the supervision of the chief resident, Dr. Peter Joseph. (After satisfying his military obligations as an army physician and after serving the community as a family practitioner, he decided to do a residency in surgery.) A tour through the hospital made me realize that Wyckoff focused their strength on the surgical department. It was at least five times the size of medicine and obstetrics. Under such guidance I would spend my first year doing surgical pathology and radiology. First year residents were also responsible for admissions of the day, for history-physicals, and for assisting in the operating room during morning hours as needed. On the basis of the rotation schedule, afternoons would be devoted to pathology or radiology. We also covered the emergency room for surgical cases.

Mr. Brooks, the hospital administrator, mentioned that in addition to room and board I would be provided with uniforms and paid $50.00 a month. With no hesitation I signed the contract, but clouded the good prospects with the possibility of my departure because of visa problems. I also mentioned the possibility of needing a letter verifying my work in Wyckoff Hospital. Since the hospital desperately needed resident physicians, he promised to help me in every way possible.

The last day of June I bid farewell to my friends at Manhattan Jewish Memorial Hospital, packed my books and limited wardrobe, and headed for Wyckoff Heights in Brooklyn. Here my assigned room was furnished with two beds, but fortunately I was the only occupant. While resident quarters seemed to be located in various parts of the hospital, most of the surgical residents were housed on the first floor, having rows of bedrooms flanking a long corridor that had a huge bathroom in the middle of it

My normal day began at 7:00 a.m. in the operating room. Throughout the year I was exposed to all kinds of surgical experiences from removing ingrown toe nails to repairing perforated stomachs. From a large number of super specialists I learned a variety of techniques in the care of patients from the new born to the very old. Tying a surgical knot for the very first time around an artery pumping blood was one of the most exciting moments of my life. As a first-year resident participating in major surgical procedures as second assistant, my responsibilities included retracting and keeping the field open, clamping bleeders, and helping to suture wounds. In non-major procedures, like appendectomy, I helped as first assistant and occasionally performed the surgery on patients who had no private doctor.

I will always remember Dr. Cook. From the looks of his bald head and stocky build, he had to be at least 70 years old. All he did to welcome me was shake hands. I doubt that he even noticed what I looked like when I reported as his second assistant for the gastrectomy.

A 38-year-old patient with a chronic stomach ulcer was prepared for partial gastric resection. After making the skin incision, Dr. Cook exchanged places with Dr. Joseph. Such a switch was common in a hospital approved for training. Allowing a young doctor to take over may have seemed strange at first. At times, however, it was more advantageous for the patient to have a young doctor with steady hands rather than an old surgeon with a solid reputation but shaky hands.

In the middle of this procedure, as Dr. Cook supervised, he began yelling, "Nurse, Nurse! My pants! My pants!"

Very calmly the circulating nurse put her hands behind Dr. Cook's surgical gown and retied the strings around his scrub pants. Apparently this was not the first incident of such an accident. Before the doctor even finished calling for help, the nurse was solving the problem. In spite of their masked faces, Dr. Joseph, now the surgeon, and Dr. Miller, the anesthesiologist, showed their amusement by the twinkle in their eyes.

The most important lesson that I learned that day was to make sure that my scrub pants were securely tied.

106
Surgical Pathology

During my lunch hour I reviewed the schedule and noticed that I was assigned to be the junior partner of Dr. Peter Joseph, the senior resident. I was on call with him every other night and every other weekend.

That afternoon he took me to the pathology laboratory and introduced me to the personnel including Dr. Angelino, who was covering for Dr. Freedman during the latter's vacation.

"All surgical specimens," Dr. Joseph pointed out, "come here from the operating room. The people in histology will then number them and place them in order on the counter for you to examine. You then dictate a description about each one of them: what it was suspected to be, what it actually is, its exact dimensions, its color, its shape, and its consistency."

Sensing that I was overwhelmed, he added, "I will do a few. Watch me. Then you do a few and I will watch you." He further advised that I spend some time reviewing pathology records. In the process I would also learn how to use the dictaphone with plastic belts--all new to me. To my surprise, he really expected me to know all about such mechanical details. In the middle of this demonstration Dr. Joseph was called out.

I was left alone.

Around 5:30 p.m. he returned, surprised to see me still plugging away at describing gross specimens of surgically removed tissues and organs, like portions of a stomach, intestines, or tonsils. "Leave the large specimens for tomorrow," he advised. "They need to be fixed."

That I did and left around 6:00 p.m., two hours after everyone else had gone.

Within the next few days I also learned to do a lot of reading fast. Before describing the gross, I checked surgical pathology textbooks for every disease presented to me. What

Dr. Joseph accomplished in three hours, I did in six. In the evening I read more. The following morning I went to the lab early to read and correct my own gross descriptions. I was relieved and satisfied when the secretaries had no trouble understanding my dictated English.

The first two weeks in this department I hardly had time to finish the work assigned, let alone study microscopic slides of the cases. Even my evenings were devoted to day time responsibilities. It was difficult to handle such responsibilities new to me, while no one considered me his responsibility.

Dr. Angelino in charge of microscopic surgicals worked a few hours in the morning, but seldom discussed anything with me. All day long I zigzagged like lightning from admitting patients to helping in the operating room to describing specimens in the pathology laboratory to reading pathology texts-- any time, anywhere. So intensely did I study, Dr. Joseph soon had only a few suggestions about my work.

During my third week in this department Dr. Freedman returned from his vacation. "Who are you?" he asked abruptly.

"I'm Dr. Payan, the surgical resident. I'm supposed to learn surgical pathology."

"Hi. I'm Dr. Freedman. I'm the chief pathologist."

"Glad to meet you."

"OK, OK, let's get to work."

Later on as he read my gross reports, he had very few comments. He simply recommended a textbook of pathology by Anderson which I relied on for many years.

By this time even though I was examining the surgicals somewhat faster, I would go to the lab early in the morning, just to get my work done.

After becoming familiar with the intricacies of gross pathology, I advanced to the more challenging study of microscopic slides. When Dr. Freedman was ready to leave the hospital, he came to my desk. "You said you wanted to learn surgical pathology? Here, do these slides tonight. I'll go over them with you tomorrow morning." With that he pushed six trays of surgical slides toward me. That meant about 35 cases represented in about 120 slides. Once again

I was left to do things on my own.

Fortunately, I was off that night. After looking at each slide I checked the surgical pathology texts, reviewed previous cases similar to the one in question, returned to the slide under my microscope, and recorded my observations. That "evening" lasted till 5:00 a.m.

Immediately after surgery or a biopsy, the tissue is fixed in formalin, a chemical that preserves the cellular structures at the time of surgery. After gross examination and description, representative sections are cut about five millimeters thick and placed in small plastic or metal containers to be processed overnight through chemicals for proper dehydration. After this procedure the tissue is cut about six microns thick and placed on a glass slide. Properly stained for identification of various structures and characteristics of the normal as well as abnormal, it is covered by a thin cover slip and made ready for the pathologist's scrutiny. In the study of slides tissues are examined for destruction, death, inflammation or cells replaced by tumors which could be benign or malignant.

While this work wasn't exactly as sensational as surgery, it was much more scientific. This practice demanded the use and training of one's eyes, rather than one's hands.

Around 10:00 the following morning Dr. Freedman found time to sit with me. "I thought you didn't know any pathology."

"That's true. This is all new to me."

"So how did you manage to do so well?"

I explained my system of observing, reading, and comparing cases.

"Keep it up," he complimented me. "That's the best way to learn." He then dropped more work in front of me--one hundred more slides.

The next four months duplicated this pace in the pathology lab. Evenings ran into mornings and mornings came too soon. Soon I became so efficient I often finished by midnight. Dr. Freedman devoted two hours to me every morning and found most of my diagnoses correct. My self-discipline taught me not only pathology, but English. This ability to express my findings equaled the importance of knowing the medical implications.

I beamed when I heard that Dr. Freedman had told Dr. Joseph that he had never seen anyone learn so much pathology in such a short time. They both suggested that I consider pathology as my specialty, since there was a shortage of pathologists and since I seemed to enjoy the work.

107
Deep Coma

Junior residency brought about all sorts of less than delightful duties. One morning a funeral director phoned Dr. Joseph, my chief resident, about a man brought to him early in the morning. As the mortician began to work on the man, the body occasionally twitched. Before continuing his routine for the funeral, he called the hospital to send a doctor to check this person.

I was the lucky one to handle this responsibility. I went by ambulance not too far from the hospital. All along the driver kept talking. "Did you hear, Doc, that one of the stiffs in this funeral home is moving? Is that possible?"

"Maybe. A person in a deep coma may give the impression of being dead."

"That's just what someone else said. This old guy was sick for a long time. Comatose. Early this morning the family physician decided that he's a goner. Dead."

As we both walked into the building (more like a mansion), the funeral director gave me a copy of the death certificate signed by the family physician who disclosed "long standing chronic renal disease with uremia." We were then escorted to the basement to view the body lying on a marble slab. I placed my stethoscope on the man's chest. An ever-so-slight heartbeat flub-dubbed through the earpiece. That close to him I could detect shallow breathing, very shallow. Suddenly he twitched again.

Quickly we placed him on a stretcher, slid him carefully into the ambulance, and squealed to the hospital at breakneck speed.

For two more days he lay in a coma. Then he really did die. At this point his wife was determined that an autopsy be performed.

Autopsies were an integral part of medical education. No matter how old or how experienced a physician may be, an autopsy may reveal conditions undiscernible by any other means. Since the administrating staff of a hospital was medically oriented, there was never any hesitation about cost. The hospital willingly absorbed all expenses of this learning experience. According to the requirements of the American Medical Association and the Joint Commission of Hospitals, those hospitals approved for training of physicians performed autopsies on at least 20% of patients dying on the hospital premises.

During this 1954 incident, nevertheless, the autopsy followed customary regulations. The wife called the hospital, the hospital notified the department of internal medicine, internal medicine called Dr. Joseph, and Dr. Joseph insisted that I accompany him to the morgue.

"First review the consent. Make sure that it is signed by the next of kin. Then review the chart carefully and if in doubt about any detail, talk to the family physician. It's good to speak with this doctor anyway. His interest may focus on a unique problem which is not obvious in the chart."

In this case the obvious was kidney damage due to long standing chronic inflammation and an enlarged heart, evidence of hypertension frequently associated with chronic uremia. Because of his age it was no surprise to find arteriosclerosis, hardening of the arteries. Dr. Joseph's meticulous dissection revealed a large peptic ulcer of the stomach and cancer of the prostate, a condition unknown to the family doctor.

I described the appearance and pathology of the various organs as we took samples of each for microscopic examination. The pathologist studying this tissue under the microscope must have detailed information to be able to dictate the final diagnoses and ultimate cause of death.

As a matter of course, this one experience led to my doing autopsies alone--to be checked by an experienced pathologist later. What took Dr. Joseph one hour took me about four hours. Instead of Dr. Joseph, pathology textbooks were my constant companions. In the lab for microscopic examination I prepared tissue, reviewed by Dr. Freedman who also reviewed my interpretation and analysis of the slides. After my six-month rotation in pathology I had performed twenty-five autopsies.

108
Scandal

Throughout the years of medical school aspiring physicians are advised not to encourage close ties with patients. Some physicians so strongly respect this principle that they refuse to treat persons with whom they have any emotional attachment. Around the world personal relations between patients and doctors are frowned upon.

When I was in medical school in Tehran, for a few months the halls were buzzing with rumors of a scandal. A last-year medical student supposedly enjoyed sexual intimacy with a patient. For such pleasures they used her bed in the ward. In spite of their precautions of waiting till all the other patients seemed asleep and drawing the curtains around their bed, some people heard their little groans of happiness. Those in the other beds may have been ill, but they were not deaf.

At a hearing when self-righteous professors met to decide the fate of the young man several of the elderly physicians recommended his expulsion without a shadow of a doubt.

Dr. Adl, professor of surgery, however, quoted, "He that is not without sin among you, let him cast the first stone." In his very wise, self-confidant manner he looked directly into the eyes of each of the members of the panel as he asked, "Think back a few years when you and I were all young in Paris. Can you recall the pulley system our ingenious fellow students invented in their strictly male dormitory? Along the outside wall they hoisted a chair from the ground up to their room level. Do you remember the girls who sat on that chair and were then lifted into the rooms? What kind of fling did you enjoy?"

A secret ballot was taken. Unanimously the experienced professors voted to allow the student to continue his studies, but postpone graduation for a year.

During my obstetrical rotation in New York I

noticed that certain obstetricians would calm their patients in the throes of count-down contractions and various stages of delivery by patting them on the shoulder, holding their hand, or even kissing them. The little kiss, even though on the mouth, did not seem to have any emotional reference. Nevertheless, I thought this practice "Strange, certainly not one practice I will ever put into use."

One evening around 10:00 p.m. I worked my way to the cafeteria for a snack. By that time I was so hungry I picked up first things I saw--a cheese sandwich and a bowl of canned fruit cocktail, neither of which sent me to gourmet heaven. The cheese was so gummy it stuck to my fillings and the fruit made me homesick for Iran, where fresh fruit was available all day long. Dr. Rengo interrupted my daydream by scraping the chair against the floor to sit opposite me.

"Hi! How come you're here?" I asked. "I thought your partner Dr. Brasov is on call tonight."

"He's out," said Dr. Rengo, almost in a whisper.

"Out? You mean he's not on call tonight?"

"No. I mean he is out. O-U-T. Out for good."

"What happened?" I mumbled as I sipped my coffee without looking up.

"He's on his way back to Europe, to Transylvania."

Now I did look up, so dumbfounded that I spilled the entire cup of coffee all over the table.

Dr. Rengo unfolded the story how Dr. Brasov was so determined to adopt American culture, especially medical techniques, that he copied everything the other doctors did. "One day as he took care of a lady about to deliver, she was grateful when he held her hand just as she experienced one nasty contraction. 'Thank you,' she said and gave him a big smile.

"Dr. Brasov interpreted that as encouragement to calm her some more. This time he kissed her--and enjoyed this American system of practicing medicine.

"Just as he stood straight up again, the patient had a visitor--her husband.

"Now it was the husband who needed some calming down. Hand holding or kissing definitely was not the solution to his rage. He yelled and screamed, screamed and yelled, threatening to lambaste the entire hospital and everyone who have anything to do with it. He was a reporter for a local newspaper. Stomping toward the main lobby, he barged into the administrator's office, pounded on his desk, and demanded, 'That lousy foreigner should be fired at once. If not, he bellowed, 'in tomorrow morning's edition the entire world will read about this salacious incident. Furthermore you and your entire hospital will be sued.'

"Dr. Brasov was immediately called to the office and told to leave for good."

Dr. Brasov apparently had seen American physicians display such tenderness, but he failed to see that these were mere impersonal gestures extended to allay fear and nervousness, not emotional sparks.

109

Mr. Brooks

Every week the residents gathered to express their concerns and discuss their problems with Dr. Joseph, the chief resident. The agenda would often include inadequacy of the living quarters, cafeteria selections, and financial reimbursement. True to human nature, rather than offer suggestions for the amelioration of a situation, the young doctors simply used the meeting as a forum to complain or gossip.

At one meeting, however, Mr. Brooks, the hospital administrator, was invited. Honored to be the guest, he opened the session with a commentary of the statistics of the hospital. He then replaced glowing medical statistics with disappointing administrative operations. After a long half hour he was still lamenting the fact that the hospital needed more young nurses, more young doctors, reliable suppliers of equipment, and--above all--more money.

Hesitantly, I raised my hand high and interrupted the report.

"Yes, doctor," beamed Mr. Brooks.

"Sir," I began meekly, almost inaudibly, "I thought this session was for you to hear about our problems, not for us to hear about yours. Perhaps it would be better for you to present your concerns to the Hospital Board."

The silence was deafening. One would think all these doctors became comatose. Gradually the residents smiled at each other, but not one had the mettle to voice his real reason for attending the meeting. Mr. Brooks realized that they were afraid to speak their mind. So he addressed me, "Let us start with you then. What is your major problem?"

"More than half of us live in this hospital because our salary leaves us no choice. Don't you think that a physician who works 36 hours straight should at least have his own room, if he cannot be compensated with more money to provide better facilities outside the hospital? Having a roommate automatically assures the one not on call disturbances by phone calls and noises which are not meant for both."

"Unfortunately, we have no rooms available," commented Mr. Brooks. "Is there anything that I could solve?"

The last presentation began an outpouring of agitations. "Someone on my floor wears wooden shoes," began another resident. "Every night, in the middle of the night, he has to relieve himself several times. Bad enough that he cannot close his door quietly, he has to clip-clop down the hall to the bathroom in those damn wooden shoes. Could you replace his clogs with a pair of slippers, please?"

Next week Dr. Joseph opened our meeting with the same procedure: attendance, minutes, announcements. When it came time for suggestions, everyone agreed that a letter of thanks to Mr. Brooks was in order. Everyone was so happy that the wooden shoes were history.

Eventually solutions were found for minor problems, nothing major. The real accomplishment was the open line of communication between the residents and the administration.

110
Miracle

A young nurse in her early twenties complained about pain in her left knee, a problem she did not need to add to her exciting life planning a wedding and working in the Emergency Room. According to X-rays, the destructive lesion of the upper end of the tibia (the larger of the two leg bones) expanded the cortex of the bone and caused pain. The radiologist made the diagnosis of possible osteosarcoma (cancer of the bone) and suggested a biopsy.

Dr. Gerter, the orthopedic surgeon, explained the situation to Margaret, the nurse/patient. With wedding bells on her mind, Margaret listened to all these possibilities of malignancy and amputation reluctantly.

"If I do have cancer, Doctor, don't tell me about it. And I do not want my leg amputated. I could not live without a leg. If you like, however, repeat all this to Jim, my fiancé. He can decide whether or not he wants to go ahead with our marriage plans."

A biopsy was performed. The pathologist reported "osteogenic sarcoma," cancer of the bone. In the 1950's the only treatment known was amputation of the leg. In spite of such a radical procedure the prognosis for survival was poor. Dr. Freedman, the pathologist, sent the slides for consultation to Dr. Jaffee, probably the most renowned osteopathologist in the world. He confirmed the diagnosis of "osteogenic sarcoma."

Dr. Gerter shared the information with Jim.

Two months later the wedding did take place. From then on every two months Margaret reported for X-rays to monitor the progress of the lesion. After the third such routine checkup the radiologist noticed a definite reduction in the size of the tumor. Nevertheless, the bimonthly tests continued. Margaret celebrated her first anniversary with the complete disappearance of the tumor.

A few cases of spontaneous regression of cancer had

been reported in professional journals, but this was the first case at Wyckoff Heights Hospital. Ten years later, T. C. Everson in his report "Spontaneous Regression of Cancer" published in the 1964 Annals of the New York Academy of Sciences describes 130 such proven cases, six of which were osteogenic sarcomas. (vol. 114, part 2, pp. 721-735)

At one of the medical staff conferences a surgeon presented a case about a colleague having a skin lesion removed and called "malignant melanoma." Since this type of skin cancer had a poor prognosis, no company would sell him life insurance. He certainly could not do anything about this situation. He simply went on living as usual--year after year after year.

Sixteen years later with no evidence of the disease he went back to Sloan Kettering Memorial Cancer Center. The world famous pathologist, Dr. Stewart, changed his diagnosis from "malignant melanoma" to "benign junctional nevus" (pigmented skin mole). At the age of 45 he paid his first life insurance premium.

Twelve of 130 cases described in Everson's "Spontaneous Regression of Cancer" were classified as malignant melanomas. The physicians called such phenomenon "spontaneous regression." Margaret, the young nurse, called it "a miracle."

111
National Board

According to the laws of the State of New York during the 1950's and 1960's all foreign graduate doctors were required to pursue a postgraduate course in order to become eligible for State Board Examination for medical licensure. In New York City this course was offered in lower Manhattan at Bellevue Hospital, affiliated with New York University, or in mid-Manhattan at the New York Polyclinic Medical School and Hospital. Eight hours a day for nine months of two years there was a concentrated review of all subjects covered in four years of medical school.

No authority ever published the reasons for such a requirement, but the underlying purpose could have been either to eliminate foreign candidates or to ascertain an acceptable fluency in English. Some physicians suspected an ulterior motive for Dr. Ezell, the secretary of the Board of Medical Examiners of the State of New York.

After finishing a residency in internal medicine Dr. Elahi took and passed the National Board of Medical Examinations. Such success qualified any physician to practice medicine anywhere in the United States, thus eliminating the hassle of taking a test in any of the individual states. When he sent a copy of the results to the New York State Boards and asked for reciprocity, he was commended for his prestigious accomplishment, but since he was a foreign graduate, he still had to take the state examinations in New York and in order to qualify for these he must first take the two-year postgraduate course.

Dr. Elahi forwarded a copy of this response to the National Board. For some unexplained reason, Dr. Elahi's complaint went unheeded. Instead, a ruling was passed denying any foreign graduate the right to take the exam for national boards.

Since Dr. Elahi already was married, established his home in New York City, and was working in the city, he had

no choice but to sit in on these classes and waste his time for two years. Eventually he did get his license for the state of New York and lived and practiced there for the rest of his life.

112
Emergency Room

Dr. Bruno from Italy became subject to the same program as Dr. Elahi . While taking classes at the Polyclinic in Manhattan, he covered the Emergency Room in the evenings. The nights that he was on call, he was given sleeping quarters in the hospital.

What a surprise for me to discover that his sleeping accommodations were in my room.

"Goot-a evening. I'm Bruno, your new roommate."

"Oh?" my voice gestured surprise. "Hello, How do you do?" I continued mechanically in my best English.

"I sleep here ven I cover Emerdgency Room," continued Dr. Bruno.

Dr. Joseph Bruno in his heavy Italian accent explained how he worked at night because during the day he was taking the postgraduate courses for licensure. He had already completed his internship at Swedish Hospital in New York. "Hard to sleep with a baby crying all night long and hard to study during the day when I did not sleep at night." He was married to an American nurse for just a year and in spite of the inconveniences he was a very proud father.

Every other night he was supposed to cover the Emergency Room. This work, as well as his studies, exhausted him so, he slept like the proverbial log. Nothing disturbed his deep sleep. While most physicians become so conscientious about their responsibilities, they become extremely sensitive to the sound of a phone. At the first millisecond of a ring, they jump--right out of a deep sleep, if necessary.

Friday nights were so notoriously busy in the Emergency Room, those on call became human yo-yo's--up, down, up, down, up down. This Friday night Dr. Bruno was on call and I was off.

Around midnight, after turning and tossing, I finally fell asleep. The phone almost jangled itself off the hook.

According to my bedside clock it was 12:30. I knew it was for him, not me, so I didn't answer. Neither did he. The phone kept ringing and ringing and ringing. I was so wide awake, I finally picked it up.

"Dr. Bruno, please," said the telephone operator. "There's a patient waiting for him in the Emergency Room."

"One moment please," I answered in a hoarse half-asleep voice.

I walked over to Bruno's bed. "Hey, wake up. It's for you. Move it. Fast."

Groggily he reached for the phone by his bed, almost held it backwards, and muttered, "Yes . . . I'm on my way."

He put the phone down and was on his way . . . back to sleep.

Ten minutes later the phone rang again. Dr. Bruno was sound asleep again. I was the one who had to get up--again. Now that I was wide awake, I decided that I may as well see the patient myself.

That and the following night we were again serenaded by the phone. After repeating the same scenario again and again, I took his calls.

When the news spread how I was taking Dr. Bruno's calls, he was given a small room adjacent to the ER. He believed that he had been given extra privileges. The truth was that waking him was much simpler when someone could go into his room, shake his shoulders, and make sure that he was on his feet ready to move out of the room.

Once I had my room back to myself again, I was able to get a good night's sleep.

113
Arab

For many years, probably even before the dawn of civilization, Iranians and Arabs as neighbors have considered each other as "foreign" and have felt suspicious of each other. Iranians consider Arabs wild; Arabs consider Iranians useless.

The surgical residents at Wyckoff Heights Hospital included Dr. Ajeenah from Baghdad, obviously an Arab. At the beginning of the year I, as an Iranian, kept my distance from him, particularly since he did not even smile when we were introduced.

About a month later when the police escorted an 18-year-old man into the Emergency Room with several knife wounds on each arm, it was imperative to stop the bleeding from so many sources immediately. Just then Dr. Ajeenah walked by while on his way out for the evening. When he saw the commotion, he turned around to help. He clamped the bleeding vessels in one arm, while I did the other.

While he helped the patient physically, he helped me psychologically. I was relieved when all the bleeding was controlled. As we sutured his gashes, we were finally relaxed enough to socialize. As he was leaving, I said, "Thanks. I really appreciate your help. See you later."

He looked back, smiled, and said, "*En sha-Allah.* (God willing.)"

Another time on a typically busy Saturday morning an autopsy became the priority of the day. The family physician urgently wanted to know the cause of death of a 10-year-old because three other siblings were also ill with a similar fever. Dr. Ajeenah volunteered to work with me performing the autopsy. Thanks to such cooperation, we finished the work in half the time. Extensive inflammation of the lungs (pneumonia) was found. Culture and sensitivity tests were done. The family physician was then able to adjust the antibiotic therapy.

During his rotation through urological surgery at

one of the weekly meetings Dr. Ajeenah presented a case of a 70-year-old patient. Prostatic cancer had metastasized to the spine involving the nerve roots. The man suffered excruciating pain, controlled only by nothing but the highest dose of analgesics.

After the meeting I invited Dr. Ajeenah to look at the microscopic slides of the patient's biopsy. He complimented me on my ability to detect such infinitesimal differences among the cells and arrive at the exact diagnosis. He did not have pathology training during his residency as I did.

"Whatever happened to the patient" I asked.

"The patient was terminal, of course, and he knew it. Dr. Hammond--his private physician, a urologist--explained the situation to him. Because of the severe pain, the elderly gentleman frequently begged Dr. Hammond to help him terminate his life as soon as possible."

"Oh, man," I gasped. "That's illegal."

"It certainly is, but as he was discharged from the hospital, he was given prescriptions for a month's supply of pain killers and sleeping pills."

A few days later the man died in his sleep. His death was attributed to "cancer of the prostate with metastases."

Mercy killing . . . euthanasia . . . has been around a long time. Privately many physicians are in agreement that the terminally ill should not have to lie in misery with no hope in sight. Whoever prefers to end his hopeless existence should be able to get help to do so. Since this is emotionally unpleasant, it is politically incorrect. Publicly, no one will advocate such a practice.

Dr. Ajeenah recalled an incident in Iraq of a man bitten by a rabid dog. "The man was violently ill, screaming and sobbing from excruciating pain. No one could do anything for him. Not only sick, he was dangerous and disturbing. By scratching or biting others, such a patient may transmit hydrophobia. He was considered such a threat to other patients that he was locked in isolation, as though he were insane. The medical director of that hospital had two orderlies restrain the man while he injected enough morphine to calm him down forever."

As Dr. Ajeenah and I worked together from time to

time, we soon became friends. I was somewhat surprised to find him intelligent, conscientious, honest--even civilized. I soon realized how labels erroneously influence one's impressions. What I interpreted as his snobbery or disdain was really reserve. One day as we sat down together for lunch, he sheepishly confessed that he had exactly the same feelings for me.

114
Congressional Bill

"My husband knows a friend of a Congressman who is introducing a bill to get both him and me a permanent visa."

I stared at Dr. Eberhart, the young German intern, as she matter-of-factly mentioned this aspect of United States government just as nonchalantly as we spooned our soup.

"How could anyone do that?" I asked skeptically.

"Well, the pharmaceutical company where my husband works wants him to stay in the United States, " she proudly answered.

"Oh?" my mind began to go back in time. "I have a letter from the hospital where I did my internship and they want me to stay."

"Use that for a congressional bill. Talk to your lawyer. I bet he knows all about such things."

The next day I was ready to see the lawyer hours before I was ready to leave the hospital. As soon as I reached Mr. Avocat's office in Manhattan, I repeated every detail that Dr. Eberhart shared with me.

"Such strategies are the domain of big companies who contribute considerable financial support to lobbyists in Congress who support their cause. The individual congressman then solicits the support of his colleagues to vote in his favor. He, in turn, supports them when they need additional votes."

To me this sounded illegal--and I wanted no entanglement with the law. "Bribing officials is very common in Iran. Isn't that *contribution* the same kind of bribe?"

He smiled, "No, it's not. That money is what a politician spends for his election or reelection. A proposal can be killed or simply left to die a natural death. In fact, the vast majority of bills never make it out of committees. About one-third of all bills are private bills. The other two-thirds are public bills."

"How much money would be expected for the support that I need?" I wondered.

"Maybe a thousand dollars. For that amount Senator Javits could easily get you that bill."

Instantly I strained my mind with phantasms. I could not even visualize holding one thousand dollars, let alone giving it away.

He continued, "Don't worry about it. Eventually, I will get you a visa, but if you want it sooner, let me know. Just bring the money."

We shook hands goodbye and I agreed to return in a few weeks--with or without more money. To clear my head I cleared my lungs with a sigh of relief. I was happy to know that such a bill is possible. "Now, where in the world am I going to get $1,000.00?" I worried.

As the subway train click-clacked its way to Brooklyn I recalled a practice of the Iranian Army. To encourage home ownership, for a small price, each officer was offered a small parcel of land in an undeveloped area north of the city. It was just adequate for a modest house. This lot had cost me 800 tumans (about $800.00), which had taken me four years to pay. Even though I had since left Iran, the land was still mine. Immediately I wanted to phone my brother in Tehran and ask him to sell this property so I could have money for my visa. One such three-minute phone call, however, cost at least $90.00. The only alternative was a letter. As I thought about it, the letter was even better, because it left no room for confusion or misinterpretation. Everything was specified--black on white.

Four weeks later my brother informed me that my land appreciated to about 2,000 tumans and he would like to buy it himself. Would I consider his payment in installments? How could I refuse!

When the first installment of $500.00 came through a bank note at Chase Manhattan, I hurried to the lawyer's office with my fortune. I had no bank account of any kind. With a monthly salary of only $50.00 I couldn't even afford the cost of a checking account. Nor did I have any money to invest in any kind of savings account. At this time $25.00 of every $50.00 was going to the lawyer toward my payment for his services. As I pulled out the bills from my coat pocket, he stared at me in disbelief.

"Never," he repeated, "never walk around with this much cash in your pocket."

Almost breathlessly, I explained how I came directly from the bank because I wanted my visa as soon as possible.

One month later my brother sent me another $500.00 and I dutifully delivered it to Mr. Avocat--in cash.

Another month later a bill in Congress was introduced on my behalf. "For the next twelve months the Bureau of Immigration has your file dormant. No one will bother you. I, however, will continue working on your case. One way or another you should have your visa by the end of the year."

When we reviewed the details of the spelling of my name and my current address, he suggested that I move from Wyckoff Hospital in Brooklyn back to Jewish Memorial Hospital in Manhattan, because that was the institution that had stipulated their need for my service.

"I have at least six more months before I finish my first year of surgical residency," I mentioned.

With that new problem I left. This time as I rode the subway train and let my mind wander, I realized that I really found pathology exciting. Maybe I could apply for that residency at Jewish Memorial.

The next Saturday that I was off I visited Dr. Elahi at Jewish Memorial Hospital. In the circle of a few friends I shared my news about the bill in my name. I also told them that Mr. Avocat asked about my intentions of ever getting married. They all laughed.

Someone added, "Are you one of those who is going to ask your family to send you a bride from Iran?"

"Well, right now with $50.00 a month, I can't even rent a room. How am I going to support a wife?"

Someone else commented, "There are many girls in the United States who support their husbands until they finish school. That kind of wife earns the degree PHT: Putting Hubby Through. Think about it. Having an American wife would make getting a visa much easier. I'm not suggesting that you marry someone you don't like, just for the sake of a wedding tomorrow, but think about it."

A divorcée about 40 years old who was now going out with a divorced pediatrician offered, "If you want me to marry you just for the sake of getting the visa, I will be glad to help you."

"Thank you," I smiled, "I'll think about it." I never heard of a woman proposing to a man before. How could anyone do such a thing? This I would never do, I thought. This certainly is not عشق (*eshgh*, meaning love). Marriage is sacred. It has to be "properly" planned with mutual respect, trust, and love. I had no choice but to wait--to wait till I got my visa, finished my education, got a license, and got a job. Only then could I think about getting a wife.

Back in my room in the hospital I soothed my emotional wounds with the poetry of Omar Khayam and the symphonies of Beethoven.

Six months later I did go back to Jewish Memorial Hospital and Mr. Avocat continued to work on my visa problem.

* * * * *

After I became a citizen, after I received a license to practice medicine, after I spent a lifetime practicing pathology, after I retired, I decided to write these memoirs. Thanks to the Pittsburgh Carnegie Library system, I found page 6693 of the CONGRESSIONAL RECORD--HOUSE for 1955. On the bottom of the page a private bill on my behalf is listed--with my first name misspelled.

PRIVATE BILLS AND RESOLUTIONS

Under clause 1 of rule XXII, private bills and resolutions were introduced and severally referred as follows:

By Mr. ANFUSO:

H. R. 6385. A bill for the relief of Dr. Husham Mofakham Payan; to the Committee on the Judiciary.

115
Pres. Eisenhower

One late afternoon while I was reviewing microscopic surgical slides in the pathology laboratory, Dr. Messina--one of the surgeons--dropped in to review some of his own. He chose that particular time in order to show me a front-page newspaper picture of the Shah of Iran and his wife Queen Soraya. The caption reported their unofficial trip to the United States.

Dr. Messina asked, "You're from Iran, aren't you?"

"Yes, I am."

"The Shah and his wife are a very handsome couple," he observed. "They have a pretty good command of English too. Have you any idea what they are doing here?"

"Visiting President Eisenhower," I guessed.

"Do you know him?" wondered Dr. Messina.

"Sure, all Iranians know the Royal Family."

"Does he know you?" Messina continued.

As I wondered how to answer that question, Dr. Freedman looked up from his microscope and came to my rescue. "Does Eisenhower know you?" he asked Dr. Messina.

116

100%

When it came to a discussion about marriage, Dr. Pirez, an intern from Mexico, vociferously vowed that he would never want an American wife. "These women always talk about fifty/fifty. They all expect half of everything I have--even my clothes, I guess, since they wear pants just like a man. In Mexico, even if I marry the daughter of *el presidente*, it will be 100% for me and nothing for her." In spite of his negative attitude toward women in the United States, he had no hesitation about dating them.

A young nurse's aide who worked in the medical department with Dr. Pirez soon showed signs of pregnancy. "Dr. Pirez is the father," she told everyone and added that they were to be married soon.

Soon it was June, time for the wedding, but the groom was nowhere to be found. Everyone surmised that he had disappeared into Mexico to avoid legal entanglement, suspecting that she could sue him for child support.

About two years later, I stepped into an elevator already occupied by a few other people, including a young nurse's aide with a two-year-old boy in her arms. She looked familiar, but I could not quite place her. Most people in uniform look the same anyway.

Nevertheless, it was exasperating not to be able to recall the name of someone who looked so very familiar.

When George opened the elevator door for her on the fourth floor, he turned to me and commented in no uncertain terms, "That little boy looks just like his father, doesn't he?"

"Who's the father?" I asked, more bewildered than ever. I couldn't even recognize the lady, yet George expected me to know the father.

When I didn't answer immediately, he turned around and stared at my puzzled face. "Dr. Pirez. Don't you know?"

117
Pathology Residency

By the end of my second year residency in June, 1955, pathology definitely had more of an intellectual challenge than surgery. Inspired by the lawyer's suggestion to move back to Manhattan, I returned to Jewish Memorial Hospital. Since I still did not have a valid passport or a visa, I again told Mr. Miller, the hospital administrator, that I may have to leave suddenly to return to Iran.

As there was no other applicant for the pathology residency, he welcomed me, "That's ok. Just let me know as soon as you can."

About a month later the administrator received a copy of the directive sent from the American Medical Association to all training hospitals. Any physician from Iran who is a member of the Imperial Iranian Army should not be accepted at the hospital for any residency. Mr. Miller showed me the letter and naturally asked about my status with the Iranian army.

"Yes," I admitted, "I am a first lieutenant."

"Well, now that you are here, you are hired. It's ok. Next year, though, we will not hire you."

"Ok," I accepted and left his office.

A year later no one remembered the AMA notice. By that time not only my knowledge of general medicine (particularly laboratory medicine), but my English, had improved considerably. I became so at ease with both disciplines that new residents, like Dr. Firestone and Dr. Kim in medicine and surgery respectively, came to me from time to time with questions or observations about their patients. In regard to autopsies the house staff all came to observe my findings. Soon I earned the reputation of being well informed and intelligent.

One day I bumped into Mrs. Gintho, the uncouth nurse who believed that all foreigners are good for nothing. What could I say, but "Hello, Mrs. Gintho."

"Hello," she answered almost passing me as though I weren't there.

"How are you?" I asked.

"Fine, how are you?" she answered, recognizing me at last. "Oh, you're Dr. Payan. Everybody's talking about how smart you are. A couple of years ago you didn't know anything. How did you get so smart? Did you read a couple of books or something?"

"Yes, yes," I answered. "I read a lot."

Before she had a chance to tell me any gossip that spread around the hospital community, I continued walking away from her, even backwards, and smiled my goodbye.

118
My First Car

After two years in the United States I was beginning to feel quite affluent. My brother paid me for the land I had in Tehran and my salary reached $50.00 per month. I had enough money to buy an old English Hillman for $400.00, exactly what I earned in eight months.

Now that I made a down payment on this light blue little car, the size of an early Volkswagen, it seemed like a good idea to learn how to drive. An American friend recommended AAA, the American Automobile Association, whose office in mid-Manhattan offered one hour of class instruction and four hours of on-the-road practice--all for $25.00.

Since I worked until 5:00 p.m. every day and was on call every other night, the five hours of training had to be spread over two weeks. Between 5:00 and 6:00 p.m., the peak of rush hour traffic, I sat behind the wheel of an enormous Chevrolet, while my instructor sat in the passenger seat next to me behind a set of duplicate controls. In comparison with my Hillman, this car was a bus. Up and down the avenues, across the streets east and west, I careened around numerous delivery trucks, endless tourist buses, policemen on horses, and waves of humanity rushing as though they themselves were on fire--all this in a cacophony of screeching brakes, screaming taxi drivers, honking horns, and the clipclop of festooned horses pulling decorated carriages.

After two sessions the instructor felt that I was competent enough to pass the test with flying colors. Together we filled out the application. At the examination site I had to be interviewed by an officer who dealt with foreign born applicants to make sure that I did understand all the English of all the street signs.

"Do you know what construction is?" he asked as he sat behind his desk.

Not too sure of what I heard in this New York

accent, I began, enunciating carefully, "If you mean construction, that's a building process. If"

"That's all right," he interrupted me.

But I continued, "If you mean constriction, that's a narrowing, like constriction of the arteries, or narrowing of the veins, preventing the normal flow"

"That's all right. That's all right," he repeated, louder this time as though I were deaf.

But I had to finish. "of blood."

He looked tired. I really could have told him more, but he interrupted me with his yelling, "I believe you. I believe you." He handed me a set of questions for the written part of the test, abruptly ending the interview.

A few days later I took the road test. One week later I had my driver's license.

Now I really was ready to pick up my Hillman from the car dealer. "There's not much gas in it," the salesman warned. At the nearest station I filled up the tank for one whole dollar.

Behind the wheel of that car I really felt Americanized, even though the car was British and many of my friends referred to it as a toy. The next time I had a Saturday off I drove to Long Island to visit friends at Queens General Hospital. They too were excited with my success. On the way back to Manhattan by way of the Triborough Bridge I sailed along on Cloud 9 at 60 miles per hour, never noticing that bridge speed dropped to 40 mph. In my euphoria I passed everybody and everything, including a police car.

I was hardly an inch in front of him when he flashed his lights, screamed his siren, and zoomed out of his lane into mine. Near the toll booth I stopped.

He stopped behind me, got out of his car, slammed his door, and marched his 6'6" frame toward me.

"Didn't you see me?" he asked.

"No, sir," I meekly answered, still subconsciously very fearful of policemen. "If I had, I certainly would have slowed down."

"Well, too bad. Next time look. Here's your ticket. Mail it with your $5.00 to the department. The instructions and address are on the back."

119
Womanizer

Thirty-year-old Dr. Rodriguez from South America came to Jewish Memorial Hospital for his first year residency, even though he had done a few years of obstetrics and gynecology in Venezuela. Residencies in foreign countries are not recognized in the United States. In order to become a specialist in the United States, he had to repeat the training. Consequently, since he was familiar with the procedures of obstetrics and gynecology, during this training in Jewish Memorial Hospital he felt very much at ease with all sorts of equipment and supplies. He never had anything to complain about. In fact, he hardly ever contributed to any conversation. He was very quiet--even somewhat reserved.

He had the same demeanor around women. Since he was often seen with a young girl talking in the residents' quarters and then going into his room, behind his back the all-male occupants of these living quarters called him a lady's man. Gossip really got hot when his companion seemed to be a different lady every time. After a couple of hours, he would leave the room with the young girl hanging on his arm. It was amazing how often he changed girlfriends. When people noticed a strange aroma, like alcohol, near his room, he was also labeled a "heavy drinker."

One cold January evening the hospital administrator accompanied by two policemen came to the residents' quarters, looking for Dr. Rodriguez. They knocked at his door, but there was no answer. Again and again they knocked to no avail. Equally impatient and uneasy, Mr. Miller had the head nurse come with the master key to let the visitors in.

Arranged neatly in a drawer of the doctor's dresser lay medical instruments ready for a curettage. In a corner of his closet behind his long white coats was a box concealing bottles of alcohol, obviously ready to clean these instruments.

In another box they found a stack of clean gauze, sheets and towels stamped with the initials of the hospital. As they checked every other closet, drawer, and notebook, they found $4,000.00 cash. Further investigation showed that Dr. Rodriguez had performed eight abortions in the past three months.

When his most recent "visitor" hemorrhaged, her mother took her to Bellevue Hospital Emergency Room. Routine questioning unfolded her episode with Dr. Rodriguez in his room. The emergency room physician then notified the police who went looking for the entrepreneur at Jewish Memorial.

At an emergency breakfast meeting Mr. Miller informed all the board members of these escapades. Unanimously they voted to discharge Dr. Rodriguez immediately and notify everyone else that no female guests were permitted in the residents' quarters.

That night Dr. Rodriguez had a room in jail.

This was 1956. In the state of New York abortion was illegal.

120
Life in the Morgue

By 7:00 a.m. I was having breakfast with Dr. Firestone, the medical resident. Christine with her motherly attitude came with the orange juice, bacon, eggs, buttered toast, jam, cereal, one container of milk, and another of coffee.

The night before, Dr. Firestone had a 40-year-old cardiac patient with all the symptoms of a heart attack. In spite of the morphine, oxygen and complete bed rest, the patient died two hours after being admitted. The doctor already had the autopsy permit signed by the wife and expressed an interest in observing the autopsy.

As we pushed open the door marked "Research--No Admittance," Frank, the caretaker, sat in a corner. He seemed to be mending something.

"What's he doing?" wondered Dr. Firestone.

"We'll see," I answered him.

To Frank, I said, "Good Morning, Frank. Are you patching your socks again?"

"Hello, Doc. Just another thing I have to do."

"We have an autopsy this morning. Did anyone tell you?"

"Not yet, but I suspected so. There's a young man in the cooler."

"We'd like to start in an hour."

"Don't worry. I'll have everything ready, but first I have to get Mr. Miller." Since neither Mr. Miller nor his wife drove, Frank served as their chauffeur whenever convenient.

Dr. Firestone couldn't believe how spotless the morgue was. "Everything sparkles as though it were brand new--or just shined. You'd think this was the operating room."

"Isn't it wonderful," I agreed. "Since Frank's wife passed away, he spends a lot of time in this hospital, keeping the morgue scrupulously clean. It's his pride and joy. His only other interest is his old Buick which he keeps in the same condition as this room."

By 9:00 a.m. lights were flashing on all floors, signaling physicians that an autopsy was in progress.

This autopsy revealed a complete blockage in the left coronary artery. To the dozen or so physicians observing the procedure, Dr. Firestone presented the history of the case and I explained and demonstrated the pathology. After all questions were answered, we left the morgue, knowing that Frank would take care of everything else.

During the night shift around 2:00 a.m. two young nurses brought a dead person to the morgue in the basement where coolers accommodated four bodies. At gurney level they pulled out one of the drawers, slid the body onto the eight-foot tray, and closed it.

Just as they were about to close the door of the morgue behind them, one suddenly realized that they forgot to turn the light off. Before they even had a chance to turn around, a male voice yelled from the morgue, "Turn off that god damn light!"

The nurses screamed . . . and ran. The elevator couldn't come fast enough. On the first floor they ran to the office to tell the telephone operator about their experience.

Instead of getting excited, she simply giggled. "Don't be upset. That's Frank. He sleeps down there all the time."

121
Bizarre Triangle

January, 1955 I started my rotation in radiology. Tony Pozio, the chief technician in the department, was married to a psychiatrist. Socializing with many of his wife's colleagues, he felt comfortable with physicians and often spent his lunch time with them, rather than with the technicians.

One day at lunch he introduced me and Dr. Ajeenah to his cousin Bernice Bertucci, who worked as one of the daytime telephone operators. She was an attractive brunette in her late twenties, about 10 years younger than Tony. Unlike the other telephone operators and clerical workers, she appeared well dressed and quite sophisticated. By the time we had dessert I found out that she too, like her cousin Tony, was a chiropractor. While they both worked in the hospital the usual forty hours a week, they shared an office together in the late afternoons and evenings.

As friends of Dr. Ajeenah's, they often came to visit in the residents' lounge.

Later I found out that Tony was born in northern Italy and came to the United States six years later with his parents. Upon graduation from high school he was married. Upon graduation from college, his wife was accepted into medical school, but he was not. As an alternative later on while his wife practiced medicine, he enrolled in a chiropractic institute. So did his cousin Bernice.

Their work intrigued me, because there were no chiropractors in Iran. The word itself was interesting as "chiro" stems from the Greek *cheir* meaning *hand* and *praxis*, *to produce*, thus defining "chiropractic" as hand manipulation of the body, different from massage. In this occupation such practitioners believe that health and disease are life processes related to the function of the nervous system. Any mechanical, chemical or psychic irritation to it can cause disease. Thus, manipulation of the neuro-muscular system and/or the removal of any noxious substance offers treatment in a very conservative manner.

In the State of New York chiropractors were not recognized as medical professionals. Unlike physicians, to conduct their practice all they needed was a business permit. Even though they were neither trained, nor recognized, as physicians, Tony addressed himself as "doctor." As a licensed physician, his wife Mary objected to this habit. "It's Mr. Pozio, not Dr. Pozio," she constantly reminded him.

The real Dr. Pozio hardly had time to say even that much to her husband. Her practice of medicine, her eight children, and her continual pregnant condition consumed most of her time and enthusiasm.

With so little time with his wife, Tony had a lot of time with Cousin Bernice. They not only attended chiropractic school together, they opened an office together, worked in the same hospital together, and even socialized together. Their friendship developed stronger than a normal relationship between cousins. Bernice became very dependant on Tony, almost as though he were her husband. Since she did not know how to drive, Tony served as her chauffeur--and preferred it that way.

One Saturday night Tony invited Ajeenah and me to his house for dinner. For our host we bought a bottle of champagne wrapped artistically. I felt very Americanized. At the door Tony's attractive blond wife Mary introduced herself as Dr. Pozio and added, "Please call me Mary." Bernice was right behind Mary to welcome us. As the evening went along, Mary told us that she was an assistant professor at a medical school.

During our visit their eight children, ranging in age from one to twelve, were entertained in another part of the house by their maid. When we did meet them briefly, Bernice seemed to be very familiar with the children and the household. Apparently, she too lived in the Pozio house.

From then on Ajeenah and I were often invited to Tony's house for coffee or holidays like the children's birthdays. As friends of Tony's and Mary's, Ajeenah and I were also invited to the homes of Tony's parents and even Bernice's parents. The older generation spoke English with an Italian accent.

Bernice and Ajeenah seemed interested in each

other, always engrossed in conversation. Somehow I doubted that they ever went out together. Perhaps being reserved and formal was part of Ajeenah's Middle Eastern Culture.

As a result of some friction with Dr. Fernandez, the new chief resident, Ajeenah left the United States in July of 1955. To those he supervised, Fernandez was arrogant and demanding; to his superiors, however, he was obsequious. Dr. Zoller, the chief of surgery, interpreted Fernandez' flattery as true admiration and respect. The attitude of both men irritated Ajeenah *ad nauseum.* With patience and tolerance exhausted, Ajeenah returned to Iraq. Even though his training at Wyckoff ended, his interest in Bernice did not. He invited her to go to Iraq to visit him.

To avoid any possible confusion with the Bureau of Immigration, in July, I too left Brooklyn to return to Manhattan, where I continued my second year of residency, but my first in pathology at Jewish Memorial Hospital.

Tony often called me from Brooklyn and I often accepted dinner invitations on weekends with him and his family. With Ajeenah in Iraq, I was often the only guest.

Near the end of April in 1956, the Immigration and Naturalization Bureau informed me that I had to leave the country within two months. Otherwise, I would be deported. Under those circumstances I would never be able to return to the United States.

Naturally I was disturbed--quite a bit disturbed. I found an American expression quite apropos, "This is it!" I thought that I had no choice but to leave. Immediately I called the lawyer about seeing him later that afternoon.

He explained that this letter was routine because no action was taken on the bill within the mandatory twelve-month period. "You need not worry," he reassured me. "I will get your visa. If worse comes to worse, I will go to the Immigration Bureau, give the clerk fifty bucks, and get your file. For the next six months, let them look for it. In the meantime we will have your visa."

It was reassuring to listen to him. I felt somewhat better, but not too sure that Mr. Avocat could live up to his promises.

On the train to the hospital all the things he said rang in my brain like some haunting melody. "The average person in the Immigration Bureau makes $200.00 a month. Most of the employees could be bribed. I worked there for two years." I thought bribing officials was unique to Iran. Obviously, it was not.

I went back to my room in the hospital to sooth my nerves with poetry of Omar Khayam and the music of Beethoven. I also called Tony to tell him about my progress with my visa problems.

My next weekend off I was invited to his home again. When the two of us were alone, he commented, "You know, Bernice will marry you so you can get your visa."

"Oh?" I wondered. "Let me think about it."

"What's there to think about?" he almost shouted. "She really has no intention of getting married, but as a friend she'll go through with it to help you."

"Well . . . let me talk to my lawyer about this."

"No, no," he got excited. "If you want to do this, you better not tell anyone else. Just get married, consider it real, and then tell the lawyer and everyone else. Bernice is willing to go to the Immigration office or to the lawyer or wherever is necessary."

"One thing you must not do is to explain why you decided to marry. Think of it as real."

Since I wasn't allowed to talk about this marriage, I wanted at least a couple of weeks to think about it.

I decided to go ahead and marry Bernice, since no harm would come to anyone anyway. I had hoped to get closer to her as a result of matrimony and maybe even become friends some day to the point that this marriage may even work. I was trying to convince myself that my intentions were sincere. If there was a problem, it was Bernice, not me. I still wondered why a thirty-year old attractive, educated woman would be willing to do this for me since we were hardly friends.

Early afternoon on June 12, 1956 I went to Brooklyn. Tony had arranged everything. At a church not far from Tony's house I met him and Bernice. A priest and a couple of others were also there. So few people attended, the place looked deserted. As we exchanged vows with the ring that I bought for fifteen dollars our words echoed. We were married, but this was so different from other weddings

I had seen. As I kissed the bride on the cheek with a hesitant peck, I wondered what went through the mind of the priest.

Outside the church, I thanked Bernice for doing this for me, shook hands and went back to my room in the hospital in Manhattan. I couldn't shake my doubts about the prudence of the whole project.

In July, 1956 my second year of residency in pathology started at Queens General Hospital. I moved to Queens, which was closer to Brooklyn, where Tony lived. A few weeks later I took Bernice and the marriage certificate to Mr. Avocat.

As he congratulated us, he remarked, "Where did you meet such a good looking girl?"

"Bernice works in the hospital in Brooklyn."I answered.

Recording pertinent details, he assured me, "I am still pursuing the original strategy that you are needed by Jewish Memorial Hospital, but this marriage will definitely speed things up."

The marriage definitely improved my relations with Bernice, Mary, and the rest of Tony's family. I visited them often, but was never alone with Bernice. The only time we were alone was during visits to a lawyer or the Immigration Bureau.

On one of these occasions I tried to tell Bernice that I did like her and if she felt the same toward me, we could improve our friendship. I thought the marriage may just work--for real.

She smiled at the suggestion, but just nodded, having no comment.

Two days later Tony phoned me just before lunch while I was reviewing surgical slides with Dr. Paris. Instead of his usual cheery greeting, he almost yelled through the receiver, "Every man should have a woman to sleep with, so he doesn't chase after someone else's."

Not knowing Tony's frame of mind at the moment, I tried to calm him down and apologized for not being able to listen to the rest of his problem. I was at a conference with the chief. I wondered if my conversation with Bernice was relayed to Tony. Maybe that's what freaked him out.

For a couple of weeks I was so busy, I called neither

Tony nor Bernice. He, however, called me and apologized for the temper tantrum. Before we hung up, he invited me to his house again and I accepted again.

From then on, however, any time I reported to Immigration with Bernice, Tony would drive her and then wait in the car till our session was over. It was obvious he made sure that she and I were never alone. I was really too busy to be bothered by the growing infrequency of our visits.

In mid-1957 Mr. Avocat informed me that my visa application had been approved. "In order to get it, however, you have to travel overnight to Montreal."

This did not make sense, but if rules are made, they must be followed. I was in no position to question such practices in the United States.

On August 12, 1957, I flew to Montreal. Bernice and Tony drove there and stayed in a hotel different from mine. The next day the three of us went to the American Consulate, where I received my papers and "green card." The following day we returned to New York--one by plane and two by car. Finally after four years and $1,600.00 I had a permanent visa. No longer did I fear policemen in the street. Being very busy during the next 12 months, trying to get a medical license, my visits with Tony and Bernice became farther and farther apart.

About a year later I had a phone call from a stranger who introduced himself as a friend of Tony's. "Sometimes we are friends, sometimes we are not. I know that you are married to Bernice, but separated. I'm interested in Bernice and I would like to marry her. However, I would like to ask you a question."

"Yes," I said slowly, wondering who he was and what he wanted.

"Was Bernice a virgin when you married her?"

"I'm sorry," I answered. "This is very personal--for me, as well as for Bernice. I do not discuss anyone's personal matters. If you are going to marry her, you should approach her with such a question."

Later that evening I told Tony all about this weird phone call. "What's this all about?" I asked.

"Oh, don't worry. This guy is nuts. He already has a wife and a few kids. Now he thinks he's in love with

Bernice. He was getting a little too close for comfort, so I told him to bug off. He thought he was going to marry a virgin. I told him that she is married to you, and even before the wedding she wasn't a virgin."

How did he know, I wondered. It sounded as though Tony enjoyed this game of playing with men who came around for the sake of Bernice. As soon as they became somewhat friendly, he jumped in to clear the territory for himself. Life was getting too complicated. This game was not for me. I wondered about getting a divorce from a marriage I didn't have. My next problem was how to mention it to Tony, who was obviously in control of Bernice's life.

About a week later Tony phoned just as I was trying to solve this dilemma. "I'm coming over with Bernice to see you," he announced. "It would be better if we talked in your room--privately."

"Sure," I agreed. "I'll be free around four o'clock." As I hung up, I couldn't imagine what tricks Tony had up his sleeve this time.

Four o'clock exactly Tony and Bernice appeared. With hardly a hello Tony began, "Bernice and I have been in love since the days we attended chiropractic school. Even though we're cousins, we don't care. Couple of times I tried to divorce Mary to marry Bernice, but neither wants that kind of scandal. Mary doesn't care about my relations with Bernice either, even though she is now pregnant with our ninth child. Bernice has been more of a mother to those children than their own mother. Mary's too busy with her medical practice to have any time for me or them."

"Why did you urge Bernice to marry me?" I almost screamed.

"Well, you needed a visa, not a wife, and she was not going to get married to anyone anyway. So, she was the answer to your problem. Now that we did you a favor, we need one from you."

"Oh," I said suspiciously. "What?"

"Bernice and I would like to have a child. As we are all Catholic and can't get a divorce, we would like to do this under your name and marriage. Afterwards, you can get a divorce and I will adopt the child."

"We need your approval and cooperation for about a year," Bernice added.

No sooner I cleared up one mess (the visa), I was asked to fall into another. Tony's proposition seemed totally irrational. My legal wife has a love affair with another man, yet they want my approval to get pregnant. I knew that Americans are broad minded, but this seemed crazy. "What about the child?" I asked. "Since no one can bring him into the discussion, I will speak for him. The answer is 'No'."

Before these two dreamed any other bright ideas, I began investigating divorce procedures. Actually, my so-called marriage probably wasn't even legal, since it was never even consummated. Nevertheless, I did have a legal marriage and I needed a legal divorce.

The next day I conferred with Attorney Levy, a specialist in divorce. "The State of New York does not grant divorce frivolously. The only acceptable reason is proven adultery." This law didn't make sense to me either, but once again I was only a cog in the wheel of life.

The lawyer offered me a package deal:

1. Early one morning board a chartered plane for El Paso, Texas.
2. From there take the bus to Juarez, where a Mexican court will grant the divorce.
3. Within an hour, reboard the bus.
4. Then take the plane back to New York.

"How much?" I hated to ask.

"$700.00--cash."

Four weeks later I propped myself up against my pillows piled at the headboard of my bed and read, "*Poder Judicial Del Estado De Chihuahua.* Whereas the divorce . . . December 22, 1958 . . ."

122
Dr. Kohan

In the 1940's in Iran there were no state laws for or against abortion, but Moslem tenets have always prohibited the procedure. Unless a pregnant woman's life is in danger, most physicians will be reluctant to do any curettage.

Roxanne felt that four children were enough for her to handle. When she discovered a fifth baby on its way, she mulled over the pro's and con's for about four months before she consulted a physician to terminate her pregnancy. Since she was in her second trimester, none of the reputable gynecologists would even discuss the possibility. Roxanne was willing to pay anyone any amount of money. As the daughter of the owner of Cinema Iran and the wife of a prosperous pharmacist, she did not worry about cost.

Finally she found Dr. Kohan, a gynecologist who agreed to perform the abortion in his office, rather than in a hospital. This way there would be neither records nor involvement of hospital personnel. The only witness would be his practical nurse, trained to administer ether for anesthesia.

The following morning the abortion was performed.

Within an hour the patient was sent home. Later Roxanne began to bleed. Shen then hemorrhaged so profusely, her husband phoned Dr. Kohan to report the situation.

Following the doctor's instructions, the husband then drove his wife to a private hospital. The bleeding continued. Her pulse became rapid. Her blood pressure dropped. Her mouth became dry. Roxanne was in a state of shock. To control the problem, she was given intravenous saline solution, since transfusions, unfortunately, were not readily accessible in the 1940's in Iran. To eliminate the source of the problem it was decided that a hysterectomy be performed. Soon after surgery the patient died.

Roxanne's husband then sued Dr. Kohan.

At this time in Iran no doctor carried professional insurance, as no one would even think of suing anyone--particularly a physician who was considered by society tantamount to God.

Within six months in the middle of the lawsuit Dr. Kohan disappeared.

Most people believed that he had gone to France, where he was trained.

Years later when I was a resident in New York City, while I sipped my morning coffee, my attention was riveted to first-page news about a gynecologist in Brooklyn, being sought by police for questioning.

> Yesterday afternoon Susan O'Connor, a sixteen-year-old pregnant girl, was brought to the office of one Dr. Kohan, while her parents waited for her in a coffee shop across the street. In the process of the anesthesia and curettage the girl went into shock and died. The doctor and his practical nurse panicked, exited the building by a back door, and left the parents wondering about the delay.
>
> When no one came out of the doctor's office four hours later, the parents went to the office, only to find the door locked.
>
> The parents immediately found a phone to notify the police. When they came to investigate, they had to force the door open.
>
> To their horror, they discovered furniture and equipment stained with blood which led them to an opened trash can. Inside they found their daughter's mutilated body, cut into dozens of pieces.

I couldn't decide whether I was more shocked or more surprised. Could this be the same Dr. Kohan that I had heard about in Tehran? Did he come to the United States only to continue his illegal practice in New

York City? Abortion was still illegal in New York.

Two months later, when Dr. Kohan and his nurse were eventually found in France, he declared that he honestly believed that what he did was for the benefit of the patient. If he had refused, the woman may have contacted a medically untrained abortionist. He felt that it is better that an abortion be done by a gynecologist in his office, rather than by a nonprofessional person in a cheap hotel room. The doctor and nurse were extradited to New York and sentenced to jail.

123

Mr. Ozar

Mr. Rostam Ozar owned a transportation company in Tehran. Since he assumed the responsibility of buying and repairing his own buses, he was able to reinvest much of his profit into improved service, rather than in wages. During WWII, however, his business suffered a setback, because the Allied Forces bought all available vehicles to be used for carrying war supplies and army equipment from southern parts of Iran to the northern parts of the country, occupied at the time by the USSR.

Mr. Ozar had no choice but to rely on horse and buggy. An excellent entrepreneur as he was, Mr. Ozar then bought a fleet of the wagons, animals, and everything else necessary to provide the best service in town. As he devoted more and more time to this new venture, he spent less and less time with his family.

With the children grown and gone, the wife felt somewhat lonely. Trying to get attention through sympathy, she complained about her symptoms of menopause. Such a topic of conversation didn't exactly excite him or challenge his sense of business. In order to be spared such drivel he decided to find himself a second wife and discussed this probability with his wife.

"I don't care if you have 10 more wives," she commented. "Go ahead, do what you want to, but don't bother me anymore."

Two weeks later he married the twenty-year-old daughter of one of his business associates. It did not take long for the second wife to get pregnant.

By the time the war ended, the economy began to improve. Within a year or two, he worked so hard improving his business, he repeated his habit of neglecting his family. As he enjoyed remarkable financial success, he decided to go to the United States in search of business connections and additional buses, especially those with more comfortable seating and air conditioning.

Unfortunately, he did not speak English. How could he communicate these grandiose ideas? Relatives reminded him that he had a grandnephew Farhang, who had gone to New York just before the war and was now a practicing physician in Manhattan. By letter he notified this nephew of his plans.

After Mr. Ozar gathered ideas about landmarks in the United States, he got his Iranian passport and a United States visa. He flew SAS between Iran and France, and then took a huge ocean liner to America.

Aboard ship he struck up a friendship with a 19-year-old Iranian college student who spoke English quite fluently. Since the older man anticipated a need for help with immigration, customs, and a possible phone call to his nephew, he made sure that he stayed near the young man as they disembarked.

Sure enough. Among other things, the immigration officer asked, "Do you have a wife?"

"Yes," answered Mr. Ozar. "Two of them."

Speechless for a moment, the officer asked, "What?"

Assuming that the officer did not understand the young man who was translating, Ozar repeated in Farsi, "Two of them. Two wives," and held up two fingers.

Somewhat dumbfounded, the immigration officer sought the help of his supervisor who decided that Mr. Ozar be detained on Ellis Island.

Now it was Mr. Ozar's turn to be dumfounded. His young new-found friend tried as best he could to explain what had been decided. At least he was allowed to call his nephew to explain the predicament. After doing all that he possibly could, the young man went on his way.

Now Dr. Farhang Parsa, the nephew, had problems. After a week and a half or so, the Iranian consulate finally managed to unite these two relatives. The nephew had to sign papers promising to care for his uncle, while the uncle had to sign papers limiting his stay in the United States to a maximum of two months.

Mr. Ozar was very happy to be released from this detainment center. As was the custom in Iran, he was very eager to stay with his nephew as a house guest.

The nephew informed the uncle that he and his American wife just had a baby and were rather cramped in a very small apartment. There was no extra room for a guest. Therefore they went to a hotel around Times Square and got a room for $7.00 a night. Before parting, the nephew advised the uncle to rest and just walk around town the following day till he would come for him around 6:00 p.m.

"6:00 p.m.?" gasped the older man. "What are you doing all day long?"

"Working," the nephew replied.

"Oh, heavens. Can't you take a few weeks off? I'm going to be here for only two months."

As they walked along toward the restaurant closest to the hotel, the nephew tried to explain that in the mornings he had patients to see in the hospital and in the afternoons, more to take care of in the office.

"Who is going to take care of me?" asked the uncle accusingly.

The nephew realized the merits of delaying an answer to this question. No sense of opening up the proverbial can of worms. Instead, he suggested, "Why don't you get some rest now. We will talk about it tomorrow night."

"Tomorrow night?" wondered the uncle. "Where will you be when I wake up?"

"In the hospital," answered the doctor calmly. "Good night."

Reluctantly, Uncle Rostam murmured, "Good night."

The next day the doctor left his office as soon as he could. He met his uncle in the lobby and then drove him to his apartment where his American wife had prepared dinner. She spoke no Farsi; the uncle spoke no English. Just as he did not recognize the sounds she made, he did not recognize the food she served.

Sensing the awkwardness of the situation, the nephew hurried the meal along and took his uncle to his office not far from home. Now that office hours were over, they could sit down without interruption and discuss some strategy to handle the uncle's business concerns. The office was on a second floor of a multistory old building with many other offices. The main entrance to the building, which was on a side street, was open. They took the elevator to the second floor and walked into the office By this time it was around 8:00 p.m.

What they did not notice was that across the street two burly young men sat in a car and watched their every move. As the lights in the office were turned on, the black letters on the window showed up clearly, "F. Parsa, M.D." The men in the car knew exactly where to go.

Five minutes later they entered the almost deserted building, climbed the steps quietly, and without a sound opened the door to the office. They both wore ski masks over their faces and carried guns in their hands. "OK, Doc," threatened one man, pointing the gun at the doctor. "Just give us your money and nobody will get hurt."

Mr. Ozar immediately fell on his knees as he would in a mosque, touching the floor with his forehead. He remained prostrate and in Farsi prayed, "*Ay, Khoda! Ay, Khoda!* (Oh, Dear God! Oh, Dear God!) don't let me get killed in this country. I promise to lie down and die voluntarily for your sake if you just help me get back to Iran and see my own house--just one more time."

The masked man stared down at the man bent over on the floor and kept yelling, "Shut up. Hear me? Shut up."

Since the uncle understood no English, he certainly did not understand such orders. Dr. Parsa tried to explain to the burglars, "He doesn't speak English. He speaks Farsi."

"I don't give a damn what he speaks. Just tell him to shut up."

In Farsi, the nephew translated, "Uncle Rostam, please stop praying. These men just want your money. They are not going to kill you. Please, stop praying."

The uncle could not believe his ears. Was his nephew really telling him to refrain from practicing his religion? What could have happened to such a nice boy since he left Iran?

"Oh, God, please don't let these men hurt me," prayed the man in the language that sounded like gibberish to the attackers. Shaking uncontrollably and sobbing with hiccoughs, the man then pulled out a wad of money from his pocket, a waterfall of one-dollar bills.

Then the masked man raised his eyes to the ceiling and somewhat exasperated intoned, "Dear, God, help me get this idiot to understand." Then he faced the doctor and demanded, "Open up the drawer. Give me the money you collected today."

Fearfully he obeyed.

"Now lie down, both of you, face to the floor. Keep counting from one to one hundred. Don't even move till I tell you so."

As Dr. Parsa translated all this to his uncle, he naturally had to move as he talked.

"Lie down and shut up," yelled the masked man. "Don't you understand English either?"

As the doctor lay counting in English, the uncle began yelling even louder and wiggled frantically. "Oh, dear God, I have to go the toilet. Oh, God, how I have to go to the toilet."

Three days later Uncle Ozar was aboard the Queen Mary en route to France, where his plane tickets waited for him to fly back to Tehran.

124

Complete Blood Count

Because of a shortage of laboratory technicians right after World War II, people with minimal training were certified to perform tasks in the laboratories that did not require professional expertise. Whatever they did was always supervised by the college educated technologists. At a small community hospital the chief technician was most satisfied with the efficiency of one such technician in the hematology lab.

"The trouble with this 20-year-old Bob," complained Bertha, the senior technician, "is that he is constantly talking about going to medical school and specializing in gynecology. He devotes every spare moment to reading gynecology textbooks."

One late afternoon, while Bertha and most of the laboratory personnel were on their dinner break, Bob was left to cover the lab. Just then a young lady walked in with a request for a CBC (complete blood count).

Bob took the prescription from her, confirming the details about her name and age. "Please remove your panties and lie on the floor," he instructed.

Somewhat reluctant, holding on to the desk with one hand, she lifted one leg out of her underwear and then the other. Staring at him from the corner of her eye, she complied nevertheless and carefully dropped on one elbow at a time to stretch out on the floor.

Bob slowly moved her skirt higher and higher to the upper part of her body, exposing her lower abdomen. Then he ever so slowly adjusted her legs to put her in gynecologic position.

As he started a vaginal examination, just as the gynecology texts illustrated, Dr. Schwartz went by in the hall. He could not help staring through the glass doors. Instantly he entered the lab and screamed, "What is going on here?"

Bob immediately got off his knees and started to

make excuses.

The patient slowly got up, brushed off her clothes, and sobbed. After being comforted by a female technician, she consented to have her blood drawn for the test according to the normal procedures.

Within the week Bob was arrested and was admitted as a psychiatric patient. The girl's family sued the hospital.

125
Queen's General

Since my one-year approved residency at Jewish Memorial was coming to an end, Dr. Schwartz asked me, "Where are you going for your residency next year?"

"I have a few applications to fill out, but I haven't submitted any as yet," I answered.

"Would you consider Queens General Hospital? It's a very busy place with Dr. Angrist in charge of the pathology department and Dr. Silverman in charge of the residency program. They're my friends. I'd be more than glad to make an appointment for you."

"I'd appreciate that," I decided right then and there.

The following Wednesday I worked my way through heavy traffic a little more than a half hour in upper Manhattan, across the Triborough Bridge, along Grand Central Parkway, and then into Queens. The hospital grounds were so extensive, many drove from one building to another. Around 11:00 a.m. I introduced myself to the parking lot attendant and explained that Dr. Silverman was expecting me.

He directed me to the pathology building--not department, but building. I drove past the 800-bed hospital and eventually found a parking space in front of the two-story building which housed the medical examiners' office, the morgue, and department of pathology including clinical laboratories. As I walked toward the entrance, next to all these American cars and this sprawling complex, my little Hillman looked like a toy indeed.

On the second floor the secretary led me to a thin gray-haired lady in a lab coat. "Hello, Dr. Payne," she smiled. "I've been expecting you. Do sit down."

"Thank you."

"How do you pronounce your name?" she looked at it quizzically.

"Pa-yan," I answered in distinct syllables. "Pa, like

the u in 'puck' and yan the same way."

"I see from your application here that you did one year of surgery and another of pathology. Why did you change?"

"The half of my surgical year spent in pathology was so interesting, I decided to switch."

"That's interesting. I know several other physicians who did exactly the same thing for exactly the same reason. In our laboratory we process about 10,000 surgical specimens a year. Most come from Queens General which has 800 beds, while a small number come from Triborough Hospital which has 600 beds at the north end of the property. Triborough concentrates on respiratory disorders. At one time it dealt with tuberculosis exclusively. Even though that disease is no longer prevalent, a few cases do occur. Nowadays a lot of chest surgery is performed here. We also provide autopsy services for both hospitals."

"How many autopsies do you have?" I asked.

"About 800 from the two hospitals. The medical examiners do about 1,200. Since none of them are pathologists, we are often called to help."

I was surprised to hear that these medical examiners were not pathologists.

She continued, "They do have some gross pathology background. Dr. Segrim, the chief medical examiner, is a neurosurgeon. Of the three others, one is an internist; one, a general practitioner, and one, a thoracic surgeon. Dr. Segrim is here between 9:00 a.m. and noon every day, while the other three are here for only one day a week." She then explained how twelve residents work while they are in training. "Unlike Jewish Memorial Hospital approved for only one year, we are approved for both anatomic and clinical pathology for four years. First-year residents earn $50.00 a month; second-year, $75.00; third-year, $100.00; fourth-year, $150.00. Naturally, you will be provided room and board," she added. Every year three new residents replaced those who had completed their four-year training.

By this time we sensed that it was time for lunch. Like everything else about Queens General, the dining room was huge. Here you were just one small cog in the wheel. You picked up a tray, stood in line, selected your own food, and after eating, carried your tray back to the designated area adjacent to the kitchen. (There was no Christine to bring the food to you and smother you with motherliness.) As Dr. Silverman and I ate, we discussed my medical education and experience, especially in regard to surgical pathology and autopsies.

After lunch we toured the residents's work room, the conference room, and the morgue. Here too, the place was larger than anything I had ever seen before. It had twelve autopsy tables, thirty-six coolers for bodies, and a room exclusively for postmortem conferences.

As we passed one of the residents at work, Dr. Silverman introduced me to Dr. Kenichi.

"What kind of case is this, Ken?" Dr. Silverman asked.

"Myocardial infarction. He was seventy years old, watching boxing on TV. He got a bit excited and a few minutes later had severe chest pain. After a few days in the hospital he died."

"Straight forward case," she said.

"Absolutely."

A few tables down, Dr. Segrim was studying the lungs of a 30-year-old man who had been found dead in his apartment.

When George, the eldest of the six morgue men walked by, he asked, "Doc, do you want me to clean this table with Lysol?"

"Why?" wondered Dr. Segrim.

"It's TB, ain't it?" he stared.

At that point Dr. Segrim hadn't determined the cause of death. "Gert," he called Dr. Silverman, "Would you mind looking at these lungs?"

"Of course not," she obliged. With her I walked closer to the table. After an educated look she instantly concluded, "Oh, yes, this is miliary tuberculosis. Just take a few sections from the lungs and close it up." Her tone of voice suggested that he do so quickly, immediately.

As we walked away, I mentioned my surprise at the way George made the diagnosis while Dr. Segrim did not.

"George has been here more than 30 years," she said reluctantly. "Dr. Segrim is a neurosurgeon, not a pathologist."

She almost apologized for the doctor, but said no more. It was obvious that she never engaged in small talk, let alone mention anything personal about anybody.

Together we walked to the administrator's office, where one of his assistants gave me a contract to sign in accepting the position. As I signed my name, she waved, "See you in two weeks. July 1st."

126
Professor of Pathology

As a child I was positive that teachers knew everything. As a child in Iran, I was taught to respect a teacher as the highest authority after my parents and God. All three are infallible. Such inculcation convinced professors that because of their status in this world, their word should never be doubted. No one dared. No one even considered such a thing!

One day my professor of dermatology lectured on vitamin deficiencies. Feeling very superior with his French medical school background, he asked, "Are there any questions?"

One of the students raised his hand, "Are there any deleterious effects from an excess of any of the vitamins?"

For a moment the silence in the room was deafening. Since the possibility never occurred to the professor, he had no answer for the student. Instead, he shouted, "That's a stupid question." Not only was the student embarrassed, so was the teacher.

On his own, my classmate checked a reference on therapeutics, where he learned, "Excessive intake of water soluble vitamins is not harmful because they are easily discharged through urine. Oil soluble vitamins, on the other hand, could accumulate in the body and cause complications." (Years later it has been established that excessive doses of any vitamin may create toxicity.)

Even though he satisfied his own curiosity, he dared not report his findings to the professor. In that culture such an approach would be considered disrespectful on the part of the student and humiliating on the part of the teacher.

During my early years of training in the United States I flinched every time a student at any level would discuss a topic as though he were on the same intellectual level as the teacher. By the end of the third month of my residency at Queens General Hospital I presented a case of Christmas Disease. At the time not much was known about this bleeding disorder and simply identified by the name of the first patient in whom it was diagnosed. Only a few articles about it were published. Since I had to make this report to the medical staff, I had one of the secretaries type my summary of these reports in multiple copies.

In the audience sat Dr. Angrist, the previous director at Queens General Hospital Laboratories, now professor of pathology at Albert Einstein Medical School. When I had finished my presentation, he said, "I don't know anything about this disease. Would you please tell us all you know?"

For a moment I was almost in a state of shock. How could a professor of pathology confess to not knowing something about his specialty? Furthermore, how could he stoop to asking a young resident for such scientific information? After I gulped in disbelief, I repeated everything that I had read and gave him a copy of the summaries. With utmost sincerity, he thanked me profusely.

It took me years--many, many years--to realize that no one knows everything about anything, that there is nothing wrong with not knowing, but there is everything wrong with pretending to know. The most serious problem, however, is not knowing what one does not know!

127
Kissable Heart

Dr. Angrist had just been appointed chairman of the Department of Pathology at the new Albert Einstein Medical School in the Bronx. In spite of the prestigious position he continued to come to Queens General Hospital two days a week--Monday afternoons for a five-hour autopsy conference to review the most recent cases and Saturday mornings to review the surgical pathology slides of the week's work.

At the Monday conference about sixteen cases of all-gross autopsies were reviewed. One case focused on a 60-year-old man having chest pain and shortness of breath while spending a long time in the bathroom because of constipation. The man was brought to the hospital and treated for myocardial infarction. For about a week, he did fairly well. At that time the physician noticed a systolic murmur, a strong hissing sound on the left ventricular area. The patient suffered a perforation of the interventricular septum, which separates the left and right sides of the heart. A few days later died of heart failure.

Dr. Angrist listened most attentively to the presentation. Gross examination of the specimens revealed a very small opening involving the interventricular part of the heart. Such perforations due to myocardial infarction are indeed rare. With his typical exuberance he looked and almost screamed, "This is so beautiful. I could kiss it!" His reaction amused everyone.

Dr. Angrist was so respected, his presence at any of these conferences attracted a large number of physicians. His infectious enthusiasm inspired other physicians to appreciate the importance of pathology. When he could not attend, neither could many of the others.

His life was totally absorbed by his professional love for medicine, particularly physiopathology, the study of disease. Rumor had it that on his honeymoon a few gross specimens were found in the trunk of his car. Eventually his wife became accustomed to finding specimens and slides in their home.

So many stories were told about the man so long that they may have been embellished as they were retold. One such incident described Dr. Angrist opening the chest of a man and finding the heart weakly beating. Since the man was not breathing and there were no other signs of life, he cut out the heart and continued with the rest of the autopsy.

Mrs. Angrist often told many people that her husband was married to medicine.

128
Multilingual

Until Ali Tofigh was 12 years old, he lived in Azarbaijan and spoke Turkish.

During his high-school years he lived in Tehran and spoke Farsi.

When he attended medical school in Geneva, he spoke French.

For his residency in internal medicine he came to the United States and spoke English.

He met every challenge with enthusiasm. As a senior resident, for the weekly clinical-pathological conference, he presented the case of a 60-year-old patient who had been admitted to the hospital because of myocardial infarction. The patient who did not have a heart murmur on admission developed one by the third day of his stay in the hospital. Within a week he died.

A heated discussion about the cause of the murmur followed Dr. Tofigh's presentation. It was Tofigh's contention that the patient had developed a fistula between his two ventricles. As he tried to clarify his position, he spoke with such conviction that he became louder and louder, gesticulating like a windmill. In such a state of excitement, oblivious to the world around him, he switched from English to French, then to Persian, pretty soon to Turkish and back to alternating among the languages.

A few of the physicians understood French; fewer, Farsi; none, Turkish. Since Tofigh did have an accent when he spoke English, many people in the audience assumed that it was his accent that prevented the explanation from being understood. It became more and more stressful for his listeners to be polite and pretend to listen with undivided attention. They began to squirm in their chairs and shuffle their feet on the floor.

Finally, I could stand the tension no longer. I raised my hand and asked, "Would you please speak English so everyone can understand you?"

129

Trip to Paris

As Turaj, Hushang, Ali, and Jamsheed circled Paris aboard Air France, they couldn't wait to land at Orly and begin their long awaited vacation for a change of pace from the grueling studies at the medical school in Geneva, Switzerland. The sight of Notre Dame, Hôtel Dieu, the Eiffel Tower, the Seine and all the winding streets increased their anticipation with every second's delay. Each young man had such a litany of things to do and see, one would think they had a month to mingle with the French.

When they touched ground at Orly, the anticipation turned to irritation. The lines at the passport control just did not move fast enough. When they finally reached the immigration officer and presented their passports, the word IRAN seemed to turn into a flashing red light. For some unknown reason only they were directed to a room different from that of the other passengers.

Assembled in isolation they were subjected to a strip search as though they were heinous criminals, not mature students about to be physicians. Interpreting such a request as an insult, they refused to comply. Instead of removing their clothes, they removed themselves from the customs area and boarded the next plane back to Geneva.

The following day at breakfast they digested their croissants along with the news in Le Monde. The headlines reported "**Princess Ashraf Arrested.**" The day before they had their odd experience at Orly, the princess Ashraf, the sister of the Shah of Iran, met with an incident even more unexpected. With extreme self-confidence she deplaned and went through the routine immigration procedures, assured that her political passport would screen her from the usual delays and possible impertinence of government employees. Unfortunately, heroin was detected in her luggage.

That's why all Iranians were detained at Orly.

130
Hemorrhoidal Veins

To prevent discomfort and illness all parts of the body need attention and care. Otherwise; otherwise.

Most young people dwell on features of their body that encourage admiration, but disregard those parts that don't command attention--until something goes wrong. For instance, they completely disregard hemorrhoidal veins of the anus until painful swelling and/or bleeding occurs.

Hemorrhoids in young people who are not pregnant are usually associated with infection which follows improper, mostly compulsive, cleaning. Rubbing the mucosa and the adjacent skin over and over by paper (especially poor quality) causes minute superficial erosion, susceptible to infection.

About a year after I had arrived in the United States from Iran, I noticed rectal pain and bleeding. Since I no longer had immediate access to a water cleaning system when I used a men's room, I had to rely on toilet tissue. I became aware of the fact that several young patients from the United States and male patients from the Middle East had the same problem. In Iran the only young people with hemorrhoids were pregnant women.

The experience of Dr. Adl, a professor of surgery in Tehran, supported this theory. While interning in the hospital Hôtel-Dieu, he participated in a study of several hundred charts of young female patients with hemorrhoids. The research indicated that the incidence of hemorrhoids in prostitutes was significantly lower than that of non-prostitutes. Apparently, the use of water from a bidet, rather than toilet tissue, is gentler on delicate mucosa, even though the reason for the habit was concern for odor, not necessarily hygiene.

Out of sight, out of mind may be a truism about uncommitted lovers, but when it comes to hygiene the attitude could be catastrophic.

131
Tuberculosis

Three years in a row (1950, 1951, 1952) tuberculosis inflicted one more pathology resident at Queens General Hospital. The most recent victim interrupted his program, because he had to spend a year in a sanatorium.

Although the incidence of tuberculosis was diminishing by the early 1950's, occasional cases still occurred. To prevent further contamination there was an all-out attempt to eradicate all possible sources. Even samples of dust were taken from every inch of the Pathology Building for bacteriologic study. It was no surprise when some of the cultures came back positive.

As tuberculosis is a contagious disease, everyone had to be extremely careful to protect himself--even if he had minimal contact with the least insignificant item involved. During autopsies of such cases, the pathologists and morgue attendants had strict orders to wear disposable gowns, hats, boots, and double gloves. They were also ordered to limit the autopsy to just enough of an examination to make a diagnosis with no more than necessary handling.

One day the ambulance brought a 50-year-old executive. The pain and discomfort from his headache, nausea, and vomiting were so intense, he checked into the hospital. Just as his wife was registering him, his hand dropped from the gurney and he died.

By law all unexpected deaths must be autopsied. As the wife signed the consent papers for the autopsy, she mentioned her husband's recent business trip to Africa. A few of the doctors suspected some acute infection, such as miliary tuberculosis (a very acute form seldom recognized until the autopsy examination).

In the morgue the resident followed the rules, taking all necessary precautions by dressing appropriately. After the autopsy and microscopic examination, the pathologist realized that all these preliminary precautions had been an exercise in futility. This patient suffered from cerebral malaria, not tuberculosis.

Till this day, precautionary measures are exercised for cases of hepatitis, AIDS (acquired immune deficiency syndrome), or tuberculosis.

132
Land of Opportunity

Right after World War II the reputation of the United States as the land of opportunity was even greater than it is today.

In 1956 after four years in this country I had just finished my second year of pathology residency, earning a salary of $100.00 a month, and had finally been granted my permanent visa. A letter from my brother had me in hysterics when he shared the news about mutual acquaintances. According to the tales exchanged by my classmates in Iran, I was earning $100,000.00 a year. My brother congratulated me on this astounding financial success and naturally expected a share of my wealth.

To myself I muttered out loud, "I wish, I wish."

A few days later I was called to the phone.

"Allo," I heard in fractured English. "I . . . am . . . Dr. Mossaded. How . . . are . . . you?"

"Oh, Hi. I am fine. How are you?" I continued in Farsi.

"Do you remember me?" he wondered.

"Yes, of course I do. How could I ever forget the day you tripped a good-looking girl, a stranger simply passing by?"

He continued to explain how he was accepted to pursue a medical course at the Brooke Army Medical Center in San Antonio, Texas. He wanted the specifics about staying in the United States. Naturally, I recounted most of my experiences and cautioned him to be patient and prudent. After I went through all these suggestions, he behaved as though he hadn't heard a word I said.

"Talk to them," he said. "Tell them to give me a job for $100,000.00 a year and a permanent visa for me, my wife, and my son. We all definitely want to stay in the United States."

Stunned, almost speechless, I tried to tell him how his request, as important as it is (especially to him) cannot be granted in a matter of minutes. I tried to have him understand that only after four years did I finally obtain my own permanent visa, was earning only $100.00 a month, and still did not have a license to practice medicine.

Minor detail. He had no interest in my problems. Again he reacted as though he were deaf, "That's OK. Go ask them. Get me the job earning $100,000.00 a year. Don't forget the visa for my family. My father wants to come too. Tell them that he can repair old antiques."

With a sigh, I eventually was able to hang up. I never heard from him again.

133
Accident or Murder

The city ambulance pulled to a stop at the entrance to the city morgue. As the driver clicked open the back door, the morgue attendant came to his side to help wheel a body into the cooler.

James Brainer, a 25-five-year-old man, was found dead in his apartment not far from Queens General Hospital.

At the autopsy Dr. Segrim found nothing exceptional, other than a peculiar two-inch long track of infection involving the left temporal lobe of the brain, right behind the eye socket. The meninges (membranes covering the brain) were also infected in the same area. The entire brain was swollen.

Upon the suggestion of the police who found the body, James Brainer's girlfriend went to the hospital.

"When did you see your boyfriend alive last?" asked Dr. Segrim.

"Saturday night, three nights ago."

"Was he all right?" continued Dr. Segrim.

"Yes, he seemed ok."

"Did you go out with him Saturday night?" pursued Dr. Segrim.

"No, the two of us had dinner at his place."

"Did he drink a lot?"

"A lot?" She thought for a moment. "We both had a few drinks. We never got drunk or anything."

"Did anything unusual happen?" asked Dr. Segrim, totally stymied.

"Well, we had a little argument about my poodle or something. James hit me, so I picked up an ice pick and hit him back. When the ice pick went into his eye, I pulled it out immediately. Fortunately that did not hurt him. He just had a drop of blood in the corner of his eye. Otherwise, he was perfectly o.k. when I left him in his apartment. He was just a little mad at me."

Now Dr. Segrim understood the reason for the peculiar infected track in the brain. Instead of offering the explanation to the girlfriend, he called the police from the lobby into his office.

The officer advised the young lady to call a lawyer and not to leave town. "This looks like murder, not necessarily premeditated first degree. Nevertheless, it's murder."

Dr. Segrim reminded everybody, "That pronouncement is up to the judge."

134

Pat on the Back

6:00 p.m. in January is almost as dark as midnight, but I never mind early darkness because I am a night person. While most people slow down as the day goes along, I function in reverse. I pick up speed.

One day when I had an autopsy on my schedule, I decided to take care of the matter right after dinner, rather than wake up early the following morning to take care of it before my routine work. Dressed in scrub suit, gown, and gloves, I picked up the chart and proceeded to the morgue.

The night attendant was sitting behind his desk, registering the two corpses just brought in. "Is my case on the table, Mr. Bernard?" I asked.

"Yes, Doc, everything is ready. Call me if you need help."

"Thank you." According to normal procedures I started cutting the Y-shaped incision. As I tried to remove the chest plate (the sternal bone), pulling the muscles of the shoulder, I felt someone behind me, tapping me on the back. No doubt Mr. Bernard, I assumed.

When I turned around though, no one was there.

I continued, struggling with the sternum. Again I felt something touching me. I never did believe in ghosts, but now I had my doubts.

The third time I felt this nudge and the third time saw no reason for it, I went to the office and asked Mr. Bernard to give me a hand. Actually, I didn't need him for the autopsy. I needed him for peace of mind.

"What would you like me to do, Doc?"

"Cut the muscles of the chest on the left, as I am doing on the right."

"OK, I'll try."

Whenever he pulled on the muscles, the stiff arm of the body swung up and patted him on the back.

I felt like doing the same thing for a job well done.

135

100-year-old Physician

Dr. James J. Ronald finished medical school in New York at age 25 and passed his state board examination that gave him a license to practice medicine. He soon passed his specialty boards and practiced dermatology in a prestigious office building shared by many other physicians on Fifth Avenue in Manhattan.

About 25 years later he invited his son to work in his office. By this time James J. Ronald, Jr. graduated from college, but was not accepted into any medical school. Since he was not gainfully employed, he reluctantly accepted his father's offer with the stipulation that he quit as soon as the nurse returns from her vacation.

Working close to his father, he soon enjoyed everything he learned. Being a rather intelligent young man, he soon learned a lot. Within a few months he was able to make a proper diagnosis and determine the treatment. Every time he met a patient with a problem different from what he had seen so far, he would borrow his father's medical books and become completely engrossed in the subject.

Ten years later he was still working for his father in spite of the fact that the nurse had returned to work and had since retired. The son now seemed to know just as much as his father. While the father practiced as the professional, the son became a "practical dermatologist." Unwittingly, nurses, secretaries, and patients soon referred to him as Dr. Ronald. And neither Ronald objected to the practice. The son became so proficient, he was able to manage the office in his father's absence. He cared not only for management, but for patients as well. He even attended a few of the dermatology meetings--first with his father, later by himself registering as the Dr. Ronald, dermatologist.

By age 75, the real Dr. Ronald suffered from hypertension, coronary heart disease, and emphysema. The younger Ronald became more and more responsible for the activities at the office. The last five years of Dr. Ronald's life, his son represented him at conferences, registering under the older man's name and license. The practice became so routine, he never stopped to think that he really was not a physician. Assuming the role of his father was actually illegal.

Twenty-five years later, when Ronald, Jr. was 75 years old, officials of the Board of Health and Education made a routine random check on physicians' credentials. As they reviewed the application for renewal, they noticed that the physician was 100 years old. Investigations soon had the office closed and the "practical dermatologist" arrested.

136

Mixed Marriage

As the saying goes, "Show me who your friends are and I'll tell you what you are." Subscribing to this adage, Mary Margaret's parents invited her fiancé Kouros and a few friends to a picnic at their home on Long Island. While the older brother Tim flipped hamburgers and hot dogs on the grill, the younger brother Michael was deeply engrossed in Sports Illustrated. The guests sat around on lawn chairs, enjoying the freshly mown lawn, cool breeze, and shop talk of their fellow doctors and nurses.

Mrs. O'Toole, the mother, was especially interested in the conversation as she wondered about her future son-in-law's background. She did not exactly approve of his dark skin, Moslem religion, and his grating foreign accent. She had many questions about his family, childhood, and his home in Sharifabad, Iran, from which he could view the mountains from the roof of his house where he slept on hot summer nights.

The only thing that seemed to interest Mr. O'Toole was the Irish whiskey which he sipped nonstop. At the mention of sleeping on the roof, however, his bushy white eyebrows went up into an upside down V. His red cheeks got redder and only accentuated his snow white hair. He mumbled, "What kind of people would sleep on a roof?"

Just then the telephone rang. Mrs. O'Toole sprinted into the house to answer it.

"Michael," she shouted from the opened window, "telephone."

Michael, the youngest brother, seemed like a clone of his father. They both had a handsome shock of hair, penetrating blue eyes, ruddy cheeks, and a comatose attitude. To answer the phone, though, he did jolt out of his chair, bouncing on the plastic webbing.

No sooner had he reappeared and sampled a hamburger on the grill, the phone rang again. The mother sprinted again. "Michael, telephone," she shouted again. Michael jolted away from the crowd again.

Mary Margaret explained to everyone that the prom was coming up in a few weeks and all the girls keep asking Michael to be their escort. They seemed to be calling him all day long.

After five more such calls, Mrs. O'Toole stomped into the house, not caring how many times that phone would ring. We could see the outline of her body in the front room, moving most deliberately. She disappeared from view as she probably bent down, then jerked up to a standing position with something dangling from her clenched fist. As she yelled more forcefully than ever, "Michael, telephone," she threw the phone out of the window onto the lawn.

All along, Kouros leaned back comfortably in the chaise longue and observed his future relatives with utmost curiosity. "Doesn't my future father-in-law do anything but sip liquor and snooze? Doesn't my future mother-in-law ever have a moment of tenderness? What will life be like spending more time with such people? Will my future wife ever behave like either of her parents?"

137
Studebaker

A year after I had bought the secondhand English Hillman it began to show its age, wear and tear. While I tried to drive the car, it was driving me out of my mind. Every time I stopped for a red light, it would groan, stall, and stop. After a few twists on the ignition key and heavier pushes on the gas pedal, it usually started again--with a few sputters (automotive obscenities, perhaps). Too often it simply refused to budge.

Fortunately, the Hillman was small and light weight. As a strapping young man, especially once I got my adrenalin up, I could put the gear in neutral, push the vehicle out of the line of traffic, and run for help.

It didn't take long for this car to exhaust my patience. I sold it for $200.00.

One lunch time as I was chanting my complaints about this Hillman, Dr. Wessley offered to sell me her 10-year-old Studebaker that she was about to trade in on a new Chevrolet.

"How much?" I asked apprehensively.

After a pregnant pause, she scratched her head, pursed her lips, and offered, "Two hundred bucks."

"It's a deal. That's all I have anyway."

I drove that Studebaker for two years without ever taking it to a garage for any maintenance, not even lubrication. Occasionally I glanced in the rear view mirror and saw black smoke. After a little more than a year, when I had gas added in the back of the car, I had oil added in the front. It wasn't long before I would stop at a station and tell the attendant, "Fill up the oil and check the gas." The gas station attendants always gave me a strange look.

By 1960, when I had a real job, I sold the Studebaker for $20.00 and bought a brand new car--a big, 8-cylinder Pontiac for $1,700.00.

138
Englishman

One winter day in 1957, two new interns joined Dr. Ron Mendelssohn and me in the dining room. One was British.

Ron, who fulfilled part of his military obligation in India, was telling us how some young American soldiers would kick the deprived natives or their animals over the cliff and then laugh it off as a joke as they drove off in their trucks.

I bristled over such inhumanity and interjected, "Such repulsive behavior is not uncommon. I saw many American, British and Russian soldiers doing things in Tehran during World War II that they would never even try to do in their hometown. Many would urinate in the middle of a crowded street. Many would get so drunk that they would get into a fight with each other. MP's would pick them up quickly and haul them off to their base to make sure that they would not be subjected to forty lashes in the public square, punishment according to Moslem law."

Dr. Patrick, the chubby intern from London, mentioned how many foreigners have taken up residence in England since World War II. "Some of them are obnoxious. The Egyptians are all thieves."

"Are you sure?" I asked in disbelief.

"Yes, I am," he answered most emphatically.

"How many Egyptians do you know?" I wondered.

"Quite a few. Quite a few."

"Like one?" I challenged him.

"Perhaps two," he admitted. "Look what they did to the Suez Canal."

"Oh, you're talking about the president of Egypt. It's Nassar that you don't like."

Then he softened his tone, looked at me, and asked, "Are you Egyptian?"

"No, I'm not," I assured him. "But I do know that Egypt has twenty million people. Do you honestly believe

that every single one of them is a thief?"

To break up this argumentative discussion Ron Mendelssohn glanced across the room, looked at his watch and said, "It seems that the kitchen help is ready to close this place. We better leave."

139
Iranian Bandits

After a hectic day in the lab I was almost the last dinner customer in the hospital cafeteria. Right behind me came Dr. Walter Rustic, a thoracic surgical resident from Triborough. With a tray of food in one hand and a newspaper under his arm, he pulled out the chair across from me. "Boy, does it feel good to sit down. I sure earned my $5.00 today."

"How were you so overworked?" I asked to give him a chance to let off steam.

"First thing in the morning I had a pneumonectomy which took until 1:30 this afternoon. That delay made me late for afternoon clinic. All those patients were automatically likewise delayed, and now so is my dinner." We sat together as we ate our meals and commiserated over the hectic activities of the day.

Suddenly we changed the subject to the world news of the day. "Wait till you see what I have to show you," he added as he shook the newspaper to unfold in front of my eyes.

Americans Killed by Iranian Bandits

Jokingly he scolded, "Look what your countrymen are doing to Americans."

I had no idea what he was talking about. Then I read that three Americans were killed by a group of bandits in the mountains of Baluchestan in southeastern Iran. One of the three was a woman. Mr. and Mrs. Kevin Carrol and Mr. Brewster Wilson were the Americans, all of whom worked for the International Cooperation Administration. The name of the legendary outlaw was Dadshah. He was being pursued by the state police under the command of General Gol-Piera.

"Obviously," I said, "these people were in the wrong place at the wrong time."

"What do you mean?"

"Would you and your wife walk around Harlem at two o'clock in the morning?" I asked.

"Oh," he mumbled and took the page from me, "OK, OK. I get it."

He then turned the page and shared tidbits of other news items. Another story gave the account of an assault by an 18-year-old boy on an old rabbi in a park in Brooklyn. The young man clubbed him to death with a baseball bat. When the judge probed for a reason for such heinous behavior, the boy answered, "For the heck of it."

"Which of these two is worse?" I asked Dr. Rustic. "The uneducated mountain recluse turned bandit or this Brooklyn high-school graduate turned murderer?"

He had no answer to my question, but he did notice that the victims in both cases did not belong in that particular area. They were strangers, foreigners in the land.

"How could the rabbi be considered a foreigner?" I wondered.

"Many consider Jews 'foreigners'. Did you ever notice those who dress differently and use non-English words? They are victims of prejudice. Many people, especially WASPS (White Anglo-Saxon Protestants) hold such opinions."

The next day when I glanced at the first page of the New York Times, I learned that Premier Hussein Ala of Iran may leave his post because of the killings. I doubted that the kidnaping had any bearing on his departure, but a few days later he did resign.

His replacement, Dr. Eqbal, happened to be the professor of infectious diseases at the University of Tehran. In addition to his interest in medicine, he was likewise interested and involved in politics. Earlier that same year while he was in New York City, all Iranians in the area were invited to come to shake his hand. Most people suspected that he was being groomed by the Shah to be in the public eye and be seen with the educated, especially those educated in the United States. In Iran such exposure was favorable to the political system.

140
Swiss Graduate

At Queens General Hospital out of 120 interns and residents, about 30 were foreigners. Of the 90 Americans, 30 were graduates of foreign medical schools. Since European medical schools right after World War II had very low enrollments, those Americans not accepted into medical schools in the United States would go to Europe. With the help of the GI Bill the majority seem to have studied in Switzerland or Italy, where $150.00 a month would cover all their expenses (including tuition).

Ron Mendelssohn was one of those Swiss graduates. At one of the meetings about rheumatic heart disease, when he made a comment about the mitral valve, he pronounced "mitral" "meet ral," as the French would.

Dr. Silverman, Canadian native as well as Canadian graduate, commented in disdain, "The second you pronounce the word *meet ral,* everyone identifies you as a foreign graduate."

No one else breathed a reaction. Almost half of the doctors in the room had some foreign background.

Being a foreigner seems to be an automatic stigma. According to the laws of the state of New York, graduates from the United States, Canadian and British medical schools qualified to take the State Board examination to get a license after one year of internship. In addition to the internship, before qualifying for the examination, graduates from French, German, Swiss or Italian schools had to take a one-year postgraduate course which covered a concentrated review of all medical school subjects. Physicians from any other country had to take two years of postgraduate courses. Only then could they take the test. Even if a foreign graduate already had a license to practice medicine in a different state in the United States, New York did not grant reciprocity.

Neighboring states, however, had no such

prejudices.

It appeared that such rules were encouraged by Dr. Ezzel, the Secretary of the New York State Board of Medical Examiners in Albany. Years later, when he no longer held this position, the rules were no longer in effect.

141
Dinner in Manhattan

One Sunday evening Dr. Marquis, one of the senior pathologists, invited four of the residents, including me, to dinner with her. Before enjoying a meal at a restaurant on Broadway, we were to wait for each other in front of the Singer Sewing Machine Shop on 42nd Street, east of Broadway, near the subway station.

Ten minutes ahead of time I was at our appointed meeting place. Since it was after shopping hours in that neighborhood, the stores were closed and the crowds were gone.

October in New York can be rather chilly, so I wore my new gray flannel suit. It was my first American major clothing purchase. (It cost me $40.00.) I felt good because I was well dressed and many of my friends made a point to tell me so.

As I stood at the entranceway to this Singer store, a young, well-dressed man went by slowly, begging, "Can you spare a dollar, so I can get a drink?"

He looked healthier, stronger, and better dressed than I. "No," I answered and turned my head away from him.

But he came closer to me, stopped for a second, and spat. He let go such a long stream of saliva that it flew high above my head against the plate glass window and made a slimy stream all the way down to the edge near the sidewalk. The incredible amount of saliva convinced me that he was a drug addict. At the same time my four friends were crossing the street toward me. I was glad to see them for more reasons than hunger.

About 2 ½ hours later we decided to walk around Times Square before returning to Queens. As we watched the tourists crane their necks to watch the moving tickertape and the animated billboards on this most sparkling intersection in New York City, we were equally dazzled by people rushing in all directions to gift shops, restaurants, theaters, even pawn shops.

Before we started for home, Dr. Marquis recalled that she had to make a phone call. While she went into a cafeteria in search of a public phone, the rest of us waited outside on Broadway.

We soon realized that it was taking her an awfully long time to make a phone call. When we tried to enter the cafeteria, the door was locked and nothing but the night lights were on. When we pressed our noses against the glass, we could see her still talking in that phone booth with the door closed.

She did notice us and she too realized that she was on that phone a long time. So she hung up.

At the exit, however, she could not open the door. Above it was a large transom partially open. Unfortunately, in order to reach it, she would have to be twice as tall as she was. "What am I going to do?" she screamed in panic.

We communicated with gestures and finally decided to get the help of a policeman. At least this was no problem. Downtown Manhattan seems to have at least one policeman patrolling every block. The one we found couldn't believe Dr. Marquis' predicament. He couldn't get her out either.

From the phone box on the light pole he notified his department, who in turn notified the fire department, who in turn sent an engine with ladders. After one fireman climbed a ladder, he slid another through the opening. He then opened the transom wider, climbed down to the interior of the store, and helped Dr. Marquis to leave the way he entered--up, through, and down. Police cars came to keep the peace and photographers came to get some news.

By midnight I was never so happy to be on a subway train.

The following morning the story appeared in most of the New York papers with pictures of the fire truck and everything. As she requested, however, her picture and name were not included.

142

Price for a Visa

After an internship in Tokyo, Hiroshi Sogetsu, a handsome Japanese young man, became engaged. Upon the completion of his pathology residency in the United States, he was to return to Japan for the wedding.

During the first year of his four-year absence, Hiroshi's girlfriend soon grew tired waiting for him, so she married someone else. He was devastated. He decided to stay in the United States, never to return to Japan. Such an easy decision, however, was difficult to realize. The easiest way to get a permanent visa was to marry an American citizen. But Hiroshi did not want an American wife; he preferred a Japanese.

Handsome and sociable as he was, he had no difficulty dating any of the nurses, especially since they knew that he just wanted company, not a permanent relationship. One day one of his friends suggested that he marry her sister on a temporary basis. "Once you get your visa, you then get a divorce. You should know, though, that she is about six years older than you and not exactly gorgeous. She is very smart, though. She's a self-supporting accountant and has her own apartment in Queens not too far from the hospital."

Out of sheer desperation, Hiroshi agreed to meet her. At first sight he found her quite homely and introverted. A few months later Hiroshi discovered that her personality outshone her looks. Nevertheless, they both agreed to the "temporary marriage."

Soon they became more than friendly and Mrs. Sogetsu became pregnant. This state of affairs depressed him to the point that he spent most of his time reading or working in the hospital. He even slept in his room there, rather than at home. Nine months later Hiroshi became a father to a little boy who looked just like him. Even this event did not improve his attitude.

Hiroshi's hair became prematurely gray and made

him look older than he was. Even with this appearance of added years, his wife looked older yet. He never attended any social functions with his wife. He never even introduced her to any of his friends. Behind his back his friends often commented, "What a price to pay for a visa!"

Years later this marriage ended in divorce.

143
Charmer

Dr. Miller, a dermatologist, often came to the pathology department at Queens General Hospital. Unlike other physicians, he seemed to have an inordinate curiosity about the diagnosis of each skin lesion of each of his patients.

One day in order to look at a few slides through the microscope he sat next to Dr. Erica Hunter, one of the young female pathology residents. In fact, had he moved one centimeter closer, his hundred-pound thigh would have been on her lap. Instead of discussing the disease, he was telling a joke. His voice boomed so that no one had any doubt about the topic of this conversation.

"One old couple took a vacation to India, where the wife became fascinated with snake charmers. With the magic of his flute one of them made a thick cord stand straight up for at least five minutes. Amazing. More so was his confidence that anyone could play the flute and produce the same results. The husband, however, could care less. His lack of enthusiasm was no surprise, because absolutely nothing excited him these past few years.

"Nevertheless, the wife paid the snake charmer $25.00 and bought the flute. They continued their vacation, eventually returned home, and resumed typical activities of their lives.

> "One night when they should have been sound asleep, the wife began to play the flute. Lo and behold, the sheet over her husband lifted--right above his middle. She was so excited, she dropped the flute and jumped into bed to snuggle next to her husband. When she lifted the sheet, perfectly erected was her husband's pajama string."

Dr. Shirley Hunter needed no such titillating humor, definitely not from a married man who was not her husband. She simply smiled and went on with her work. Everyone else laughed as a matter of courtesy and wondered why this old "coot" didn't concentrate on his own wife. Eventually Dr. Miller got the message and stopped coming around the lab.

No one even heard about him till three years later. At the age of 68, Dr. Miller divorced his wife to marry his 22-year-old secretary. Their honeymoon came to an abrupt ending when he was unable to consummate the marriage.

His impotence distressed him so, he sought help from a urologist. Physical examination disclosed a large, firm prostate. The biopsy confirmed his physician's suspicions of cancer. The only treatment was total prostatectomy, total disappointment for such a man.

Not long after his discharge from the hospital, he went to the house he was having built for his new wife on Long Island supposedly to check on progress. When the second Mrs. Miller went there to see what was keeping him so long, she found him lying on the living room floor with one hand on his wispy gray hairs and the other stretched alongside his breathless body with the gun only inches away.

144
Sputnik

Rumor had it that in the 1950's after WWII many German scientists who wanted to pursue their professional interests had no other choice but to move to the USSR or the USA. Jokes told how the Russian unmanned Sputnik and the American unmanned Explorer were circling the earth. As one artificial satellite passed the other, they both commented, "We can speak German now, there are no Russians or Americans around."

145

Liver Conference

Every Friday afternoon between 4:00 and 5:00 p.m. about one hundred male physicians of the house staff of Queens General Hospital gathered in the conference room. Since many of them celebrated the end of their work week with a hearty drink of beer, they called the meeting "Liver Conference" since liquor affects the liver adversely. Even a few sips gave some of them a license to lose all inhibitions and try to top each other with dirty jokes or accounts of sexual exploits. Sometimes they discussed and complained about their low pay as interns and residents. Most of the time was spent socializing, getting better acquainted to feel free to approach one another when they really did need to communicate.

The last two years of my residency every member of the house staff of every major hospital in New York City was assessed five dollars a year. For a fee of $1,000.00, the money collected from the doctors, a lawyer sued the city for paying the physicians less than the janitors.

By order of the court the city then had to pay each physician at least $500.00 a month. Unfortunately, the ruling went into effect the month *after* I had finished my senior year of residency that awarded me $150.00 a month.

146
Sex in the Garden

At the "Liver Conference" a speaker occasionally entertained the house physicians. With the announcement of the topic "Sex in the Garden," every doctor made sure that he attended that Friday's session. Even though all 120 people were encouraged to attend, all 120 were not expected. For one thing, the conference room wasn't large enough to accommodate such a crowd. That weekend, however, the room was bulging.

Dr. Dole began, "Sex is always exciting to everyone. After self-preservation, reproduction is the most important function of all living things. In the evolutionary realm genes which are not reproduced are replaced by those which are. If a person could reproduce by oneself, not only would he propagate his own genetic material, he could eliminate a tremendous waste of time and energy which accompanies sexual attraction and reproduction.

"The advantage of sexual reproduction, however, is the combination of genetic material from different sources which is important in the natural process of evolution. Colorful and beautiful flowers that please so many are the genital organs of the bushes and trees. These flowers exist in order to attract the agents, like bees and butterflies, who facilitate cross pollination. Certain orchids produce an aroma and color to mimic the female of certain species of bees and thus attract the male."

As the speaker went on and on and on, projecting illustrations and graphs, it became obvious that his subject had nothing to do with the pleasures that the physicians anticipated--in or out of the garden. One by one, these young men in their twenties disappeared from the audience just as quietly as the butterflies in question. When the lights flooded the room after the presentation, every other seat in the conference room was empty.

147
Argument

From time to time I would accept invitations to parties. The people you saw at work were the same people you saw at the parties. Within minutes the conversations turned to shop talk, the same old thing you would discuss in the hospital anyway. To such gatherings came interns, residents, student nurses and their guests (usually spouses, sometimes friends). They all mixed to eat, drink, dance, listen to the music, or just chitchat. In spite of the drinking, the guests were mature enough to behave discreetly--usually.

At times it seemed that some of these people had no inhibitions about anything. In regard to behavior there seemed to be no difference between male and female. This was in contrast to women in Iran who were very submissive to any male in the family.

One night, Dr. Mark English, a handsome intern with the reputation of being a womanizer, brought Nancy, his latest acquaintance. Like him, she was extremely good looking and pleasant.

As the drinking and dancing continued throughout the evening, their admirable demeanor turned ugly. Their shouts almost drowned out the music. Suddenly the girlfriend stopped dancing in the middle of the floor, stomped her foot, clutched her bosom, and pulled out both of her falsies. "Here," she screamed, "if this is what you want, take them!"

"Damn it," he mumbled, "I thought that was the only real thing you had."

"Oh, yeah?" she retorted. Louder and louder she screeched with each word, "Take me home. Now. I want to go home. Now. Now."

"I'm not ready to leave," he answered most assertively. "The party just began."

The shouts and insults volleyed until Dr. Leonard Smith politely suggested that he drive her home.

"No," she yelled louder than ever. "I came with that S O B and he has to take me home."

Dr. English was not to be outdone in the screaming field. He shouted obscenities back at her--until a few people gently walked him out of the room.

Eventually the girlfriend did listen to reason and let one of the nurses take her home.

I knew that Americans speak their minds, but this woman was beyond belief. A few American men who talked about the incident considered her to be out of line.

148

Elections

While Kennedy and Nixon debated national issues on television, the rest of the Americans debated among themselves about which one would win this presidential election. The way people argued during the lunch hour, it's a wonder that indigestion didn't become the national health problem. Arguments flew in all directions.

"The force behind the Kennedy campaign is Joe Kennedy, the father who spent millions of dollars," said Dr. Firestone.

"Actually," commented Dr. Powell, "What is against him is the fact that he is too young and too Catholic."

"Did you hear the joke?" asked Dr. Fishman.

"What joke?" I wondered.

"Apparently some reporter asked Kennedy if it is true that he has adrenal cortical insufficiency. Kennedy responded, 'Compared with President Eisenhower's brain cortical insufficiency, that's not bad'."

At this time Dr. Erica Hunter, a pathology resident who seldom participated in political discussions publicly declared, "I am going to vote for Kennedy."

"Are you really?" asked a few of the listeners at the same time like some chorus.

"How did you reach that decision?" I asked, impressed with her political assertiveness. I wondered how she found the time to keep abreast of political issues and study the background of the candidates.

"Well," she pursed her lips and thought for a moment, "he's rich and he's handsome. What else do you want?"

This prompted a chorus of laughs.

Years later I read that President Nixon had the same opinion of his opponent. In his memoirs he stated, "I considered Kennedy's biggest assets to be his wealth and appeal of his personal style."

149

License to Practice Medicine

Armed with my permanent visa (green card), I had to declare my intention of becoming an American citizen within the next five years. Since I intended to do so, I had to find a job to be able to live like one. Like every other foreign graduate, I had to comply with the rules of the state of New York. First I needed information about eligibility. As a physician from Iran, I was required to take postgraduate courses to be eligible for the examination. I immediately wrote to Dr. Ezell, the secretary of the Board of Medical Examiners of the State of New York, asking for the necessary forms. I also applied to several other states, because I doubted a favorable response from Albany. Some states required citizenship that I as yet did not have. In Connecticut, Illinois and Virginia, however, I was eligible.

As expected, the response from Dr. Ezell's office repeated the ruling. I had no choice but to take a two-year postgraduate course either at New York University or at the New York Polyclinic Medical School and Hospital, both in Manhattan. New York University supposedly was very strict about daily attendance and charged a thousand dollars each year. At Polyclinic, on the other hand, attendance was not checked as thoroughly and the tuition was $800.00 a year. Without any hesitation I chose Polyclinic.

The New York State Board of Examiners further demanded that I take and pass a high-school equivalency test to prove that my communication skills were adequate to take the medical exams. At this examination, questions covered mathematics, physics, chemistry, biology and English. The only difficult part was English, which seemed to concentrate on Shakespeare. I was positive that I had not made an acceptable grade. To my surprise, however, came a large envelope containing my "High School Equivalency Diploma, #9638."

Hiroshi and I started the first year of the

postgraduate course September 15, 1959. Every day Hiroshi and I took the subway from Queens to Manhattan. Parts of the review were interesting, but most were a waste of time for me, covering the basic essentials of what I already knew well. The hour's ride each way provided the opportunity for me to read. Rather than tote a heavy textbook, I had cut up Anderson's Pathology into chunks of several pages which I could bend and squeeze into my breast pocket. (I wondered what my mother would say if she saw me tearing my brand new book apart.) While riding the New York subways, I read the entire book twice.

In order to support myself while I attended class that first year, I worked nights and weekends. Dr. Silverman, head of the department of pathology at Queens General, who knew me well by this time, was short of residents, especially for such coverage. As a compromise to pursue the course during the day, I worked those odd hours at night. Because of the work I was able to still live in the hospital and earn $150.00 a month.

It was about this time that physicians became aware of the importance of pap smear tests, early diagnosis of the cancer of the cervix, and subsequent treatment that saved many lives. This discovery made front page news and became a popular subject for politicians. The United States Department of Health and Welfare provided generous grants to doctors, hospitals, and laboratories to make this test available to all female patients. Along with money to pay for the tests, funds were available for preparing the slides by gynecologists and reading them by pathologists.

In charge of the money allocated to the department of pathology, Dr. Silverman divided it among the senior residents willing to spend extra time learning the technique and reading the microscopic slides. On an average day the lab processed about 10 trays involving two hundred slides. For each patient there were two slides: one vaginal and one cervical.

For one year this grant money promised me an additional hundred dollars a month for diagnosing pap smears every other night. Although this took several hours that I usually devoted to study time, it paid for the course at Polyclinic and taught me much cytology.

It was during the first postgraduate year that I took the state board in Connecticut. I went to New Haven by train, a short ride from New York City. The examination consisted of basic sciences for two days and six months later, medical sciences for three. Answering multiple-choice questions was one more new experience for me. My Connecticut license, #9394 dated April 21, 1959, was my first license to practice medicine in the United States.

I really had no intention of leaving New York City, because by this time I was familiar with the area, established meaningful friendships, and enjoyed professional relationships. Nevertheless, this license made me eligible to take the examination that would qualify me as a board certified pathologist.

At the end of the first year of the postgraduate course I already was a board eligible pathologist and had a license to practice medicine in Connecticut. Under those circumstances I requested permission to take the State Board examination for a license to practice medicine in New York at this time, rather than after another year of repeated postgraduate course.

Dr. Silverman suggested that I get a letter of recommendation from Dr. Angrist, who knew me from my first year at Queens General Hospital and my frequent visits to Albert Einstein Medical School. She even offered to call him and urge him to do so.

The following Monday morning I went to Albert Einstein Medical School with other residents to participate in a pathology conference about electron microscopy as a diagnostic tool.

After the meeting I stopped at Dr. Angrist's office to ask for the letter of recommendation. He thought a bit, looked at me, and said, "I have written too many of these this year. Since Dr. Silverman recommends you, I will write this one too, but when you write too many of these, the people in Albany only disregard them." True, he did not know me well, but he gave me the impression that my unusual name and my accent created a negative impression.

Two weeks later a letter from Dr. Ezell's office denied my request because I needed another year of the postgraduate course.

"Bureaucratic minds do not change easily," I thought.

Because of the continuing shortage of residents during the second year of the postgraduate course, Dr. Silverman accepted my request to stay another year as senior resident at Queens General Hospital.

As an added service I volunteered to organize a surgical-pathology conference every morning. Once again Dr. Silverman graciously agreed to my plans and offered to help in anyway possible. From then on, in addition to the pap smears, I read the surgicals every night. Out of a daily 50-case average I selected the 10 most interesting. These led me to research the topics in question to such an extent that I could discuss them with confidence the following morning. These daily conferences not only helped me with all the examinations I was taking, but created so much enthusiasm for the residents, that when I left a year later, Dr. Silverman decided to continue the practice.

When the pap smear grant was awarded to another resident, I was offered a part-time job at Booth Memorial Hospital. Every afternoon between 1:00 and 5:00 p.m. I helped Dr. Ancel with gross and microscopic surgical specimens. For these four hours a day I earned an annual salary of $6,000.00 and vast invaluable experience in surgical pathology.

Booth Memorial, a new nonprofit hospital with 250 beds in one building and 50 in another for unwed mothers, was managed by members of the Salvation Army who offered their services for very small remuneration. Those employees who were not members of the Salvation Army earned wages typical of the same work elsewhere. Members, however, enjoyed pension plans, modest apartments and free medical care. Much of the practice concentrated on private patients. As in religious oriented hospitals, poor patients were taken care of with no question of payment.

About the same time the American Medical Association along with a few other institutions, like the American Hospital Association, had formed a council and devised an examination for foreign medical graduates--ECFMG (the Educational Council for Forcign Mcdical Graduates). By testing English communication skills, as well as medicine, it would qualify foreign trained physicians to do residency in the United States. Even though I had completed my residency program, I was among the first to take this two-day exam in New York. (I felt like a professional test taker.) A few months later I received one more certificate, this one dated March 16, 1960 and numbered 4328.

My next exciting venture was on a national basis. On April 21, 1960, I flew Braniff Airlines to Memphis, Tennessee for $57.37. Three nights at the Good House hotel cost me $27.78. My greatest expense was the three-day pathology board examination--one hundred dollars, the most expensive examination yet. Given twice a year, it changed venues each time.

Memphis in April was a wonderland of flowers at their peak. I rode through the streets in awe, but had no time to enjoy the natural beauty of the area.

I was surprised to see Dr. Angrist, professor of pathology at Albert Einstein Medical School, old enough to retire, taking an exam for the newly created specialty of Forensic Pathology. (In Iran it was rare for an adult to pursue an intellectual challenge beyond graduation.) Angrist was so famous that one young pathologist commented, "They'll probably give it to him anyway, just because he is Angrist."

Thanks to my excellent training at Queens General Hospital and my reading efficiency forced on me by the lack of free time, I breezed through the anatomic pathology examination. Even though Queens General Hospital was approved for both anatomic and clinical pathology, none of the pathologists had any interest in clinical pathology. As a result, my training and experience were extremely limited and I found the clinical part of the exam extremely challenging. None of the physicians from Queens General passed this second part of the test.

From an academic point of view I was officially a board certified pathologist, but I was not happy with my poor performance in clinical pathology. For the next few years I read extensively on this subject and participated in every educational program that I could. When I returned to retake this part of the test, I passed with flying colors.

It was unfortunate that the AMA authorities who

approved hospitals for training did so without adequate investigation or periodic unannounced inspections for re-approval. The heads of the departments were aware of the lackadaisical approach, yet felt no need to improve their programs.

Back in New York City, I was armed with my certificate dated 21 April, 1960 of qualification--Board Certified Pathologist. It has no number on it, but it has the signatures of one president, six vice presidents, and five secretaries. Till this day I have never seen so many signatures on any one certificate. This accomplishment qualified me for the title "Diplomate."

The second year of the postgraduate course I did not attend any classes. Hiroshi signed me in and out. I went to Polyclinic only on days of scheduled examinations. I did go, however, to the graduation ceremony and received one more diploma. The course at Polyclinic ended on June 3, 1960.

At this point I had satisfactorily completed two years of postgraduate school which cost me $1,600.00 tuition.

The course may have been most insignificant, but this piece of paper was not. It made me eligible for New York's medical licensure examination, which I took and passed that following September. Certificate #84853 gave me the right to practice medicine and surgery in the state of New York.

Within a few months I flew American Airlines to Chicago to take the Illinois exam. The round-trip ticket cost $74.20 and the fee for the exam was $50.00. This last exam was one of the longest. It took five entire days. Besides the stress of such a mental ordeal, I had the misfortune of having a very noisy hotel guest in a room right above mine. All night long he would stomp across the floor and drop heavy things with a bang, creating noises that deprived me of my sleep.

On October 3, 1960, I received certificate #36-36920. Unlike no other license, this one had the name of the governor of Illinois right across the top, William G. Stratton.

For my last exam for medical licensure I went to Virginia.

When I was scheduled to take the test in Richmond, I was already licensed, board certified and employed. I really did not need another license. In that frame of mind, I enjoyed the trip to Richmond as though it were a vacation. License #15064, however, added one more certificate to my files.

Practicing pathology the next 41 years, 36 of them outside of New York, acquainted me with West Virginia, Michigan and Pennsylvania. I never did work in Connecticut, Virginia, or Illinois. The states where I did work granted me licenses by reciprocity.

Today these certificates, diplomas, and licenses are like pictures in a photo album, reminders of the good ol' days. While these mementos remind me of the importance of diligence in studying and working, for others they are just scraps of brittle paper. Once I am dead they become meaningless. They hold no memory or inspiration for anyone else. They should be burnt along with my corpse.

* * * * *

Dr. Ezell, the secretary of the Board of Medical Examiners for the State of New York, was the most difficult person that I ever dealt with. Years later I was not surprised to learn that he was arrested and jailed for accepting a $25,000.00 bribe from an Italian candidate for giving him the examination questions a few days ahead of time. The candidate apparently sold copies to ten more people and charged each one $5,000.00. Some of these went around talking, only to get everyone incriminated.

After Dr. Ezell's departure from the State Board of Medical Examiners, the postgraduate courses for foreign graduates were eliminated.

150
In Practice

As assistant pathologist at Booth Memorial Hospital, I had no problems until Dr. Ancel took a week's vacation and left me in charge of the laboratory. Should an unusual condition occur with patients, specimens or test results, the pathologist is expected to return the situation to normal.

In the midst of a busy morning, Mr. Rutz, the chief chemist, charged into my office, almost screaming, almost breathless, "Sorry if I'm interrupting you, but you better talk to this guy. I can't cope with this." His face became more flushed with each word. "An hour ago Dr. Howard ordered a stat bilirubin to be done at 3:00 p.m. I am confused. Does he want it now or at 3:00 p.m.? When I called him to clarify this dilemma, he blew his top. <u>You</u> talk to him."

I followed him to the chemistry department and picked up his phone. "Hello. This is Dr. Payan. What can I do for you?"

"This is Dr. Howard. I don't like technicians questioning my orders."

"Are you referring to Mr. Rutz, our chief chemist?"

"I don't give a damn what his name is. The point is that <u>he</u> is a technician and <u>I</u> am a doctor. When <u>I</u> order something, it has to be done. Period. Done. That's it!"

"What is it that you ordered?"

"I ordered a bilirubin on a pregnant patient stat at 3:00 p.m."

"Stat means now," I tried to explain.

"This is not an autopsy," he began to bellow at me. "This is clinical medicine. And I am the doctor, not someone who works in the lab."

The insinuation that I, a board certified pathologist, was not a doctor, made me bristle. Like never, I lost my composure. Each word as deliberate as a stab with an ice pick, I responded, "Doctor, if I knew as little clinical medicine as you, I would give up medicine and hang myself." If my words did not pierce his ear drum, the bang of the phone certainly did.

The chemist breathing more calmly by now and overhearing the entire conversation, explained, "Dr. Payan, one technician is on vacation, another called in sick this morning, and only one other person is here to help me. We don't have time to answer phone calls like this."

"That's O.K. Let me see the slip, please. He never did say why he was ordering bilirubin, anyway."

I took the slip, took the elevator to Maternity on the fifth floor and read the patient's chart. Eight months pregnant, the patient suddenly developed pain in her right upper abdomen and became jaundiced. "Who's the consultant on this case?" I asked the nurse.

"Dr. Tobin."

I then had the telephone operator get Dr. Tobin on the line. "Good morning, Dr. Tobin. This is Dr. Payan, the pathologist."

"Good morning. How are you?"

"Fine. Do you recall a Mrs. Rebecca Enceinte, a lady eight months pregnant who has jaundice?"

"Oh, yes. Is there a problem this morning?"

"Well, somewhat. An hour ago Dr. Howard ordered bilirubin 'stat' at 3:00 p.m. I wondered about the time."

"Oh," his voice trailed in surprise. "I told him 'bilirubin stat and 3:00 p.m.'."

"That's fine," I answered, thankful that the mystery was solved. "Thank you very much. Good bye." I put the slip on the desk, changed the "at" to "and," so it now read, "stat" and "3:00 p.m."

Back in the lab I explained the situation to the chemist. Dr. Tobin suggested monitoring the bilirubin in the patient's blood for possible obstruction of the bile duct.

Anticipating some repercussion from Dr. Howard, I filed a written report explaining the groundless complaint from the obstetrician.

A week later the chemist came to my office again, this time smiling. Dr. Howard apologized for his rude behavior. In fact, ever since then, Dr. Howard has been most polite to me too.

151

Delayed Publication

Suffering from hypertension and heart failure, an elderly woman consulted her doctor. For hypertension she received diuril (a diuretic); for the heart problem, digitalis (a stimulant). Since diuretics lower one's potassium level, potassium chloride tablets became necessary treatment.

For years this patient followed her doctor's orders and felt fine. One day, however, she experienced acute abdominal pain and fever. After she agonized for a day at home, the intense pain became unbearable. Her doctor admitted her to Booth Memorial Hospital, suspecting bowel obstruction.

Twenty-four hours later--in spite of antibiotic therapy--she died. Unexplained deaths, by law, had to be autopsied. As I opened the abdomen, I noticed peritonitis, general infection. Further examination revealed a three-millimeter perforation of the small bowel at the center of a one-and-a-half-centimeter ulcer, one and a half meters from the stomach. Lying in the ulcer bed was a potassium chloride tablet. Instead of being dissolved and digested, it was lodged tightly against the bowel wall. The potassium chloride appeared to have chemically destroyed the mucosa, gradually perforating the bowel.

As routine procedure the medical photographer photographed the lesion while I carefully noted the details in the autopsy protocol. This was such an unusual case, I presented it at several conferences and eventually described it for possible publication and sent it to the Journal of Gastroenterology.

One month after I had sent out my manuscript it was acknowledged as #3733. It was not accepted for publication because the editors had no precedent for such a medical phenomenon.

Never having submitted anything to any periodical, I lacked experience in the format and strategies of doing so.

I was an assistant pathologist of a hospital laboratory that dealt with real patients in a real world. I was not in an academic environment that coupled the practice of medicine with research and speculations. Somewhat disappointed, definitely discouraged, I simply filed my rejected report with other important papers.

Three years later, toward the end of 1964, the AMA Journal and Acta Shirurgica Scandinavica each published an article describing five similar cases.

Immediately, I resurrected my manuscript, rewrote the article now amended with references to these two reports, and on December 24, 1964, resubmitted it to the Gastroenterology Journal, the very same magazine I considered from the beginning. As manuscript #4895 it was published six months later. Two months later, in August, 1965, the Yearbook of Drug Therapy requested my permission to reprint the article in their revised edition about to be printed.

Four years later, July 29, 1969, the State University of New York requested permission to use the pictures and the report as part of their Report on Pharmacy, a continuing education series for pharmacists.

Neophytes in all disciplines find prestigious titles of editors intimidating. Even as early as Pericles, people obeyed authority unquestionably. So too I was in awe of such supposedly accomplished men as editors and accepted their judgment of my work as final.

Years later as I became more experienced and self-confidant, I discovered that some of the editors of professional journals making decisions about manuscripts are usually no better than an average physician.

152
IRS

As long as I was in Hartford, taking the state board examination for a license to practice medicine in Connecticut, I looked up my classmate Dr. Mahmood. Immediately after graduation from medical school he came to the United States, did pediatric residency, got a license, established a practice, married an American nurse who worked with him in the office, and became an American citizen.

That day when I visited him and his charming wife, we had a few laughs about "the good ol' days."

Years later he told me that a few days after my visit two FBI agents visited him in his office, asking questions about me. Apparently, I had become one of the twenty-five million people who had a dossier filed with the FBI in J. Edgar Hoover's office. Since the Eisenhower administration had friendly relations with the Shah of Iran, the United States Armed Forces had informed the FBI of Iranian military personnel who defied their Iranian Army orders to return to Iran.

However, since there was nothing illegal about anything I had done, my name (like many others) went to the Internal Revenue Service (IRS). My tax paper returns (Form 1040) fell under scrutiny for about 20 consecutive years. In 1960, I paid $2,093.54 in taxes out of the $14,747.70 that I earned. After the audit I was told to pay an additional $140.00. My accountant saw no reason for this additional sum, but I was in no mood to take on the IRS. Besides, the accountant's fees would probably cost me more than this $140.00.

Years later, with the help of a lawyer and the financial planning of the Aetna Insurance Company I arranged a "deferred compensation plan." Since physicians were not allowed to invest in tax-deferred savings for retirement, I had to resort to some way of saving for my old age. Naturally, my next income tax return included details of this plan.

The following summer, the IRS auditor declared it illegal. Once again I had phone calls, letters, and personal meetings with the lawyer and a representative from the Aetna Insurance Company. Six months later after I had spent $1,200.00 more on lawyer and accountant fees, the IRS official was proven wrong and I have never been audited since.

153

Without an Accent

One evening with a few others I was invited to the Ahans for dinner. By the time all the guests had arrived, Mrs. Peggy Ahan had everything ready. The only missing detail was our host: Dr. Ahan, a surgeon. He had promised his wife to be home on time, but one hour after the expected time, she had yet to see the whites of his eyes. Minute by minute, she was becoming less and less patient.

As he rushed into the house, like a gust of wind, she was happy to see him, but not too happy that he had been detained.

Dinner had hardly begun. The salad was passed around for seconds when the phone rang. Sure enough, it was for the doctor. He was called to the hospital for an emergency involving one of his patients who was bleeding. He was so upset about having his evening disturbed and having his wife disturbed even more, he slammed down the phone and yelled, "Oh, Shit!"

His wife, an American, commented, "That's the only word he can say in English without an accent."

154
Boys Will Be Boys

Shapoor and Jamsheed, like other Iranians who went to Medical School in Paris after World War II, often met each other on Sundays for a glass of beer, friendly talk, and relaxation. Some days they met at Chez Dupont; others, in the Jardin de Luxembourg.

When the studies at Faculté de Médicine in Paris became a challenge not only because of a foreign language, but for the content of their courses, the least association with "home" became a blessing. Every Sunday they made each other the priority of the day.

One humid afternoon they sat under the awning of a *brasserie*, sipping their *Bière Alsace* and watching the world go by. From their vantage point along Boul' Mich, they enjoyed the parade of students (female, of course) just as much as they enjoyed their cold French beer and ham sandwiches. The conversation soon centered on the passers-by. "You know, I have been here in Paris for a whole year. I have yet to see a French girl giving me the come-hither look. It seems as though everything we heard in Iran about loose French women was just a bunch of bull."

Jamsheed, who had been in Paris for three years, decided, "Oh, yeah. In Iran people told us all kinds of stories. So . . . when you and I go back, we too will do the same--just tell stories, only ours will be wilder than anything they had ever heard before."

Somewhat disappointed about the state of affairs in regard to loose women, Shapoor added quietly, almost remorsefully, "Actually, it was better in Iran. Persian women--even those who wore the chador--were much, much easier to get close to--if you know what I mean."

Jamsheed stared at his friend. "Hey," he scolded, "you and I were supposed to go back to Iran and tell stories about loose French girls. You're not supposed to tell me stories in France about loose Persian girls."

155
Transfusion

At 2:30 p.m. just before nurses changed shifts, Susie, the head nurse of the third floor, stopped in the laboratory to pick up the results for the patients on her floor. As she was walking out, Peggy, the blood bank technician, asked her, "Would you please take up the blood for George M. Springer? It's ready now."

"Sure," she agreed, got the blood, and left. On the floor she gave the blood to one of the new nurses and told her that it was for George M. Springer.

As the young nurse prepared the transfusion tray, she checked the name on the unit against the patient's name. Approaching the patient, she told him, "We are ready to start your blood transfusion."

George M. Springer, a 60-year-old man expecting to have bilateral herniorrhaphy the following morning, wondered why he needed blood, but decided not to question the experts. "They must know what they're doing," he surmised.

An hour later the nurse from the fourth floor called the laboratory, looking for the blood for Mr. George M. Springer.

Peggy told her that Susie had already taken it up.

"Well," huffed the fourth floor nurse, "there must be something wrong. She works on the third floor. This is the fourth. Where did she take it?"

"The third floor."

"No, no. George M. Springer is here, on the fourth floor and we still do not have the pint of blood we ordered for him."

They hung up and Peggy then checked the list of hospital patients. That day there were two patients in the hospital with exactly the same name and middle initial.

Peggy ran to the pathologist's office, where I was reviewing the surgical slides.

"Doctor," she said breathlessly. "There are two patients in the hospital by the name of George M. Springer, one on the third floor and one on the fourth. One of them is receiving the wrong blood. And I don't know what to do."

"Where is the George M. Springer who is getting the blood?" I asked.

"Third floor."

"Let's go." The two of us rushed to the third floor, where we met the head nurse of the evening shift and continued to the patient's room.

To stop the flow immediately I put a clamp on the plastic tubing. By this time, however, the patient had already received about a third or 150cc of the unmatched blood. As I explained to the patient what had happened, I recorded the incident in the chart.

Back in the office I called the patient's physician to inform him of what had happened.

Another pint of blood was cross-matched for George M. Springer on the fourth floor, the 70-year-old man with anemia.

George M. Springer on the third floor had his herniorrhaphy the following morning. Within a few days he developed jaundice, a complication of mismatched blood transfusion. That delayed his discharge from the hospital.

His physician urged him to sue the hospital and collect insurance money, as much as he could get. A settlement out of court brought him $50,000.00.

The entire incident was reported to ABBA, the American Blood Banking Association.

A month later ABBA ruled that from now on, the labels on all blood units include the hospital admission number in addition to the first name, middle initial and last name.

156
Cancerophobia

In recent years preventive mastectomies have been performed on those who have a strong family history of breast cancer.

In 1959 a forty-year-old lady underwent unprecedented surgery to have both breasts removed. When I examined the specimens in the laboratory grossly, they appeared perfectly normal. Further examination under the microscope confirmed my suspicions.

Before I signed the report, I showed it to Dr. Ancel, the chief pathologist. He too examined the breasts, both grossly and microscopically, and agreed with my diagnosis. Surely, this was a case for the tissue committee, who review the performance of surgeons.

I then signed the report. Along with a copy for Dr. Quentin, the surgeon, copies went to the tissue committee. After the members of this committee agreed that neither breast should have been removed, copies of their decision and my report went to the executive committee of the hospital.

Dr. Quentin was called to the executive committee to defend the surgical procedure. During their next meeting, he detailed the concerns of the patient. A 38-year-old very good friend of hers had died of cancer of the breast. One year later a 40-year- old neighbor had likewise died of cancer of the breast. The possibility of the same fate for her gnawed at her peace of mind constantly to the point that she could not always function normally. The surgeon's diagnosis was "cancerophobia." After a few consultations in his office he agreed to do the procedure. Afterwards she was perfectly happy and healthy.

The rationalization was not acceptable to the medical community. When Dr. Quentin's privileges at the hospital were revoked, he apparently said, "I am in charge of my patients. Nobody will tell me what to do."

After enjoying a successful practice for 30 years, Dr.

Quentin was affluent enough to snub his detractors and build his own hospital a few blocks away. Such wealth gave him control which corrupted him. He believed that he could do whatever he felt was right, rather than follow the dictates of the scientific community.

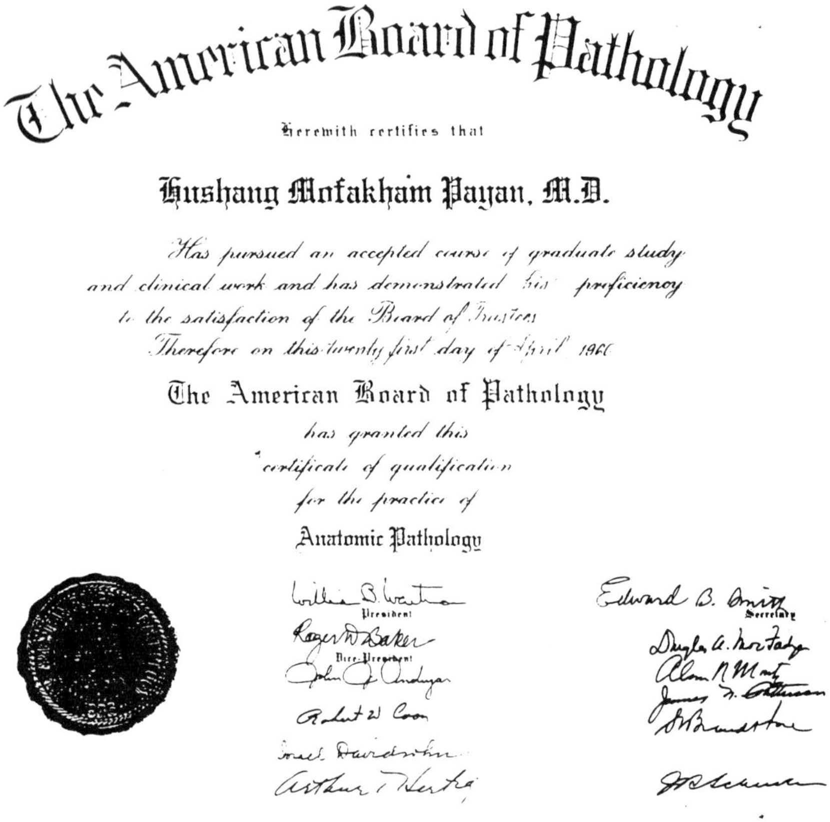

The American Board of Pathology

Herewith certifies that

Hushang Mofakham Payan, M.D.

Has pursued an accepted course of graduate study and clinical work and has demonstrated his proficiency to the satisfaction of the Board of Trustees

Therefore on this twenty first day of April 1960

The American Board of Pathology

has granted this certificate of qualification for the practice of

Anatomic Pathology

President

Vice-President

Secretary

157
Alcohol Abuse

Not all physicians are affluent or assertive. Jim Murphy, who was three years ahead of me in residency, had been married for five years already and had two children. Doris, his wife, a few years younger, was also a pathology resident. Because they both worked, Doris's divorced mother lived with them to take care of the children.

While Doris's mother loved her grandchildren, she hated her son-in-law. Because of his drinking habits her opinion of him was clouded to the point that she never saw anything positive about him. After living with this family a while, she was absolutely sure that her daughter should get a divorce.

Jim's periodic depression interfered with his work and efficiency at the hospital, as well as home. To "drown his sorrows" he would have a drink . . . or two . . . or more. Such drinking led to more depression; the depression, to more drinking. He was caught in a vicious cycle. When his friends and colleagues tried to help him, even cover up for him, he interpreted their concern as interference. Since he could not recognize the seriousness of his problem, he refused to join Alcoholics Anonymous. In 1957, when it came time for him to take the pathology boards--which are given once a year--his state of anguish impeded his performance. He failed. In 1958, when he took the exam the second time, he failed the second time. When I sat for this examination in 1959, Jim was just a few rows away from me, taking it one more time--only to fail one more time.

The destructive consequences of Jim's alcoholism escalated. Hoping to help her husband take control of his life, Doris dropped out of the residency program to be a full time wife and mother. This plan didn't work either.

The couple separated. Doris, her mother, and the children continued to live in an East Side apartment. Jim moved into an efficiency in the Bronx. This personal crisis led to devastating drinking and intensified his depression to such an extent that his only recourse was to see a psychiatrist.

A few months later, while Doris and the children were buoyed by the spirit of the holidays and the activities on Christmas Eve, Jim went to his office at the deserted medical school, where he worked as an instructor, and drank a whole bottle of whisky. Late that night the security personnel noticed smoke coming from the bottom of the closed door. When they knocked, no one answered. They then tried to open it, but it was locked. All the while, the smoke was getting thicker and thicker. By this time they heard crackling sounds. Within minutes of their alarm, the building was surrounded by firemen and their trucks.

By the time the guards and police reached Jim, he was dead. According to the death certificate, the cause of death was "smoke inhalation." Jim's friends felt sure that he died because of depression and alcohol abuse, but they were all reluctant to mention it.

158

Immigration Officer

In spite of the legal entanglements, I was determined to stay in the United States. Perhaps the difficulties only intensified my determination since they became quite a challenge. An episode now engraved in my memory that will last forever took place in the Immigration Naturalization Office in New York City. Just before I left Queens General Hospital I finalized the requirements for citizenship.

Officer (*barking without looking up from his paper*):	What's your first name?
HMP (*meekly*):	Hushang.
Officer (*gruffly*):	How do you spell that?
HMP:	H-U-S-H-A-N-G.
Officer:	Your middle name?
HMP:	Mofakham.
Officer:	What? Talk louder. How do you spell that?
HMP:	M-O-F-A-K-H-A-M
Officer (*finally looking at me*):	And your last name?
HMP:	Payan.
Officer:	Spell that too.
HMP:	P-A-Y-A-N.
Officer (*looking back at his papers*):	When were you born?
HMP:	January first, 1925.
Officer (*in a monotone*):	Where were you born?
HMP:	Iran.
Officer (*now like a robot*):	Spell that, please.
HMP:	I-R-A-N.
Officer (*looking up at me*) :	What is your address now?
HMP:	Queens General Hospital, New York.
Officer (*looking back at his papers*):	You live in a hospital?

HMP:	**Yes, sir. I am a physician, a resident.**
Officer:	**Your profession?**
HMP (*hesitating because the officer had just been told*):	**Physician.**
Officer:	**You work in that hospital?**
HMP:	**Yes.**
Officer:	**What is your salary for the year?**
HMP (*getting tired of all these details that seemed to have nothing to do with application for citizenship*):	**$1,800.00 a year.**
Officer (*staring at me, speaking slowly in disbelief*):	**Is . . . that . . . all . . . you . . . make . . . a . . . year?**
HMP:	**Yes, Sir. I'm only a resident physician.**
Officer (*looking at me from the corner of his eye*):	**But you are an M.D.?**
HMP:	**Yes, I am.**
Officer:	**Where did you go to school?**
HMP:	**The University of Tehran.**
Officer (*in a questioning tone of voice*):	**The University of what?**
HMP:	**Tehran.**
Officer:	**How do you spell that"**
HMP:	**T-E-H-R-A-N.**
Officer:	**In which country is that?**
HMP:	**Iran.**
(*anticipating his next question, I spelled*):	**I-R-A-N.**
Officer (*cocking his head in wonder*):	**By the way, where is Iran?**
HMP:	**In the Middle East.**
Officer (*looking back on his papers*):	**What is your nationality?**
HMP:	**Iranian.**
Officer:	**So you're an Arab.**

HMP:	No, I'm not.
Officer:	Then since you're from the Middle East, you're a Jew.
HMP:	No, Sir.
Officer:	So, what is your nationality?
HMP:	Iranian. Some people call Iranians Persian.
Officer:	And what would you call yourself?
HMP:	Iranian.
Officer:	Iranian? And that is neither Arab or Jew?"
HMP:	No, Sir. Iranian is Iranian or Persian.
Officer (*looking back at his papers*):	Have you ever been a beggar?
HMP (*somewhat surprised*):	No, Sir.
Officer:	Have you ever been a thief?
HMP: (*somewhat irritated*)	No, Sir.
Officer:	Have you ever been a prostitute?
HMP (*almost shocked*):	No, Sir.
Officer:	Have you ever been a Communist?
HMP (*wondering if anyone ever answered "Yes" to any of these questions*):	No, Sir.
Officer:	Have you ever been a member of a political party?
HMP (*not too sure what one does as a member of a political party*):	No, Sir.
Officer:	Have you ever been involved in an anti-American activity?
HMP:	No, Sir.
Officer:	Are you married?

HMP:
(***blurting***)
(***now feeling nervous because the lawyer stressed the importance of never volunteering any information)*** — **No, Sir, but almost. I am engaged.**

Officer: — **Is your fiancée American?**

HMP: — **Yes.**

Officer: — **Where did you meet her?**

HMP: — **In the hospital where I work.**

Officer: — **What does she do in that hospital?**

HMP: — **She's a doctor.**

Officer: — **Did you sleep with her already?**

HMP (*blushing with embarrassment*): — **No, Sir.**
(*remembering that my lawyer advised me to stay calm, no matter how stupid the questions seemed*)

Officer: — **Do you have a lawyer?**

HMP: — **Yes, I do.**

Officer: — **Then why isn't the lawyer here with you?**

HMP: — **He didn't feel it was necessary for him to be here with me. If you, however, want him to be here, I can certainly arrange the meeting for another day.**

Officer (*still not looking up from his papers*): — **No, that won't be necessary. You can go now.**

HMP: — **Thank you very much. Good bye.**

159
Citizenship

The courtroom was packed. People chattering in every language imaginable remained standing, waiting for the judge to appear.

Exactly on the appointed time the judge's voluminous black robe preceded him. "Raise your right hand," he said mechanically. As he raised his gray head and gave a sweeping look at the entire audience, he continued, "When I pause, repeat after me:

> "I hereby declare, on oath, / that I absolutely and entirely / renounce and abjure/ all allegiance and fidelity to any foreign prince,/ potentate, / state, or sovereignty / of whom or which / I have heretofore been a subject / or citizen;/ that I will support and defend/ the Constitution and the laws / of the United States of America/ against all enemies,/ foreign and domestic;/ that I will bear true faith/ and allegiance to the same; / that I will bear arms / on behalf of the United States / when required by the law; / or that I will perform/ noncombatant service / in the armed forces of the United States / when required by the law; / or that I will perform / work of national importance / under civilian direction/ when required by the law;/ and that I take this obligation freely / without any mental reservation / or purpose of evasion; / so help me God."

After a longer pause the judge again gave a sweeping glance at the group, lowered his arm and signaled, "You may lower your hands now." With a broad smile and a nod he said with enthusiasm, "Congratulations. You are now citizens of the United States."

Everyone applauded and the judge left the room. People began talking out loud, hugging each other, and even crying from joy.

Joe Rapucci and I had come together from the hospital and stood next to each other during the ceremony. This was a turning point in our lives, just as important as the successful completion of our medical residencies. We congratulated each other.

In his Italian accent Joe remarked reflectively, "You know, I think they are letting too many foreigners into this country. Pretty soon this place is going to be just as crowded as Europe. Too many people."

As I smiled, I unconsciously replied, *"khod-bin."* (selfish).

160

Lousy Foreigner

All living creatures violently react to the intrusion of anything foreign. When skin is damaged by a foreign material, like a piece of glass, white blood cells instantly erupt and surround the intrusive material to protect the skin, to inhibit further destruction and to destroy the foreign matter, e.g. bacteria. Lymphocytes, fibroblasts, and huge foreign body giant cells form an army around the site of injury. Such an event is a natural reaction of the body to defend itself from what does not belong there by encircling, eliminating, or destroying the foreign material. E. O. Wilson, a sociobiologist, describes the maximum cooperative behavior against a stranger by insiders of a group--such as wild birds, Canadian geese, and farm chickens.

In a broad context "foreigner" indicates anyone somehow different from the person using the term. Roget's Thesaurus lists endless connotations of the word: alien, stranger, outsider, barbarian, exile, outlaw, wanderer, refugee, emigre, displaced person, hostile intruder--anyone not belonging. The word "foreigner" has a negative connotation. "Lousy" adds indignation. Such derogatory expressions exist in every language of every nation. In Iran foreigners are called *kharejee kaseef* and in France, *sal étranger*--both meaning "dirty foreigner."

The fear and distrust of anything or anyone foreign is deeper than skin. For the sake of self-preservation, fear of the unknown is a basic instinct of all living things. As a group, people become one large entity with the same makeup. To protect themselves, they enact laws of immigration to control foreigners from intruding into their domain.

Distrust of a foreigner, anyone with a difference, is not new. Around 4000 B.C. the earliest Sumerian records in Cuneiform writing show the same symbol for "slave" as for "foreigner." Around 3000 B.C., under the pharaohs of

Egypt, foreigners were captured and forced into slave labor maintaining government buildings and temples.

Around 2000 B.C. Hammurabi, the king of Babylon, received his code of laws from the Sun-God-Shamsha. These laws legitimized the use of captured foreigners to remain shackled while they built roads, canals, and palaces. Punishment of crimes was harsher for these slaves (foreigners), than for the free people guilty of the same offense.

Rulers who sacrificed people to their gods preferred foreigners. King Amenhotep of Egypt (1300 B.C.) used prisoners and foreigners to be sacrificed and dedicated at the temple to the God Amon. To appease their god around 500 B.C., Druids (an order of powerful priests among the Celts in the British Isles) sacrificed foreigners taken as prisoners of war.

Averse to manual labor, the Greeks in Athens had most of the work done by foreigners. Three groups made up their work force: slaves who were unransomed prisoners of war, slaves who had been set free, and metics who were free men but foreign born. None of these three groups could become citizens, marry a Greek. or vote. Aristotle (384-322 B.C.) and Lysias the Orator (459-380 B.C.) were among the upper class metics.

Among other famous Greek personalities, even Alexander was considered a foreigner. His mother Olympias, a powerful woman in her own right, carefully guarded her daughter-in-law Roxane and her grandson. After Alexander's death in the struggle for power she ordered the death of approximately one hundred people, presumably her enemies who were at the same time supporters of Cassander, one of Alexander's generals. Cassander besieged the city where Olympias lived and threatened the inhabitants. Relatives of the victims whom Olympias had killed retaliated by stoning her to death. Cassander later poisoned Roxane and her fourteen-year-old son. He then proclaimed that Alexander was never a true heir to his father Philip because his mother Olympias was a foreigner, a barbarian.

When the Greeks were conquered by the Romans and thus used as slaves, the talented, educated ones were kept separately and shown only to the wealthy. Slave trading was such a lucrative enterprise, that wealthy Romans followed the armies, bought these people like merchandise from soldiers, and sold them the same way in the marketplace. These foreigners were exhibited with a sign hanging from their necks disclosing the country of origin, age, and intellectual achievements. The slaves were absolute property of the master.

As early as 1000 B.C. slavery also existed in Media and Persia. Here too, slaves--war captives or foreigners--were forced to do manual labor, such as farming and personal services. In Iran slavery continued as late as the mid-nineteenth century, 1848, when Muhammad Shah issued a *farman* (decree) forbidding the "importation of slaves into Iran by sea." There seems to be no mention of admitting slaves by land.

Around the time of the birth of Christ, some warring nations slaughtered their prisoners, rather than use them as slaves. Romans sent some of them, mostly captives from Germanic peoples and Gauls, to the *familia gladiatorum* (gladiator school) and trained them to fight and kill each other. Originally, such gladiatorial games (250 B.C.) were part of funeral ceremonies. Later they evolved into entertainment in front of massive audiences. At times, as many as 10,000 gladiators were involved in this popular contest for a period of 123 consecutive days.

About the same time (186 B.C.) in the Colosseum, sporting events featured contests between ravenous beasts and captive foreigners or criminals. In these pagan times early Christians, as foreigners, were often pitted against lions. To whet their appetite, animals were kept hungry. To frustrate them to the point of anger, the floor of the Colosseum was one enormous maze in this arena measuring 280 feet by 175 feet.

Around 640 A.D. Arabs used captured foreigners as domestic slaves or soldiers. Salman Farsi (Ruzbeh), a famous Iranian slave freed by Muhammad, became his teacher and adviser. Some Moslem sects, particularly the Nasairis, not only respect Salman Farsi, but consider him the archangel Gabriel himself who brought the revelations to Muhammad.

In the Koran any allusion to someone different is not expressed as "foreigner," but as "unbeliever," nevertheless subject to the same ostracization.

5:82	Strongest against man in enmity to the believers wilt thou find the Jews and Pagans.
2:231	Do not marry unbeliever woman.
3:28	Let not the believers take unbelievers for friends or helpers

In religious accounts references to foreigners are not limited to the Koran. The Old Testament repeatedly urges people to be kind to strangers and foreigners. Such advice obviously had to be specific in order to control those who were not kind to foreigners.

Leviticus 19:33	And if stranger sojourn with thee in your land, ye shall not vex him.
Jeremiah 22:3	Do no violence to the stranger, the fatherless, nor the widow.

In spite of all these admonitions, there is evidence of discrimination against foreigners.

Deuteronomy 23:20	Unto a stranger thou mayest lend upon usury; but unto your brother thou shalt not lend upon usury.
Numbers 3:38	Keeping the charge of the sanctuary for the charge of the children of Israel; and the stranger that cometh nigh shall be put to death.
Deuteronomy 14:21	Ye shall not eat of anything that dieth of itself; thou shalt give it unto the stranger

that is in thy gates,
that he may eat it; or
thou mayeth sell it
unto an alien.

About 300 A.D. the Roman Empire was plagued by political decay and economic disintegration. Free rural workers abandoned the farms to the slaves--foreigners incapable of operating them efficiently. In order to have their land yield a better profit, many landlords emancipated their slaves and changed their status to *coloni*, tenant farmers. Because of the lack of slaves and/or foreigners now, services in the cities, like road maintenance, deteriorated. The previous slave-foreigners soon became restless. In order to support themselves, they joined the army which eventually attacked the wealthy, the former owners of these very same people. With direct pillaging of the well-to-do the social and economic order deteriorated as the order of *coloni* and serfdom throughout the Middle Ages flourished.

During the Crusades, Christians and Moslems enslaved each other. In spite of the brotherhood proclaimed by each, slavery flourished. In the late Middle Ages, as the population of Europe increased, slave trade became insignificant. Of these few, most of the foreigners were Slavic.

After the Black Death (Plague) around 1400 the government of Florence, Italy approved the importation of infidels as slaves--foreigners from Greece, Russia, and Central Asia.

Around the 1500's the development of colonial expansion and the commercial revolution in western Europe created a tremendous demand for human labor. The British, French, Dutch, Spanish, and Portuguese all enjoyed profitable African slave trade. In less than admirable partnerships with the Europeans, tribal chiefs in Africa increased their wealth considerably. This time the captured foreigners were Africans exported to the Americas. Millions of the young captives died at sea en route to the Americas. Most of those who did survive the passage received brutal treatment from the owners. On several occasions efforts to enslave American Indians were made, but failed. The

Europeans seemed to forget that they, not the Indians, were foreign to the territory.

As plantations developed in the South, so did the need for workers. Young Black foreigners were bought and sold and often mistreated by the slave traders. This practice continued through the 18th century, during which about fifteen million Africans endured such treatment in the Americas.

In 1807 the British Parliament outlawed the trading of slaves; and in 1833, slavery itself.

By the 1830's anti-slavery sentiment in the United States became quite strong, especially in the North.

On December 22, 1862 President Lincoln signed the "Emancipation Proclamation" declaring all slaves to be free on January 1, 1863.

Two years later slavery was abolished by the thirteenth amendment to the United States Constitution.

Since the 20th century, slavery has become illegal in most of the countries around the world. Cheap labor and abusive treatment of foreigners, however, still exist in regard to migrant workers, tenant farmers, servile marriage, and sham adoptions. The September 23, 1996 issue of US News and World Report relates the exploits of a meat packing company in Iowa which recruited illegal Mexicans (foreigners) to perform the dirtiest, most dangerous, most repugnant work refused by local employees. Some scholars of finance believe that everything filters down to economics.

Racial differences are not the only reason for prejudice. Differences in language, culture, habits, morals, dress and the last, but not the least, religion create antipathy. Just as children fear strangers (the unknown), adults fear foreigners (likewise the unknown). Human instinct, more so than reasoning, dictates man's behavior.

Anti-foreign attitudes exist everywhere. While vacationing in England we were having dinner in a medieval castle changed into a restaurant and nightclub. After realizing that most of the guests were American, the emcee made a joke about pronunciation, "This is a *costle*, not a *castle*, and it is not for sale." In Iran for the 50 years before Khomeini the educated officials tried to delete Arabic words from Farsi, like *Allah*, *salaam*, *ghamar*, and *shams*. In France within the past few years repeated attempts have been made by the government and the French Academy to eliminate the usage of English words, like drug store, parking, shopping or weekend. A Parisian friend of ours mentioned that Frenchmen constantly complain about foreigners, but since visitors bring money, nothing can be done about them.

Irene, my wife, and I have toured the province of Quebec several times. In small towns when she speaks English at some place of business, the people react as though they do not understand and ignore us. But when she repeats the same message in French, they immediately accept her and to show friendship answer in their best English. This behavior has been repeated so many times, it's obviously a signal that French Canadians have a negative attitude toward anything English.

Some 30 years ago in Paris I was with a group of Americans standing in line to enter the Eiffel Tower. An older Frenchman also came with two ladies to see this monument, but he decided to go to the head of the line as he thought himself privileged because he was French. The lady at the head of the line, however, who was quite large, wearing cowboy boots and a Texas hat, grabbed the Frenchman by the shoulders, turned him around, and said, "No you don't, you God damn old man. Get in the back of the line." All the people in the American group cheered and applauded heartily. The man left, but not without calling her *sale étrangère*.

Until recently any alumnus of a medical school outside the United States or Canada was classified by Americans as a foreign graduate. Nowadays they are considered IMG's, international medical graduates. Most people who speak a second language naturally have an accent. Most people who have neither interest nor talent for any other language but their native tongue immediately label the foreigner "stupid." The faulty pronunciation leads the natives to believe that the foreigner's education is lacking. Such a stereotype clouds most foreign graduates for most of their lives.

One evening, Dr. Kim, a native of Korea, was the surgeon on call when an obese young woman came to the emergency room with her mother, complaining of vomiting and acute abdominal pain. An ultrasound examination disclosed gall bladder disease with stones. The patient was then referred to Dr. Kim, who scheduled her to have laparoscopic removal of the gall bladder first thing in the morning.

While Dr. Kim's laparoscope searched for the gall bladder, all of a sudden he noticed the face of a fetus. The patient never mentioned pregnancy. Since she was eight months pregnant, the uterus had extended up to the area of the gall bladder. Noticing that he had perforated the uterus and the embryonic sac, Dr. Kim removed his laparoscope immediately. Within minutes a Caesarian section was performed. The gall bladder surgery was postponed.

A few days later the baby and its unwed mother were discharged.

Some people in the hospital kept talking about the horrible mistake the foreign graduate surgeon made. One of the doctors was saying, "Don't forget, laparoscopic cholecystectomy is new and the surgeon is a foreign graduate. The combination worked against the patient." When he noticed me in the room, he added, "We don't consider you a foreigner anymore."

I smiled, "Gee, thanks."

Two weeks later on a Friday, Dr. Neif--an American born, American graduate, gynecologic specialist--did an endometrial curettage on an obese sixty-year-old woman who had vaginal bleeding. After being monitored a few hours, the patient was sent home and advised to take the prescribed analgesics.

The following morning this patient called Dr. Neif, complaining of severe abdominal pain. He suggested that she double the dosage of her pills.

Monday morning the young pathologist brought me the slides prepared from the curetted tissue to show me a piece of large bowel mucosa, evidence of the perforation of the uterus and the bowel. As a senior pathologist, I confirmed her observation.

When I paged Dr. Neif to inform him of the pathology findings, he informed me that the patient was at that very moment in the emergency room in a state of shock.

The patient was taken to the operating room

immediately. The bowel and uterus were both repaired. In spite of vigorous treatment with antibiotics and steroids, her general condition worsened. The following day she expired.

An autopsy was performed. Cause of death was listed as "septic shock due to perforation of the bowel."

I never did hear physicians, nurses, technicians, secretaries, or any other hospital employee mention Dr. Neif's alma mater. I never heard anyone imply that he had even done anything wrong.

Nor did I ever hear another word about Dr. Kim's mistake or his foreign background.

Xenophobia is inherent in the nature of every living being. A complex immune system of the human body is constantly at work against a hostile environment. Skin and mucosa are excellent barriers against chemical or bacterial intruders. The body of an average person produces more than a million specific antibodies, chemicals against foreign substances called antigens. The body of an ill person--who desperately needs a new heart, for example-- would violently reject the "foreign" organ unless the immune system is weakened by drugs. The anti-foreign instinct is obviously for self-preservation. However, this too, like other human emotions, could be exaggerated to the point of becoming abnormal and/or harmful.

On the other hand, symbiosis (also created by natural evolution) permits many useful bacteria to coexist in animals and man. Deoxy ribo nucleic acid of mitochondria (a human intracellular organelle) is very similar to that of some microorganisms, rather than the DNA (deoxy ribo nucleic acid) of human cell nucleus. In other words, such symbiosis exists within each of our body cells.

So too in human societies, certain periods of history evince a kind of sociologic symbiosis. Nations form alliances and coexist for the benefit of each other. During World War II such cooperation converted British and Russians from enemies to allies. In the United States people who hated each other when they lived in Europe now live in peace as concerned neighbors.

In comparison with the size of the universe, the earth is hardly a drop of water in the Atlantic. People occupy a very small part of this earth and should be able to get along in this small neighborhood. Attempts for internationalization of the world have been made by a few religious leaders and politicians. Such hopes of internationalization of the world have been promulgated by thinkers like William Penn, Desiderius Erasmus, President Woodrow Wilson and President Franklin D. Roosevelt, Thomas Hobbes, John Locke, David Hume, Jean-Jacques Rousseau, and Karl Marx. The concept of world unification may be too logical for emotional masses to understand. Throughout the entire world there is a desperate need for massive educational programs focusing on global understanding, cooperation, and appreciation. The United Nations and the European Common market are making strides in the right direction. Among various human institutions, sciences and business do not seem to recognize borders. Volunteer groups like the Council for International Visitors are vital in promoting friendship and understanding among people who may seem different.

When I arrived in the United States in 1952 and worked as an intern and later a resident for $30.00 a month, I did not seem to disturb anyone. When I became a board certified pathologist, however, and began competing for better paying jobs, I suddenly was labeled a foreigner with an accent, a foreign graduate, and a foreign person with a very strange name: Hushang Mofakham Payan. Some of my friends even suggested that I change my name. With so many documents involved throughout my life so far, such a task would be overwhelming. In spite of such complications, my friends call me Hank.

Instead, I was determined to work harder than the average person and use every ounce of energy and enthusiasm to prove to my peers, as well as superiors, that I was equal to (if not better than) others in my field. Adopting the language came relatively easily; absorbing the culture was not. I did not enjoy American sports and had absolutely no inclination to savor beer while watching these games. I succeeded in getting the man out of Iran, but I could not get the proverbial "farm out of the man." A few times, behind my back of course, I was called a lousy foreigner. Throughout the years I became more and more American, to the point that many of my friends doubt that I could survive in the culture into which I was born.

During the infamous Khomeini hostage taking in Iran, many Iranians encountered the rancor of self-proclaimed vigilantes. These few over zealous Americans were determined to make life disturbing for anyone labeled Iranian, regardless of how long these people have been citizens of their adopted country or how repulsive they found the antics of the Khomeini regime. Some Iranian-Americans even lost their jobs for no particular reason. To avoid such discrimination many Iranians pretended to be Cubans or Arabs.

According to the system at Bell Memorial Hospital in Ishpeming, in the middle of every month I received a check for services rendered as director of the laboratories. This November morning was no different, but the afternoon certainly was. As I approached the teller's station, the lady about to wait on me happened to be one of the vice presidents. Since I had banked at this particular branch for at least fifteen years, we knew each other and greeted each other by name. In front of her I signed the check with the words "for deposit only." She looked at the piece of paper, but refrained from touching it as though it were contaminated.

"Oh," she hesitated. "I don't think we can handle your account anymore. President Carter declared that all Iranian money should be frozen."

Then I hesitated. I couldn't imagine what she was talking about. My check was not issued by anyone in Iran. I was being paid for services rendered at Bell Memorial Hospital just three blocks down the street. Within a minute I began to lose my temper. I felt flushed, but controlled my anger. Most emphatically, accentuating every syllable, I said, "This . . . money . . . does not . . . come . . . from Iran. If you . . . don't want my money . . . in this bank, . . . I will simply . . . cross . . . the street . . . and bank . . . there. I am sure . . . that they . . . will be glad. . . to reap the benefits . . . of my business. And as I do so. . . I will personally inform . . . Mr. Cohodas . . . the president of this bank . . . whom I know personally . . . about the reason . . . for my actions."

"Oh, no," she flustered, "I didn't mean for you to do that. I'm sorry if I irritated you. That law is meant for people who bring money from Iran."

"I assure you," I interrupted her, "if anyone would come from Iran with any amount to deposit at this bank, Mr. Cohodas would not mind taking it. The Iranian assets that President Carter talked about on November 14, 1979 referred to money of the Iranian government, not Iranian individual. Furthermore, I am a citizen of the United States and have been for twenty years."

That evening during dinner with a lawyer friend of mine I relayed my experience at Miner's Bank. He mentioned that there were laws protecting people like me and disciplining people like Mrs. Kroosi.

* * * * *

Seven years later I was about to retire. What a difference from the day I landed in the United States. Thanks to a shortage of pathologists by the time I finished my training, many opportunities unfolded. After feeling inferior, insecure, and apprehensive during those early years in this country, I gradually realized that I had become valuable, important, and even appreciated. I contributed not only to pathology, but to research and teaching.

Upon my retirement in 1986 my colleagues presented me with a farewell present--a plaque that signified the change of the name of the hospital library to "Hushang M. Payan Medical Library."

161
Citizen of the Universe

I no longer feel like a lousy foreigner.

From Hushang to Hank

Hushang
fearful, Iranian
studying, aspiring, questioning
mosques, Khoresh, hamburgers, skyscrapers
understanding, earning, hoping
self-confidant, American
Hank